Nov 14

Phyllis   Hamish   Virginia   André Leon   Anna   me   Tonne   Mark
Posnick   Bowles   Smith   Talley   Wintour   Goodman   Holgate

Also by Grace Coddington

Grace: Thirty Years of Fashion at Vogue

The Catwalk Cats
(with Didier Malige)

Grace

GRACE
A MEMOIR

GRACE CODDINGTON

WITH

MICHAEL ROBERTS

Random House Canada

PUBLISHED BY RANDOM HOUSE CANADA

www.randomhouse.ca

Random House Canada and colophon are registered trademarks.

Library and Archives Canada Cataloguing in Publication

Coddington, Grace.
Grace : a memoir / Grace Coddington.

Issued also in electronic format.

ISBN 978-0-307-36274-2

1. Coddington, Grace, 1941–. 2. Vogue. 3. Fashion editors—United
States—Biography. 4. Women periodical editors—United States—
Biography. 5. Models (Persons)—Great Britain—Biography.
6. Fashion—History—20th century. 7. Fashion—History—
21st century. I. Title.

TT505.C63A3 2012   746.9'2092   C2012-902069-9

Book design by Grace Coddington and Michael Roberts
Drawings by Grace Coddington

Printed and bound in the United States of America

2 4 6 8 9 7 5 3 1

For Henri

CONTENTS

INTRODUCTION   XXV

I .... ON GROWING UP   2

II .... ON MODELING   38

III .... ON THE FASHIONABLE LIFE   70

IV .... ON BRITISH VOGUE   92

V .... ON TAKING PICTURES   104

VI .... ON BEGINNINGS AND ENDS   112

VII .... ON CAFÉ SOCIETY   126

VIII .... ON STATES OF GRACE   146

IX .... ON BRUCE   178

X .... ON DIDIER   192

XI .... ON CALVINISM   198

XII .... ON AMERICAN VOGUE   204

XIII .... ON THE BIGGER PICTURE   222

XIV .... ON ANNA   240

XV .... ON PUSHING AHEAD   260

XVI .... ON LIZ   274

XVII .... ON BEAUTY   290

XVIII .... ON CATS   304

XIX .... ON THEN AND NOW   320

           Selected Work   335

           Information   373

           Acknowledgments   378

           Contributors   383

GALLERY

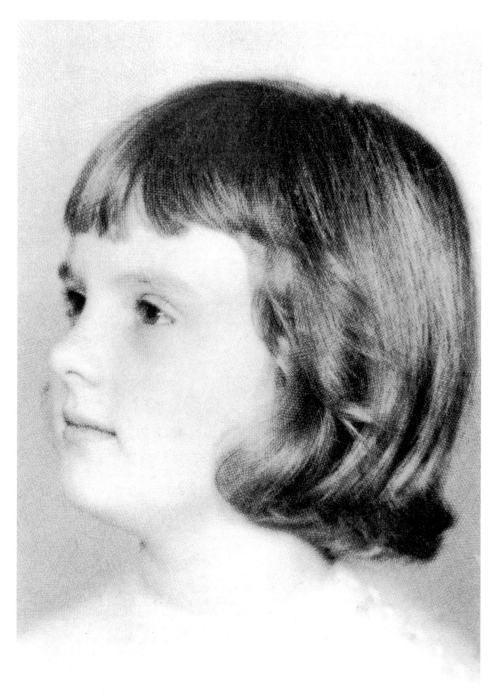

Me, the chubby-cheeked future model, aged four or five

One of many, many hairstyles, about 1954

My first model card, with the picture Vogue *loved, 1959*

My famous Vidal Sassoon Five Point Cut. Photo: David Montgomery, 1964

My very happening makeup look. Photo: Jeanloup Sieff, 1966. © Estate of Jeanloup Sieff

Guest-modeling in a YSL fashion show, Maunkberry's nightclub, London. Photo: Anthony Crickmay, 1970. Courtesy of Vogue © The Condé Nast Publications Ltd.

On a shoot inspired by Edward Weston, Bellport, Long Island. Photo: Bruce Weber, 1982

Photographers gather to celebrate my book Grace: Thirty Years of Fashion at Vogue. *From left to right: Mario Testino, Sheila Metzner* (lying down), *Ellen von Unwerth, Steven Klein, Annie Leibovitz, Alex Chatelain, Herb Ritts* (seated), *Bruce Weber, Craig McDean* (on wall), *Arthur Elgort, me, David Bailey, Peter Lindbergh. Photo: Annie Leibovitz, 2002*

Never thinner: My portrait with a borrowed cat for Italian Vogue. *Photo: Steven Meisel, 1992*

Peering into the future, London. Photo: Willie Christie, 1974

With Didier at a Vogue *party, New York Public Library. Photo: Marina Schiano, 1992*

INTRODUCTION

In which
our heroine
finds fame
on film but, like
Greta Garbo,
just wishes to be
left alone.

The first I heard of *The September Issue* (the movie that is the only reason anyone has ever heard of me) was when Anna Wintour called me into her office at *Vogue* to tell me about it and said, "Oh, by the way, I've agreed to a film crew coming in to make a documentary about us." The film was originally supposed to be about organizing the ball at the Metropolitan Museum of Art's Costume Institute, but it grew bigger and bigger. Now they would be turning up to film all the discussions, meetings, fights, and frustrations that go into creating the most important issue of the year. They would be in our office, and on our sittings, too. It was just about everything I didn't want to hear. As creative director of the magazine, I have a thousand things to deal with. And it's difficult enough putting a complicated photo session together without having onlookers hanging around! "Don't expect me to be in it," I said, sensing Anna's eyes glaze over as she looked past me out the window. She has a way of blanking people out when they are saying something she doesn't care to hear.

My reaction to this intrusive idea was naturally one of horror, because my feeling has always been that people should concentrate on their jobs and not all this fashionable "I want to be a celebrity" shit. Afterward I found out that it had taken the filmmakers almost a year to persuade Anna to say yes. I'm sure she agreed in the end only because she wanted to show that *Vogue* is not just a load of airheads spouting rubbish. By then we had all had enough of *The Devil Wears Prada,* with its portrayal of fashion as utterly ridiculous.

During filming, the crew approached me time and again, confident they could win my cooperation. They had heard that I could be difficult (and I did have a reputation for refusing interviews), yet still they knocked at my door requesting my participation. Perfectly nice they were, but I told them I wasn't interested and I didn't want them anywhere near me because it was too distracting. I hate having people observing me; I want to swat them away like a swarm of flies.

My office door remained firmly closed. I said the rudest things to the director, R. J. Cutler, and for about six months managed to keep him and his crew at bay whenever they pointed a camera in my direction. They would be filming among the racks of clothes in the hallway outside my office, and I could hear people saying things like "Ooh, I just love this red dress," and "Ooh yes, I think Anna would definitely like it," and all the kinds of superficial nonsense people come out with in front of the cameras. Then the film crew followed us all the way to the Paris collections. This was really exasperating. They were constantly getting in our way or elbowing past us to get a shot of Anna. At the Dior show, Bob the cameraman trod on my toe as he filmed her while walking backward. That was the final straw. I really let him have it. "By the way," I screamed, "I work at *Vogue,* too!" They were so intent on filming Anna's every move: sitting in the front row, watching the show, reacting to the

"The September Issue" film crew

"I'm really not interested"

" I don't want you hanging around
anywhere near me ......"

show. It all seemed so over-the-top. I noticed that she was even wearing a mike, which of course created yet another obstacle, because now she would only talk to me in a guarded sort of manner.

Eventually I thought, "If you can't beat them, join them." Besides, Anna had hauled me into her office one last time and told me, "They really are coming to film your shoot. They are going to film your run-through, and this time you cannot get out of it. There will be no discussion." So I definitely had a gun to my head. "But if you put me in that movie, you will hear things you won't like," I warned. "I can't pretend. I'll be so focused on the shoot that I will probably blurt out anything that comes to mind." (What I secretly thought was that if I said anything too bad, they wouldn't use it —which is why I'm caught swearing like a trooper throughout the entire movie.) There had been other documentaries about the fashion business that I'd been filmed for, but my contributions had always ended up on the cutting room floor.

When I saw the final cut for the first time, I was in total shock. There was *way* too much of me in the film. Later, one of the crew members told me that the forceful dynamic between Anna and me strengthened the movie. We had two screenings at *Vogue*. I think Anna didn't want to see it with the rest of us. I was down to go to the first showing with the fashion people; she was off to the second with the writers and the more intellectual crowd, whose opinion she probably valued more. Our hearts sank as we tried to remember what was said during all those months of filming because the whole thing had been out of sight ever since, stuck in the editing room for almost a year.

Now I can look at the end result and laugh. After all, I *was* rather outspoken. Nevertheless, there really is way too much of me. Once Anna had seen the finished version, I never got an opinion out of her about it. Ever. All I know is that she didn't disapprove, but she didn't entirely approve of it, either. The only thing she said was "Just let Grace do all the press," and then moved on. She did, however, attend the first major showing at the Sundance Film Festival and stood onstage afterward at the Q and A, unmoving and enigmatic in dark glasses and clutching a bottle of water while R.J. did most of the talking.

At a screening I attended in Savannah—it was the first time I agreed to do some publicity—with *Vogue*'s editor-at-large André Leon Talley, there was an extensive Q and A session with a roomful of journalists who kept saying, "Oh, we think you are so wonderful." So I grew to like that. (I'm kidding, but it was quite pleasant.) Throughout the question time, the audience was mostly trying to find out about Anna. (They are always trying to find out about Anna.) André was brilliant. He's very good at deflecting awkward moments. Whenever she was mentioned, he changed the subject and began referring instead to Michelle Obama or Diana Vreeland.

I'm always surprised that people who've seen the movie respond to me in such a positive manner. Maybe it's because I come across on-screen as so emotional. It makes me appear idealistic, in contrast to Anna, who is by nature much more determinedly and quietly controlled. Or maybe it's because I appear to be put upon. Or perhaps they are always going to react to someone who seems to be spontaneous. Or someone who dares talk back to her boss like no one else does at the magazine, as I have done and probably will again.

During the opening weeks of the film I was also asked to give a talk at the New York Public Library by Jay Fielden, who at the time was editor in chief of *Men's Vogue*. This was a particularly nerve-wracking

"Look Nicolas, he thinks we're Brad & Angelina"

situation because, out of the corner of my eye, I could see Anna and S. I. Newhouse, the owner of Condé Nast, sitting in the audience. After a while, the Q and A's became much easier. I got into the rhythm of things, hiding in the dark until the last minute—at which point you make your sudden dramatic appearance—and looking directly at the questioner. And then one day I realized I had somehow become pretty recognizable. I found groups of people regularly gathered in front of my apartment building in Chelsea, New York: fashion freaks, gays, straights, young, old, a whole mixture. It was a cross section of the neighborhood, all shouting at me from across the street—but always in such a nice way. I felt like the Beatles. Actually, better than the Beatles, because the crowds chasing them in the early days of their fame could get rough. I did once get mobbed, though. Having agreed to do a Q and A at my local cinema, I arrived right as the audience from an earlier showing was leaving. When I rounded the corner, all I could hear was "Grace, Grace. Oh my God, it's her!"

And they still haven't forgotten. Perhaps it's because I'm frequently on the street or in the subway and not discreetly hidden away in a Town Car, like Anna. It got me thinking, now that my memories had been well and truly raked up by all the questions I'd been asked, that maybe I had a bigger story to share. Which led to the next surprise—here I am doing something I never imagined I'd be old or interesting enough to embark on: writing my memoirs.

Sometime after *The September Issue* came out, I was having a quiet dinner in a little restaurant in Lower Manhattan with Nicolas Ghesquière, the designer for Balenciaga, who had flown over from Paris. "Grace, is it true that people recognize you wherever you go?" he asked me suddenly. So when we finished eating, I suggested he walk home with me. And as we strolled past the many crowded restaurants, bars, and gay nightclubs in my part of town, people kept popping out, saying, "It's Grace. It's Grace! Wow—and Nicolas Ghesquière, too." Cell phone cameras flashed and clicked. In the end we just cracked up, the both of us behaving like Paris Hilton!

Grace

ON
GROWING UP

In which
the winds howl,
the waves
crash, the rain
pours down,
and our lonely
heroine dreams
of being
Audrey Hepburn.

There were sand dunes in the distance and rugged monochrome cliffs strung out along the coast. And druid circles. And hardly any trees. And bleakness. Although it was bleak, I saw beauty in its bleakness. There was a nice beach, and I had a little sailboat called *Argo* that I used to drift about in for hours in grand seclusion when it was not tethered to a small rock in a horseshoe-shaped cove called Tre-Arddur Bay. I was fifteen then, my head filled with romantic fantasies, some fueled by the mystic spirit of Anglesey, the thinly populated island off the fogbound northern coast of Wales where I was born and raised; some by the dilapidated cinema I visited each Saturday afternoon in the underwhelming coastal town of Holyhead, a threepenny bus ride away, where the boats took off across the Irish Sea for Dublin and the Irish passengers seemed never short of a drink. Or two. Or three or four.

"Well, it could be summer or winter, but either way we're not swimming"

For my first eighteen years, the Tre-Arddur Bay Hotel, run by my family, was my only home, a plain building with whitewashed walls and a sturdy gray slate roof, long and low, with the understated air of an elongated bungalow. This forty-two-room getaway spot of quiet charm was appreciated mostly by holidaymakers who liked to sail, go fishing, or take long, bracing cliff-top walks rather than roast themselves on a sunny beach. It was not overendowed with entertainment facilities, either. No television. No room service. And in most cases, not even the luxury of an en suite bathroom with toilet, although generously sized white china chamber pots were provided beneath each guest bed, and some rooms—the deluxe versions—contained a washbasin. A lineup of three to four standard bathrooms provided everyone else's washing facilities. For the entire hotel there was a single chambermaid, Mrs. Griffiths, a sweet little old lady in a black dress and white apron equipped with a duster and a carpet sweeper. I remember my mother being quite taken aback by a guest who took a bath and rang the bell for the maid to set about cleaning the tub. Why wouldn't the visitors scrub it out themselves after use? she wondered.

Our little hotel had three lounges, each decorated throughout in an incongruous mix of the homely and the grand, the most imposing items originating from my father's ancestral home in the Midlands. At an early age, I discovered that the Coddingtons of Bennetston Hall, the family seat in Derbyshire, had an impressive history that included at least two wealthy Members of Parliament, my grandfather and great-grandfather, and stretched back sufficiently into the past to come complete with an ancient family crest—a dragon with flames shooting out of its mouth—and a family motto, "Nil Desperandum" (Never Despair). And so, although some communal rooms remained modest and simple, the dining room was furnished with huge, inherited antique wooden sideboards decorated with carved pheasants, ducks, and grapes, and the Blue Room contained a satinwood writing desk hand-painted with cherubs. A large library holding hundreds of beautiful leather-bound books housed many display drawers of seashells, and various species of butterfly and beetle. There was a grand piano in the music room (from my mother's side of the family), and paintings in gilded frames—dark family portraits—hanging everywhere else.

Guests would rise with the sun and retire to bed at nightfall. If they needed to use the telephone, there was a public booth in the bar. There was a single lunchtime sitting at one o'clock and another at seven p.m. for dinner, with only two waiters to serve on each occasion. Tea was upon request. Breakfast was served between nine and nine-thirty in the dining room—and certainly never in the bedroom. There was also a games room with a Ping-Pong table where I practiced and practiced. I was good. Very good. I would beat all the guests, which didn't go down too well with my parents.

The sand on the long, damp beige ribbon of beach in front of the hotel was reasonably fine-grained but did get a bit pebbly as you approached the icy Irish Sea slapping against the shore. You could, however, paddle out for a fair distance before it became freezingly knee-deep.

Throughout my childhood I longed for the lushness of trees. Barely one broke the rocky surface on our side of the island. Only when we paid the occasional family visit to my father's aunt Alice in her big, shaded house on the south side would we ever see them in numbers. My great-aunt was extremely frail and old, so I always think of her as being about a hundred. Her home was close to the small town of Beaumaris, which had a huge social life in the 1930s. My parents met there, as my mother lived nearby with her family in a sprawling house called Trecastle.

Flanking our hotel on one side was a gray seascape of cliffs, rocks, and bulrushes, then acres of windswept country and a lobster fisherman's dwelling, and on the other Tre-Arddur House, a prestigious prep school for boys. Once I reached the age when boys became of interest, I used to linger shyly, watching them play football or cricket beyond the gray flinty stone wall bordering their playing fields until I arrived at the bus stop and took off on my winding journey to school.

We were open from May to October but the hotel was guaranteed to be one hundred percent full only during the relatively sunny month of August, the time of the school summer holidays. Many vacationing families from the not too distant towns of Liverpool and Manchester made the effort to come and stay with us because, although it might have been easier for them to reach the more accessibly popular holiday spots of North Wales, our charming beach and village were that much more individual. At other times we were mostly empty or visited by parents who had come to join their sons for special events at the school.

Each year tumultuous clouds and fierce equinox gales announced the end of summer. A mad scramble then ensued to rescue all the little wooden sailing boats belonging to the locals that bobbed about in the bay. Llewellyn, the lobster fisherman, was in charge of having them hauled out of the sea and beached beneath the protective seawall. All winter long, while we were closed, thick mists enveloped us and rough seas pounded our shoreline. The entire place became desolate. On foggy nights you could hear the sad moan of a foghorn coming from the nearby lighthouse. It hardly ever snowed, but it rained most of the time: a constant drizzle that made the atmosphere incredibly damp, the kind of dampness that gets into your bones. So damp that, as a child, I swear I used to ache all over from rheumatism.

In the afternoons, I took long walks along the cliffs with Chuffy, my mother's Yorkshire terrier, and Mackie, my sister's Scottie. Stormy waves foamed and crashed over the gray rocks along the seafront, and if you missed your timing, you were liable to come in for a complete drenching whenever you dashed between them.

Throughout the endless weeks of winter, the hotel was so deserted it wasn't worth the bother of switching on the lights. My sister and I would play ghosts. Wrapped in white sheets, we hid along the dark, empty corridors, each containing many mysterious, shadowy doorways from which you could jump out and say, "Boo!" We would wait and wait, the silence broken only by the tick-tock, tick-tock, of our big grandfather clock. But in the end, I couldn't stand the gloom, the suspense of waiting, the sinister ticking. It was too scary, so I usually fled to the warmth and comfort of the fireside.

I was born on the twentieth of April 1941 in the early part of World War II, the same year the Nazis engulfed Yugoslavia and Greece. I was christened Pamela Rosalind Grace Coddington. My elder sister Rosemary, or Rosie for short, was the one who chose Pamela as my registered first name, which then became abbreviated to Pam by most people we knew.

Marion, my maternal grandmother, was a Canadian opera singer who had fallen in love with my grandfather while visiting Wales on a singing tour. He followed her back to Canada, where they married and where my mother and her brother and sister were born. For a while they lived on Vancouver Island, which was heavily wooded and filled with bears. Then they moved back permanently to Anglesey, where my grandmother grew more and more morose and wrote terribly sad poetry. I'm told my grandfather was somewhat extreme when it came to what he perceived as correct behavior. Apparently, he once locked my grandmother in the downstairs bathroom—which he had designated for gentlemen only—for an entire day when she had used it in an emergency.

Janie, my mother, inherited this strict, no-nonsense Victorian attitude and believed that children should be seen and not heard. She demanded absolute obedience but never lost her temper or raised her voice. It was a given that I would make my bed and tidy my room, and that I had my chores to fulfill. She was the strong, stoic one who held our family together. Photographs of her from the 1920s show a sleek and prosperous-looking woman. She drew and painted rather well in watercolors and played the piano and the Spanish guitar. Welsh—although she preferred to think of herself as English—she could trace the family lineage back to the Black Prince. (In fact, we weren't encouraged to think of ourselves as Welsh at all; more as foreigners, émigrés from Derbyshire.)

My father William, or Willie, was impeccably English: introverted, preoccupied, and oh so very reserved that you would have to draw the words out of him, as you have to with me. I remember him sitting in the hotel office for hours and hours, but I don't remember him actually doing anything. There always seemed such an air of sadness about him.

He dabbled in mechanics. His hobby was making toy boats and airplanes that he would build in the hallway outside our bedroom, using a small lathe to fashion the tiny engines. He gave me my third Christian name, Grace, in remembrance of his mother. When I eventually left home at eighteen, an old friend in London called Panchitta—who was, to me, very glamorous because she studied acting—told me she considered my third name far more useful than my first in order to succeed in the big city. "I think Grace sounds very good for a model," she enthused. "Grace Coddington. Pretty impressive."

I was a solitary and sickly child, suffering from frequent bouts of bronchitis and the croup. I was stricken so often that my doctor thought I might have tuberculosis. Because of this, I missed at least half of each term in every school year. My parents even tried building me up in those pre-vitamin days by feeding me glasses of Guinness and a dark, treacly substance called malt extract that was totally delicious. I was pale, freckly, and allergic to any significant amount of sunshine. Luckily, whatever sun we had during my youth in Wales was filtered through heavy gray clouds. Later, when I was in my twenties, if I had too much exposure, my face would swell up. But I did love the outdoors. And right through to my teens I was always more outside than in, sailing, climbing, and clambering over the rugged slopes of the nearby mountains of Snowdonia, or wandering along our island's country lanes, their hedgerows dotted with wildflowers.

Our family lived in what was known as "the annex"—the self-contained part of the building just beyond the hotel kitchen. We had our own private front door, a pretty clematis-covered porch, and a garden filled with roses and hydrangeas that was my mother's pride and joy. In the back we grew vegetables and kept geese, ducks, and chickens.

The annex was our own enclosed world within a world. It was furnished in a similar style and in the same taste as the rest of the hotel, but everything was on a much smaller, more personal scale. The paintings and tapestries on the walls, for instance, were all my mother's work. It was also extremely cluttered, because she could rarely bring herself to throw out so much as an empty jam jar. And so the clutter grew, to the point that, despite its getting piled into cupboards or hidden out of sight behind curtains, I was too embarrassed to invite any school friends back home.

It wasn't until much later that I was stunned to discover our little

Tre-Arddur Bay Hotel never actually belonged to us but to my mother's brother, Uncle Ted, a bluff military man who inherited this and many other neighboring properties from my grandfather. And it was thanks to him that we were living there at all. In true Victorian fashion, every property belonging to my mother's family—and there was a considerable amount—had been passed down to him as a male, despite his being the youngest child. Nothing whatsoever went through the female line, which in this case consisted of my mother and her sister, Auntie May.

Uncle Ted's son, my cousin Michael, stood to inherit the estate. A year older than me and an easygoing boy with a great smile, Michael and I were inseparable for a time as children. Then the family was posted to Malaysia for several years. On their return, Michael resumed his role of protective big brother. We sailed together, and when he graduated from bicycle to motorbike, I would hop on the back to ride about with him. We even vowed we would wed each other if, by the time we were fifty, we were not otherwise taken.

During the war, it was generally assumed that if the Germans tried to invade Britain, they would set off from Ireland and disembark on some part of our unassuming little Welsh beach. And indeed, in the year I was born the German Luftwaffe bombed Belfast, just across the sea from us, in the biggest air raid outside the London Blitz. So the army commandeered our hotel, closing it down but allowing us to stay on, even though we were left with no real means of earning a living.

The soldiers installed gun towers all along the coast, on headlands, and over the hills, while the area in front of the beach became a parking space reserved for army tanks. Meanwhile, every evening, as a wartime ritual, we dimmed the lights and drew thick blackout curtains across our windows to avoid detection by enemy aircraft.

Great-grandmother Sarah Williams, 1899

Grandmother Grace Coddington, 1897

My father, William, with Grandmother Grace Coddington, Leslie (with Jack, the dog), Robert,
and Grandfather Reginald Coddington, at home at Bennetston Hall, Derbyshire, England, 1912

Auntie May, Grandmother Marion Williams, my mother, and Uncle Ted, about 1911

My mother and father's wedding, 1934

My home: Tre-Arddur Bay Hotel, Anglesey, North Wales, 1964

My father, sister Rosemary, mother, and me in the garden in front of our Wendy house, Tre-Arddur Bay, 1941

With my sister, Rosemary, in my mother's knitting, beside the hydrangeas, Tre-Arddur Bay, 1945

About to go sailing in full-on Audrey Hepburn chic, and probably in love, Tre-Arddur Bay, 1955

In a modeling mood at home, wearing an A-line dress, Tre-Arddur Bay, 1954

Rosie looking glamorous, just prior to her engagement, Tre-Arddur Bay, 1955

I was about three years old when an entire troop of Americans arrived at the hotel to join the squaddies already quartered there. These GIs were barracked in temporary huts they built out front, right across the hotel grounds. They were friendly and kind to my sister and me, showering us with sweets in a time of scarcity and ration books, and helping us back onto our push bikes whenever we fell off—because we did ride fast, two daredevil young sisters racing up and down the hotel driveway, now heavily pitted with potholes thanks to the coming and going of army trucks.

In 1945, when the war ended and the soldiers packed up for home, they left the place in the most god-awful mess. They really trashed it. Floors were destroyed, mirrors broken, walls pitted with holes. For the longest time, my parents tried to get the army to reimburse us. And finally, they did—at prewar prices, a fraction of what the repairs would actually cost.

As peacetime settled in, we fixed up the hotel in a simple, affordable way and opened once again for business. Our village then carried on much the same as before. We still bought our newspapers at the general store. I continued to regularly put my pocket money in the post office savings bank run by Robin the Post, where I also stocked up on favorite sweets such as mint humbugs, dolly mixtures, and sherbet fizz. Our general provisions still came from Miss Jones's shop, which was as cramped and dark as ever, and filled with everything from sticking plasters to eggs, jam, and flypaper. Miss Jones was still so remarkably tiny that she stood on a teetering series of boxes behind the counter to serve us.

Everything would, I hoped, be as tranquil and cozy as it once was. But it did occur to me that, although we were quite affluent before—my sister kept a pony, my mother had lots of beautiful jewelry, and my father drove an amazingly luxurious French saloon car called a Delage (banished to the garage throughout the war because of petrol rationing)—we now seemed fairly poor. For instance, we previously owned a small home movie camera, I would imagine not a cheap item in those days, and I remember my sister's childhood being recorded on grainy film. Mine wasn't. I can only think it was sold to help pay for a few of the more urgent renovations or debts.

Following my mother's difficult second pregnancy—both Rosie and I were delivered by cesarean section—the doctor told her that she mustn't have any more children. There was no real contraception at that time, so my father removed himself from their bedroom. They were already sleeping in separate beds by then, anyway. My sister and I shared a bedroom because I was terrified of being alone in the dark (and still am). However, Rosie was grown up enough at this point to merit her own room, so my father moved in with me instead.

Abstinence quietly drove my parents further apart, but I didn't notice that at the time. I was just happy to have my father to myself every evening. At night he would tickle my arm and tell me stories until I fell asleep. It's strange how little I remember of him, except that I really adored him. As the years passed he became an increasingly melancholy figure. In wintertime he would sit for hours in front of the small electric fire in our room. He developed a terrible, wracking cough brought on by the packets of unfiltered Player's Navy Cut cigarettes he smoked continuously. By now he had taken to visiting the betting shops, where he lost considerable sums on the horses. He would then pawn all the jewelry he had given my mother, hoping to recover it the following week if ever he enjoyed a big win.

One early-autumn afternoon when I was eleven years old, I went into the bathroom and found my father collapsed on the floor, not quite unconscious but certainly delirious. I rushed off to fetch my mother and watched as he was immediately taken away to hospital. They did test after test but just four months later—on New Year's Day, 1953—he died of lung cancer.

When he first came out of hospital, my father told me they had no idea what was wrong. At this stage I think they were keeping the truth from him. That my mother knew, I was sure. She and I switched rooms so that she could better care for him. Over the months, he grew weaker and weaker, thinner and thinner, and was unable to make himself understood. My mother fed him little measures of whiskey to help him gather his strength. During the last few weeks of his life, she finally told me that his condition was not going to improve.

My auntie May, who had been living with us for some time, was the one who came to tell my sister, Rosie, and me that our father had died. Rosie rushed into his bedroom, while I remained in the corridor outside. My mother was standing at the bedside in tears. The instant she realized he was gone, my sister tried to shake my father back into life. She was devastated and hysterical. I witnessed all this, my mother trying to calm her screams, my aunt struggling to get my sister out the door.

I never entered the room again. It remained empty after that. Only rarely would I approach it in future years, nervously willing myself to push a toe across the unlit threshold. But I always ran off again, my heart pounding in fear of the unknown.

I did not attend the funeral. That was my mother's decision; she said I was too young. On the day of the burial, I wandered around the empty fields behind our hotel, grieving, not understanding what death was all about, feeling inconsolable loss yet wanting to be part of what was going on. I remained on my own until all the friends and relations returned for their postfuneral tea and cake.

My father was the first to be buried in the family plot of the church-yard next door to the convent I attended all through my teens. There was enough room for him, my mother, my sister, and me. But then my aunt died and took the place that had been reserved for me. In retrospect, that's fine. I plan to be cremated anyway.

From the time I began to read, children's comics transported me to cheerier places. My mother kept books, but I rarely looked at them, much preferring the traditional British weeklies such as *Beano* and *Dandy,* and a glossy new one called *Girl,* which was, naturally enough, much more girly than the rest and remained a firm favorite of mine until I graduated to fashion magazines like *Vogue.*

When I was very young, my sister used to read me all the children's classics like *Winnie-the-Pooh* and *Alice in Wonderland.* Years later, I would use Lewis Carroll's great narrative to inspire one of my favorite fashion shoots. But the stories I really loved were about Orlando the Marmalade Cat. These were a series of beautiful picture books by Kathleen Hale about Orlando and his wife, Grace, who had three kittens, Pansy, Blanche, and Tinkle. Seeing a story visually rather than in words was what I was responding to.

Most of the people who stayed at our hotel were families that returned year after year. And then there was Mr. Wedge. I nicknamed him the Shrimp Man because he liked to take me shrimping. He was a regular hotel guest, very proper, smoked a pipe, and could have been a banker. I recall his suit trousers being rolled up to his calves and his wearing a waistcoat as we paddled about the shallows with our nets. He was considerably older than I, possibly in his late thirties or forties. I was barely thirteen at the time and no doubt thought of him being as unbelievably ancient as Santa Claus. One day he came to the house, confessed to my mother that he was madly in love with me, and said he would like to wait until I grew up and then marry me. My mother was horrified. She completely flipped and then threw him out.

We still didn't have a television, but once a year, when we went to stay with my aunt, uncle, and cousins in Cheshire, we rode their pony and were given permission to watch their TV. But it was the movies that fascinated me the most. Once a week from my early teens, I was allowed to visit the local cinema for the matinee performance. So every Saturday, after making the beds, washing the dishes, and finishing the remainder of my chores, I was off, walking the mile along the seafront to the bus stop by myself, darting to avoid the stinging sea spray. Then I would take the country bus to Holyhead, passing through a no-man's-land of derelict parking lots to get there.

The cinema was a crumbling old fleapit, a small-town cliché of a picture palace complete with worn plush velvet seats and a young girl selling ice cream in the interval. Think of *The Last Picture Show,* only even more shabby. I would settle into one of the larger, more comfortable double seats in the back row—a place where the boys usually sat and smooched with their girlfriends during the evening show—and there in the darkness I would completely give myself up to the dream world of celluloid.

I remember being crazy about Montgomery Clift and James Dean. I loved all the boys with soft, sad eyes and lost souls. I loved horses, too: *National Velvet,* with Elizabeth Taylor, and *Black Beauty,* which was dreadfully sad, although not as sad as *Bambi.* When I saw that, I cried all the way through to the end. *Duel in the Sun* was another favorite—such a tragic love story. I adored Gregory Peck; his voice was so warm and reassuring. I sometimes imagined myself marrying him—well, perhaps not marrying in the carnal or conventional sense, but of being with him on a mysteriously prolonged "dream date."

I was enchanted by *The Red Shoes,* with Moira Shearer and Robert Helpmann. This was the first film I ever saw. So beautiful! Her mane of red hair! Her red ballet shoes! A few years later I saw it again and thought, "Well, there is a really dark side to this film." But I was just twelve when I watched it first with my mother and saw only the romance of the ballet.

Audrey Hepburn, too, was so chic and adorable in her skinny pants and little pumps. Watching the romantic comedy *Sabrina,* I easily pictured myself as Audrey sitting in that tree—the chauffeur's daughter, looking down yearningly at all the handsome boys, was just like me whenever I spied on my elder sister and her good-looking boyfriends. I loved Audrey, not only through her films but because of some reportage photos I saw in the magazine *Picture Post* that struck a chord. She was shown happily riding around on her bike and cooking in her tiny apartment. Everything was so clean and shiny. I aspired to live in exactly that same perfect way.

Back home I often attempted to make outfits similar to the sophisticated looks worn by the actresses on the big screen. Throughout my teens I made most of my own wardrobe—even suits and coats—on our Singer sewing machine, which you worked with foot pedals. All it took was patience, and lots of it. I would use Vogue patterns and fabrics from Polykoff's, a big old department store in Holyhead. I never made anything outrageous. My mother only allowed me to dress in relatively conservative clothes. Everything else she knitted for me. As many old photographs will attest, my mother seldom stopped knitting. She took her knitting everywhere, night and day, making things that were the bane of my life because they would become saggy, especially the knitted bathing suits: saggy and soggy.

Even when I was a child, *Vogue* was already on its way to being my magazine of choice. I used to see my sister's copy lying around the house after she was done looking through it—so in a way, it was Rosemary who introduced me to fashion. When I was older, I would make a special trip to Holyhead to buy it for myself. It always arrived rather late in the month, and there were usually only one or two in stock. Presumably, *Harper's Bazaar* was around then, too, but for me it was always *Vogue*. I bought it for the fantasy of looking at beautiful clothes, and I liked getting lost in its pages.

Leafing through the magazine, I was fascinated by the new styles, those ladylike fifties outfits implying a softer, more approachable type of glamour than that which dazzled me at my local cinema. But what I particularly loved were the photographs themselves, especially those taken outdoors. They transported me to all sorts of exotic places—places where you could wear that kind of thing. Après-ski wear under snow-topped fir trees! Beachy cover-ups on sun-kissed coral islands!

The images that stood out for me the most were by Norman Parkinson. He was one of the few fashion photographers back then who was a celebrity in the modern sense. Tall and skinny in an elegant suit with a small, bristling, old-fashioned military mustache, he was always putting himself in his pictures. I began to recognize his work for its lighthearted humor and irrepressible personality. Parkinson would come to play an important role in my life.

During the years after I turned thirteen, I spent even more time studying *Vogue,* since my sister left home to get married, and I inherited the sophisticated privacy of her room. It was very much hers when she lived with us; I wasn't even allowed through the door without an invitation. So the first thing I did was redecorate. She had painted it yellow. I painted it pink. Or was it the other way around?

My mother never questioned my sister getting married so young—she was only eighteen—because her obsession was for us girls to find husbands. My sister's, John Newick, was a lecturer at Birmingham University some years older than she who had been married before and had two children.

The funny thing was, after Rosie moved out, we became much closer. I even saw her more often. Our relationship changed dramatically: When I was younger, she had been able to push me around, and I bore the brunt of her terrible temper tantrums. But by the time she left home, I had grown a lot bigger and taller, and found I had a new way of dealing with things. The more someone gets angry with me, the calmer I become, a policy I have stuck to all my life.

Le Bon Sauveur was the name of the convent school I attended from the ages of nine to seventeen. It was run by a French Catholic order in Holyhead and was small and a little bit exclusive, being the only private school in the area. It had beautiful wooden floors, high ceilings, tennis courts, and wonderful grounds with rolling lawns and pretty gardens. Apart from the standard lessons and games, we were also taught ballet, needlework, and several other pastimes intended to prepare you for married life without a job.

My sister, who had been sent there before me as a boarder, wasn't much taken by convent life, complaining that she found the excessive amount of chapel worship hard on her knees. However, a note from my parents explaining that we were perfectly content to remain Church of

England and had no intention of converting to Catholicism cleared the way for me to skip the devotionals.

There were about sixty girls at the school. This was the first time I had been thrown into such a sizable crowd, and I experienced tremendous anxiety. I would become nauseated and even physically sick around too many new people, and while this affliction eased as I grew older, it hasn't entirely gone away. Throughout my childhood, I couldn't sit down to eat with all the other girls at school without feeling a dreadful fear-induced sense of panic. At one stage, I persuaded my mother to let me return home for lunch, despite the long ride—an hour there and back—leaving barely enough time to eat. Finally, my parents were able to organize prepaid lunches at a quiet little café in town, where I didn't have to talk to anyone. I still seize up sometimes when I have to do something that should be painless, such as speaking up during our weekly fashion meetings at *Vogue*.

my Winter school uniform

In the summer, I would cycle to school past empty golf courses and fields filled with horses, cows, and sheep in my simple uniform of a blue short-sleeved shirt and gray knee-length pleated shorts. Winter mornings, however, were quite a different matter. They were invariably so cold that I could see my frosty breath despite warming up my room with the small one-bar electric fire I was permitted to switch on for only ten minutes at a stretch. So I would get dressed in bed. I kept my school uniform—a gray worsted wool tunic with a blue flannel long-sleeved shirt and tie, a gray woolen cardigan, and thick lisle stockings—neatly tucked under the pillow, and I'd squirm into it under the bedclothes.

Pupils from the nearby state school hated us convent girls and considered us snobs. There was a lot of name-calling. "Posh," they all hissed in my direction as I sat there in my school beret and gray raincoat, protectively hugging my satchel on the morning bus and hugely outnumbered by my persecutors.

At recreation times we girls were expected to converse in French. We called our headmistress, or head nun, "Ma Mère." The teachers were called "Madame," because they were all married to God. I think very few of the nuns actually were French, but they were certainly quite groovy, even if they did wear the obligatory severe-looking black habits and white wimples. The convent had an extensive area of flat roof, and in the hour-long break after lunch they went roller skating up there, flapping about in their robes like crows on wheels. Very good some of them were, too. They didn't exactly kick their legs up high, but they did pirouette.

My one special friend was Angela, although I didn't see much of her outside school because she lived twenty miles away at the other end of the island. Our occasional adventures involved slipping off to the mainland by train, across the Menai Straits to Bangor, in order to take ballroom dancing lessons for which we always seemed to be partnered by boys so short they barely reached our chins. My only other friend, Mary, was bright and the "rebel" of the class. For a fourteen-year-old, she also had the most enormous breasts. On our way home, we often chatted at the bus stop, which was next to the local garage. A cute mechanic worked there, and Mary the rebel soon became pregnant.

The moment the news swept through class, we were all transfixed with excitement because the school taught no sex education whatsoever. Obviously, you couldn't ask your parents or the nuns any questions. So we

one two three, one two three .... ouch!!

were thrilled to get every bit of information right here, firsthand. At break, there we were, breathlessly gathered around Mary, asking urgent things like "So what did you do?" and "So what did he do next?" and "So what did it feel like?"

I was fifteen when I fell madly in love for the first time. His name was Ian Sixsmith, and he was the middle son of one of the families who stayed with us each summer. Ian was lanky and handsome with dark, shiny hair combed straight back. His younger brother was a pupil at the prep school next door to us.

Our family was never one to get together to discuss love, life, and sex or anything. With us, there were no touchy-feely moments. I don't even remember hugging or kissing my mother apart from the odd peck on the cheek. This, however, didn't strike me as at all odd, because it seemed to be the way all families behaved.

Ian and I had our first kiss on my front doorstep. I prayed that my mother wouldn't see. My sister had previously suggested I should "Put some lipstick on, make yourself more attractive." So I did. But Ian and I never slept together. Young girls—apart from hopeless cases like Mary—didn't sleep with young boys in those days until after marriage. Then, all of a sudden, Ian was gone. Conscripted: called up to join the RAF and packed off overseas to Cyprus. I went to say goodbye at the railway station, and it was like a scene from the eighties film *Yanks*. There I was in my printed frock (which in all likelihood I had made myself), waving him on his way, so handsome in his uniform, the train whistle blowing, steam clouds swirling. My heart was broken. We wrote to each other every week for some time. But eventually, I fell for someone else, and we lost touch. Absence, I guess, did not make the heart grow fonder.

Ten miles from the hotel was an air base called RAF Valley—its motto was *In Adversis Perfugium* (Refuge in Adversity)—which housed a branch of the Fleet Air Arm (and was later attended by the Queen's grandson Prince William). These were seventeen- to eighteen-year-old kids, only a few years older than I, young boys sent out to the Welsh countryside to learn how to fly in battered old training planes and master the incredibly difficult tasks of piloting blind and taking off and landing on an aircraft carrier anchored offshore—terrifying feats that occasionally ended in tragedy.

During the season, the young fliers grouped together on Saturday afternoons and came over to the Tre-Arddur Bay rugby club to play against our local team. Now in my midteens, I helped out at the club, making cups of tea for them at halftime. They looked so heroic, covered head to foot in mud.

Each one seemed to possess a sports car that he drove really fast during time off. Bob Holiday, my pilot boyfriend of the moment, had an open-top Austin-Healey that he sped about in fast and furiously, often hitting around 100 mph, taking corners too tightly and going into a spectacular spin. He was a tall, good-looking blond, forever in trouble with his superiors. He grew his hair longer than regulations allowed, which landed him in hot water when someone in authority spotted it poking out beneath his flying helmet. After a while he became serious about me, and we almost got engaged. Then Bob transferred to Devon. His best friend, Jeremy, drove me down one day to join him. Jeremy owned a vintage MG, had a sunny personality, a smart family town house in Kensington, and was great fun. Halfway there, we realized we quite fancied each other. And that was the end of Bob.

By the time I turned eighteen, I knew I must leave my tiny Welsh island. Although I had nothing like a good alternative plan, there was no choice if you stayed in Anglesey. You could end up working in either a clock factory or a snack bar.

All through my teens, people had remarked upon my height, saying that I was tall enough to be a model (probably because most Welsh girls are pretty short). My old school friend Angela always encouraged me, saying, "Let's go to London. You can go to modeling school, and I can get a job as a secretary, and we will see where it leads." So, before I left home, I cut out and posted a coupon from the pages of *Vogue*. It was a tiny snippet, a paragraph in the back of the magazine promising, for twenty-five guineas, a life-transforming two-week course at the Cherry Marshall modeling school in Mayfair.

Modeling seemed like an amazing escape into a world of wealth and excitement, a chance to travel to new places and meet interesting people. At the very least, I reasoned, it could lead to a greater social life, a respectable home, and marriage, all of which would make my mother deliriously happy. Besides, I loved seeing beautiful clothes in beautiful photographs and dreamed of being part of it.

II

ON MODELING

In which our
heroine leaves
home, lands a job,
learns how
to walk, runs
naked through
the woods,
and discovers sex.

aving arrived back at my American *Vogue* office in New York after the Paris collections, I find myself inundated with paperwork. Because I categorically refuse to squint all day at a computer screen, a snowdrift of printed e-mails has buried my desk. Budget estimates for upcoming fashion shoots and their ever-spiraling costs wait to be whittled down. Photocopies of model hopefuls—referred to nowadays as "the new Daria" or "Kate" or "Naomi" and never as girls in their own right—litter my in-tray. Urgent notes summoning me to write introductions to photography books and requests for me to design a special bag covered with my cat drawings for Balenciaga clamor for my attention.

After a week first stuck in Paris traffic en route to noting the clothes in more than thirty ready-to-wear presentations, followed by a swift shoot in the South of France with my favorite model, Natalia Vodi-

My first modeling job

"I know the leaves are falling Parks, but did my clothes have to fall too?"

anova, and the actor Michael Fassbender (I still blush after seeing him in *Shame*), during which I became trapped in the hotel lift and had my luggage misplaced on the journey home, I am exhausted. Now I am expected to address requests to design the shop windows at Prada to coincide with the annual Costume Institute exhibition at the Metropolitan Museum of Art and to trawl through heaps of film stills of the actress Keira Knightley in a new production of Tolstoy's *Anna Karenina,* as she is the possible lead for our October issue.

At the same time, I have to try to find a day that works for both Lady Gaga and the photographers Mert and Marcus to shoot the cover of our all-important September issue, which this year, even more importantly, celebrates 120 years of *Vogue* and is more than 900 pages thick.

"Multitasking," I think they call it. Whatever, it's a far cry from the carefree fashion career I envisioned as a coming-of-age teenager appraising *Vogue*'s photographs of girls draped across country gates gazing dreamily at the cows. And an even longer way from the world I would discover after setting off from home for pastures new over half a century ago.

Early in 1959, I arrived in London by train one afternoon with my few belongings packed in a smart new blue fiberglass suitcase. The capital city, so steeped in history, was well on its way to becoming the hugely overcrowded metropolis it is today. The area I was about to move to, Notting Hill, was crammed with recently installed black tenants, mostly arrived by boat from overseas British territories such as Trinidad and other Caribbean islands. Terrace upon terrace of tall, elegant, white-painted Victorian houses, each with its own impressively grand front door and porch, had been recently subdivided into warrens of small rooms that the landlords were renting out to large immigrant families and hard-up students at inflated prices. There was a great deal of racial tension in the air.

My friend Angela and I shared a bed-sit in one of these converted row houses in Palace Gardens Terrace, a large stuccoed room on the second floor with two narrow single beds and a washbasin. There was an open fireplace in which stood a gas fire on a meter and a little electric ring for boiling an egg or warming up uncomplicated things like baked beans, and a pay phone on the wall in the outside corridor for general use. Our rent for two was four pounds a week. The last bus home was at ten-thirty, and if I spent the evening out or was delayed on the late shift at work, I would be highly nervous returning alone. This was around the time of the notorious Notting Hill race riots, when resentful gangs of blacks and whites lay in wait for each other armed with cutthroat razors and petrol bombs.

I worked as a waitress at the Stockpot in Basil Street, Knightsbridge, a literal stone's throw from the vaunted halls of Harrods department store. My actress friend Panchitta, who worked at the Stockpot part-time, set up a job interview for me with the owner, Tony. It was a bistro, the kind of continental-looking place where they usually stick candles thickened with dripped wax into picturesque Chianti bottles wrapped in raffia, and cover the tables in red-and-white-checked tablecloths, except this one had lacquered pine tables and banquettes. All the smart girls of London used to work there—demure young ladies from respectable backgrounds in the home counties, fancy girls from fancy families talking about fancy clothes, and pouty debutantes with beehive hairdos and pale pink lipstick, each reasonably pretty and all hand-picked by Tony, who thought himself God's gift to women.

We didn't have a uniform as such but wore a navy-blue-and-white-striped cotton apron over our street clothes. The Stockpot was informal and inexpensive. Close to the cash register was a counter and a hot plate

"I'd really like you to meet Norman Parkinson ...
oh, and one Italian cheese omelette please ....."

where omelettes were prepared, each flavored to the customer's liking with exotic fillings such as Italian cheese, tomatoes, and ham. This was called the Omelette Bar. I was sometimes put there to work but did it reluctantly because my cooking was always considered suspect, and up to this point I had never made an omelette in my life.

We, the girls of slender means dreaming of potentially glamorous lives and debonair boyfriends with smart foreign cars, were generally overworked and underpaid. There were also two Cypriot chefs, both with fiery tempers, who thought us all terrible waitresses (which, for the most part, we were). So on occasion they would angrily hurl their chopping knives at us across the kitchen. Despite this, the hours were good and allowed many of us would-be models and aspiring actresses (I think the British film starlet Susannah York was one) time to attend auditions and go-sees.

Between shifts at the Stockpot, we would meet up and go to the soda fountain at Fortnum & Mason, the grand department store in Piccadilly that also carried the proud title of officially being By Royal Appointment, greengrocer to Her Majesty the Queen. There we would sit, sipping our afternoon tea, as a fashion show went on around us. It was our fashion fix! I was so amazed at how the models walked—with that precarious slant, as if they were about to topple over backward—and how they could pause, turn, and move around the little tea tables so elegantly and hold their gloves in a certain expensive manner.

I was soon deeply immersed in my two weeks of evening classes at the Cherry Marshall modeling school in Grosvenor Street, W1. Down the road in one direction, Ban the Bomb demonstrations were being orchestrated at nearby Speakers' Corner in Marble Arch by earnest Cut Nuclear Defence members in horn-rimmed glasses and duffle coats. In another, Lady Docker, the richest woman in the land, would swan

Working girl.

around Berkeley Square in her gold-plated Daimler with zebra-skin upholstery. Within barely a fortnight, I would be taught how to apply my makeup, style my own hair, and walk about elegantly in spiky stiletto shoes. In those days it was called deportment, although I don't think we balanced books on our head to keep ourselves more erect or anything like that. We also learned how to curtsy, which was useful if you were a debutante but not exactly something needed if you were not. Finally, we learned how to walk the runway, how to execute a three-point turn, and how to properly unbutton and shrug off a coat while at the same time gliding along and smiling, smiling, smiling. This was something I was never much good at. My coordination and synchronization have always been a problem. And yet somehow, at the end of my fortnight, I was signed up and placed on the agency's books.

Unlike now, when everything is done for them, a model back then had to apply her own eyeliner, shape her brows, and put on her lipstick. She also had to set and style her own hair, back-comb it and fold it into a neat chignon, or make the ends curl outward in the look of the time, the "flick-up." Makeup artists and hairdressers who specialized in photo shoots were completely nonexistent. Each model was expected to own a model bag, and what she put into it was terribly important. There was no such thing as a stylist, either, so the better your accessories, which you carried in your bag too, the more jobs you were likely to get.

My bag was huge, about the size of one of those big nylon holdalls-with-wheels that you haul onto planes these days, except, of course, mine didn't have wheels and I had to drag it everywhere. In it I put all my makeup, wigs and hairpieces, hairpins and hair lacquer, gloves of all lengths, fine stockings in beige and black, safety pins, a sewing kit, false eyelashes, false nails, nail varnish, an *A to Z of London,* a large bottle of aspirin, pennies for the phone, a book, some kind of knitting or a tapestry to while away the tedious hours of waiting, an apple, a sandwich in case there was no time for lunch, and maybe even a cheap bottle of wine if the shoot went on into the night. I carried stiletto pumps, pairs of which were likely to be beige or black (you could always tell the poorer models by their badly scuffed shoes). And I had a huge selection of costume jewelry. I always included a push-up bra, which helped me look a little more busty, and heated hair rollers. You had these if you were madly up-to-date and avant-garde, which I was.

But however well equipped you might be, as with most situations in life, friends with influence are much more useful than face powder and rouge.

A man called Tinker Patterson was often a customer at the Stockpot; he was tall and very good-looking, with a pale complexion, sandy hair, and freckles. He was a London painter as well as an in-demand part-time model, and although he already had a girlfriend, he was to become my very first affair.

Tinker invited me to spend the weekend in his delightful little rose-covered cottage in Kent. I could hardly contain my excitement at the prospect of getting out of town for a few days. We drove there on a Friday evening, chugging through the countryside in his little Austin 7, a compact British car from the 1930s that had become popular again in the economy-conscious 1950s and contained so little legroom, it would make a Mini seem spacious. When we arrived, he cooked a beautiful candlelit dinner for two, after which I was shown up to what I thought was the guest bedroom.

I undressed, put on my nightie, pulled down the top sheet, and there, neatly laid out on the pillow like one of those little chocolate mints you find in boutique hotels nowadays, was a condom. "What is this?" I wondered. I really hadn't a clue. Moments later, to my surprise, I was joined by Tinker carrying a steaming cup of cocoa and looking adorable in his stripy cotton pajamas. But his air was not that of someone about to read me a bedtime story.

Tinker regularly worked for the fashion photographer Norman Parkinson, whose pictures I had pored over back in Wales, and he told "Parks," as he was known, that he should see me. So I dressed up in my smartest Kiki Byrne two-piece, which had a cropped jacket and a box-pleat skirt that I pouffed out with some nice crisp petticoats (my secret was to wash them in sugar water to make them stiffer), and off I dashed to meet him at his studio in Glebe Place, Chelsea. When I arrived, I asked if he would like to see my portfolio (I was told by my agency that this was the thing to do). He replied, "No, I don't want to see other people's pictures of you. I'm only interested in *my* view of you." And then he said, "I have this little job at the weekend on my farm in Pishill. It's a nude photograph, if you don't mind."

Well, I only registered the word "photograph," I don't recollect why, but I guess it didn't occur to me that he meant I should take off all my clothes. Later on I did wonder whether it was the proper way to behave. Not that I was embarrassed by my body (which, now that I think of it, Tinker probably told him was pretty good), just worried about what my mother would say. To Parks, however, all I said at the time was "Okay" and off we went to take pictures of me running through the woods naked. He demonstrated what I should do. "This is what I want!" he shouted, mustache twitching as he leaped through the air from behind a

tree, a tall, gentlemanly figure wearing one
of his lucky little woven Ethiopian skullcaps.
And that was that. I think it was for an arty
fashion catalog called something like *Leaves
from the Autumn Collections*. Anyway, I had
a lovely time. It was my first modeling job.
And afterward we all went home for tea.

A model competition ran in British *Vogue* in
1959, publicized with a picture of a pretty
young girl, Nena von Schlebrügge (later to
be Uma Thurman's mother), and a caption
asking, "Could this be you?" Someone at the
Stockpot said to me, "Why don't you try this
route?" and so I did. There were four catego-

*meeting Parkinson in
my Kiki Byrne suit*

ries for entrants—one for the more mature model, called Mrs. Exeter;
categories for models in their twenties and in their thirties; and a junior
category called Young Idea. Because Cherry Marshall had previously
arranged for me to visit a photographer's studio and pose for a model
card, I had a picture of myself in pigtails wearing a big sweater and a
straw boater, so I sent that in. A few months later, a letter arrived from
Vogue informing me I was on the list of finalists and thus invited to a
formal tea party at Vogue House to meet everyone involved in the competition.

So off I trotted to Hanover Square, anxious as hell because, as I've
mentioned, I'm nervous even on the best of days. There was a long table
with tea served from giant urns and piles of cucumber sandwiches cut
into perfect little triangles. All the finalists were there, as were all the
senior editors and *Vogue* photographers, including Norman Parkinson

and an American, Don Honeyman, who, a couple of weeks before the party, had hired me for what I would call my very first fashion job. In this picture, taken with a group of girls standing on top of a vintage car, I was actually wearing clothes.

A little later it was announced which of us had won in the various categories. I won the Young Idea section. Our prizes included a photo session with *Vogue*'s top photographers, and we were allowed to keep any piece of clothing we wore in the pictures. I was photographed twice, once wearing a lovely cocktail dress and a second time fishing in rubber waders. Somehow these items never came my way.

Suddenly, everyone began asking for me. I was a success! It was truly a Cinderella moment. My mother was over the moon with excitement. I didn't go back home to visit too often in those days, but whenever I did, she proudly showed me photographs of myself snipped from various magazines. In fact, quite a few were not of me at all but of other, similar-looking girls. "That's not me," I'd tell her. But she would say, "Oh well, it's a nice photo and I like it anyway," and pop it back into my file.

My editorial rate for magazines and newspapers was two pounds a day, and my advertising rate was five pounds (although I must say I didn't get many advertising jobs). As we were often paid by the hour, we had to arrive fully made up and ready to roll. Funnily enough, though I'd only recently mastered the art of professionally applying cosmetics at Cherry Marshall's, I was booked for a *Vogue* shoot by Frank Horvat. This internationally renowned photographer preferred almost no makeup at all for the models in his pictures. If my first lesson in modeling was to "expect the unexpected," this was further confirmed when another photographer, Saul Leiter, booked me. He famously used a long lens and specialized in fashion photographs that felt uncannily like reportage. After dressing in Vogue Studios, I was told to go out into adjacent Hanover Square, where he was waiting for me. After walking around the square several times, I went back into the dressing room, distraught at having somehow missed him, only to be told that Mr. Leiter was very happy with the picture he had taken.

My contemporaries were girls like Bronwen Pugh; Sandra Paul, a classic English beauty who married a politician; and Enid Boulting, whose daughter, Ingrid, also became a famous model and went on to marry John Barry, who composed much of the music for the James Bond movies. Another contemporary, Tania Mallet, who herself was cast in a Bond film (only to be killed off after a fleeting appearance), and many of the other girls ended up marrying lords. There was a kind of *Upstairs, Downstairs* feeling to things at the time. I suppose that's why my mother didn't object so much to my going to modeling school. But the models-pursued-by-aristocrats phenomenon was not destined to last. The Profumo Affair, a sex scandal that hit the British headlines in 1963, was a sordid sensation involving government ministers, aristocrats, Soviet spies, and two call girls, Christine Keeler and Mandy Rice-Davies. They were referred to in the popular press euphemistically as "models"—which gave our profession a terrible name because, to the British public, the word "model" became pretty much synonymous with "prostitute."

Not so long after, while the establishment still reeled from the Profumo Affair, along came the snap, crackle, and mod of the sixties youthquake. Social barriers came tumbling down, and it became far cooler to go out with cheeky East End boys than public school toffs. Everything wasn't solely about privilege, title, or money anymore—although I saw it happening financially for these East End boys, too, because the ones I knew were all driving around in Rolls-Royces and Bentleys.

This was a sensational twist to the status quo. The working-class boys were much more fun. And they looked up to women. I befriended the cockney photographer Terence Donovan, who, along with his mates Brian Duffy and David Bailey—the ringleader and certainly the most famous of the three—were the likely lads at the head of the pack.

Donovan had a little studio in Knightsbridge opposite a pub called the Bunch of Grapes, and the first time I arrived on a go-see with my portfolio, he informed me he had just gotten married that day. I was so surprised that I asked, "Then why are you sitting in your studio?" To which he replied, "Well, I still like photographing pretty girls." I really adored Terry. He was funny and outrageous, cheeky and yet so wise. As he grew into a national personality, he also grew in size and became a black belt in judo. He remained a very close friend until the day he died. At his funeral, Bailey made a great speech. At one point he said, "All us working-class lads love a posh girl," then turned and looked directly at Princess Diana, who was best friends with Donovan's widow, a classy woman called DiDi.

I had a little crush on Bailey, too. It was just after he split up with the great model Jean Shrimpton. But he had a harem of pretty girls available to him and a wildly promiscuous reputation. "David Bailey Makes Love Daily" was the famously racy saying of the day, which gave us all fair warning. And yet he was so skinny and undeniably attractive, even better-looking at the time than the Beatles.

Early on, my agency sent me to Paris for an introduction to Eileen Ford, the American doyenne of all model agents. She was in France setting up deals with other agencies to expand Ford throughout Europe. Some of the better girls were sent over to meet this small, intimidating woman. I was chaperoned by my agent.

When I entered the room, the first thing she wanted to know was why I didn't possess a waist cincher (a wide elasticized belt), followed by the

With my original eyebrows in a picture taken on winning the British Vogue *model competition. Photo: Norman Parkinson, 1959. © Norman Parkinson Limited / Courtesy Norman Parkinson Archive*

LONG SHORT EVENING DRESS
IN WHITE WITH
A PINK AND WHITE
CHECKED APRON SASH

Dress, copied from
an Esterel model, 25 gns.,
Woollands. Shoes to order,
Woollands. Dinner jacket
from Connock & Lockie,
54 New Oxford St., W.C.1

An early job for British Vogue. *Photo: Frank Horvat, 1960. Courtesy
of Vogue © The Condé Nast Publications Ltd.*

With the Chelsea Set in British Vogue. *Photo: Frank Horvat, 1960.*
Courtesy of Vogue © The Condé Nast Publications Ltd.

Dressed to the nines in couture for British Harper's Bazaar. *Photo: Richard Dormer, 1962. Courtesy of Harper's Bazaar UK*

On British Harper's Bazaar'*s cover. Photo: Richard Dormer, 1962. Courtesy of Harper's Bazaar UK*

My first British Vogue *cover. Photo: Peter Carapetian, 1962. Courtesy of* Vogue © *The Condé Nast Publications Ltd.*

Playing a fashionable mum for British Vogue. *Photo: Frances McLaughlin-Gill, 1962. Courtesy of Vogue © The Condé Nast Publications Ltd.*

Feeling sophisticated in British Vogue. *Photo: Helmut Newton, 1964.*
Courtesy of Vogue © The Condé Nast Publications Ltd.

With my new Vidal Sassoon haircut in a Paris hammam for Mademoiselle. *Photo: Marc Hispard, 1965*

Giving a wink on French Elle's *thousandth issue. Photo: Fouli Elia, 1965. Courtesy of Elle France*

A futuristic look in Queen *magazine. Photo: Marc Hispard, 1967*

Meeting Eileen Ford

oh these English girls, so unprofessional,
no sweater bra, no waist cinch. FAT! FAT! FAT!
...and off with those eyebrows

whereabouts of my sweater bra, which is a bra without seams to keep a cleaner line under your clothes. She then told me she didn't think I had what it took to be a successful runway model anyway. To see if I could possibly look any better in fashion photos, she personally came at me with a pair of tweezers and plucked my eyebrows (they used to be dramatically heavy) into a thin arch—only to afterward declare me unfit material for fashion photographs as well. For goodness' sake, I was five feet nine, with an eighteen-inch waist, thirty-three-inch bust and hips, and long legs—and *Vogue* loved me. How bad could I honestly be?

Back at the London agency, they at least recognized that I had perfectly nice hair. I was sent to a celebrity hairdresser of the 1950s called Teasy-Weasy, who was famous enough to make cameo appearances as himself in several British films of the period, had a camp pencil mustache, and whose real name was Raymond. He said he would make me fabulous. He didn't; he dyed my hair white-blond, cut the sides short, and left the back long, all of which gave me a frumpy, lopsided look. It was awful. I was then sent to Snowdon (known in those days as the society photographer Antony Armstrong-Jones and just about to become engaged to Princess Margaret) to do some test shots. After that, Teasy-Weasy dyed my hair yet again—a kind of red this time, which looked even worse than before. At this juncture it began to fall out and had to be cut very short to get rid of the color. Abandoning Teasy-Weasy, I defected to Vidal Sassoon in Bond Street, which was the best thing I ever did.

Vidal was an East End boy who had been brought up in an orphanage from which he kept running away. He had spent time on a kibbutz and later paid a voice coach to get rid of his incomprehensible cockney accent. By now he had transformed himself into a hip and happening hairdresser with neat hair and shiny shoes, fastidiously groomed in a

Beatles-style suit, who had recently opened his own sensational new hair salon—a cool, jazzy place with big plate-glass windows so that people passing by could see the clients inside having their hair styled—all of which back then was shockingly different. He also employed a lot of uncouth lads in the salon who, after cutting the customers' hair, took them upstairs and attempted to shag them.

In the fifties, hairdressers had been very, very gay. Vidal changed all that. He employed hip young people like Leonard and another called Rafael, who was outrageous and within minutes had his hand up your skirt.

I was a "character" rather than a pretty model, and I suppose that's exactly what I look for in the girls I now select to put in American *Vogue*—the ones who are quirky-looking. English girls have so much individuality. I can't stand all the sappy blondes, or athletic girls with too much of a tan. I like freckles. I like girls such as Karen Elson from Manchester, with her amazingly pale face and mass of red hair that reminds me of . . . well, I can't think! I pick my models as if I were casting a film, because I'm choosing a girl to play a role. I don't like it when they complain, but I'm happy to look after them when they don't. I do feel for them if it's too hot or too cold. I always check to see if they are too tired to continue. Some are okay in a group. Others fall to pieces if there's another girl in the picture. I try not to put them in dangerous situations—like when some stupid photographer tries to pose them on a wall with a hundred-foot drop on the side.

What makes it difficult today is how hard it is to get time on the caliber of girl I'm going for. They all have huge, lucrative advertising contracts they can't get out of, and even the lure of *Vogue* simply can't compete. Some, like Daria Werbowy, hate modeling. But she's so stunningly beautiful, I have to catch her when she's in the mood to work. Unfortunately, she loves sailing and doesn't put into port too often. The Russian model Natalia Vodianova is a dream, with her faraway gray-blue eyes. Inconveniently, she keeps having babies—although I'm always happy to utilize them as beautiful props in my pictures when they are old enough.

Linda Evangelista was always a fantastic model, although when she famously said that she wouldn't wake up for less than ten thousand dollars . . . well!! She was always a little militant, organizing the other girls, telling them to walk out if the conditions weren't right. But you must admit that Linda is special, because even now, twenty years after her supermodel heyday, she still looks amazing and brings the same enthusiasm and something extra to all her photo shoots.

I first met her way before she cut her hair short, a move that skyrocketed her career, then dyed it blond or red at the drop of a hat. Then, she was just a long-haired Canadian brunette working with the French photographer Alex Chatelain. One night we all went out to dinner and I took along my nephew Tristan, who at the time was a sixteen-year-old schoolboy. He became so besotted with Linda that he and Alex were both coming on to her long before the meal was over.

Naomi Campbell is a beautiful enigma, difficult sometimes but unique. She was fifteen when I first met her. I brought her from England to America to work with the photographer Arthur Elgort for a session based on dance because she was said to have had formal ballet training. But Arthur, who is something of a balletomane, was having none of it. "This girl has no more had ballet training than I have been to the moon," he said, and kept up a string of complaints about her stance and poor footwork and the way she scrunched her shoulders. Afterward she met Steven Meisel, and the rest is history.

my beatnik look
with beehive hair-do

Kristen McMenamy was another great star, a model who has sustained remarkable longevity. With her cool, stately looks, she has the stylized quality of a 1950s couture model, but in front of the camera she always manages to look truly modern. Christy Turlington was and still is an out-of-this-world beauty from whichever angle you photograph her. She is probably the most beautiful model I have ever seen.

I also love the Puerto Rican American model/actress Talisa Soto; Twiggy, of course; and the strange-looking American girl Wallis Franken, who married the eighties fashion designer Claude Montana and suffered a mysterious death. The model turned Academy Award–winning actress Anjelica Huston was an all-time favorite, with her wicked sense of humor. And Uma Thurman, another fifteen-year-old infant model, like Naomi in her time, was a beauty with incredibly wide-set, hypnotic eyes and very strong opinions.

I think it was the photographer John Cowan who nicknamed me "The Cod." You know, Jean Shrimpton was known as "The Shrimp," so therefore . . . I thought it was quite charming at the time because usually, only a model as iconic as Shrimpton was given a nickname, although I must say that "shrimp" sounds a lot better than "cod." Cowan worked in a reportage style and is best known for the fashion pictures he took in the sixties of his athletic-looking blond model/girlfriend Jill Kennington doing amazingly risky things like perching on the tip of an iceberg or standing on top of a high statue. I worked with him quite a bit at the beginning, and he photographed me waiting at a bus stop in a bikini or arranged on the cold marble of a fishmonger's slab.

I was appearing in a lot of British hair shows for Vidal Sassoon who, in a short span of time, had become internationally famous for his abstract geometric styles. I went to him all the time and was one of his muses for the Sassoon Look. He even created one special, super-modern style on me called the Five Point Cut.

We used to drink and dance till dawn in those early days but had the youthful stamina to bounce back in the morning. I would quickly change out of my fancy dancing dress, then rush off to do some job hauling my enormous bag of accessories. James Gilbert, an account executive and keen amateur aviator, was now my boyfriend, and he took me flying practically every weekend. He flew flimsy open-top biplanes called Tiger Moths, with me in the passenger seat in front of the pilot wearing a flying helmet and goggles as we popped across the Channel for lunch, often to the small French coastal town of Berck. Or he would take me through a series of hair-raising dives and loop-the-loops, shouting, "This is rather fun!" while I sat there staring at my terrified face, distorted by gravity, reflected back at me from the speedometer. He never did any of this on the journey back from France, though, for fear of losing his meal. Then one day, just as my career started seriously to take flight, we had a terrible car accident.

It was twilight and raining. He went through a red light in Eaton Square, Belgravia, one of the most exclusive residential areas of London, and rammed straight into a passing delivery van. I smashed my face in the driving mirror, and my left eyelid was sliced off. Luckily, they found my eyelashes.

I must have been thrown clear of the wreckage because I woke up on the side of the road in the arms of a policeman, bleeding all over him. My leg was injured, too, and losing blood, so they had to cut open my favorite skinny pants to treat it. I was rushed to the emergency room and remember hearing the wail of the ambulance siren all the way there. At the hospital, they wouldn't let me look in the mirror. When James saw me, he nearly fainted.

I was taken into the operating theater to be sewn up, and although I was still in deep shock, I remember chatting with the doctor and telling him I was a model. At which point he decided to take out all the stitches he had already sewn into my eyelid and start again, making them much smaller and neater. I was horrified. Even if I wasn't a model, shouldn't I be getting the best treatment possible?

After that I didn't really work again for two years. I lived on very little, which was okay because I'm quite frugal. My friends were extremely generous and they all looked after me, and my mother even managed to send me a little extra money. I did odd jobs for John Cowan around his photographic studio. Terry Donovan was particularly kind. He gave me any small modeling assignment he could, shooting me from the side or the back.

I had five plastic surgery operations over two years. I hid my scars behind huge dark glasses—fortunately, Jackie Kennedy was making them popular at the time, so I didn't look too out of place. But perhaps because they remind me so much of that painful period, I now have a total aversion to wearing sunglasses.

Little by little I started working again. I developed a new look for my eye makeup, using large quantities of black eye shadow, shading and blending it into the sockets. And people liked it, although, admittedly, it was a form of camouflage, a way of hiding the damage.

Eventually, I did a few fashion shows, dancing the twist along the catwalk for Mary Quant. By now she had a new shop in Knightsbridge.

It was very small, but she would hold her presentations there anyway. You had to come down a flight of perilously steep stairs and onto a runway that was all of four feet long. I did more hair shows for Vidal Sassoon, too, who required us girls to shake our heads like little wet puppies to show how his revolutionary technique allowed the hair to fall back instantly into place. But James's insurance company had by then gone bankrupt, and I couldn't afford to pay my doctors' expenses.

Things had not worked out quite as I had planned.

III

ON THE FASHIONABLE LIFE

In which
England swings,
France goes
yé-yé, miniskirts
rule, discos go
kapow, and pop
art makes
a lovely seat.

Although my position as creative director allows me to do fashion shoots in practically every corner of the globe, I've rarely taken the opportunity to return to London since moving to New York almost thirty years ago. In fact, I can think of only a handful of occasions when I've developed a fashion story that specifically had to be shot back in Britain. Do I somehow suffer from a mysterious aversion to my British past? Certainly, these days I seem to spend far more time arranging photographic sessions just across the Channel, where Paris always makes for a delightful location.

Recently I did, however, crisscross the ocean several times to work in the English countryside, once to do a story based on the remake of the film *Brighton Rock,* and then for a fashion story in Cornwall inspired by Steven Spielberg's film of the hit British play *War Horse.* And I must

" St Tropez here we come ! "

admit I was overcome with unashamed nostalgia for the landscape's wild, romantic beauty. There really are nothing like English fields, woods, gardens, and flowers for providing a background with magical effects. On the last occasion, I also revisited the Kings Road in Chelsea, which in the early sixties had been my home territory and the center of my fashion universe. From World's End to Sloane Square, this sentimental journey led me past the building where, as a young model, I first graduated to my very own flat, the pub where my social group—the Chelsea Set—regularly hung out, and the places once occupied by the bustling Italian restaurants and coffee bars that fueled us all between boutique spending sprees. The quaintness is no longer there, the pavements have been widened, and much of the shop frontage has been modernized—and not in a pretty way. Yet in the little side streets I could still detect quirky pockets of charm and character.

As we walked on, at one point it became obvious that I was being stalked by two whispering schoolboys. Fidgeting and nervous, they kept pace with us, throwing long, meaningful glances over at me and nudging each other. It surprised me, not just to think that my five minutes of fame brought about by *The September Issue* also resonated in England, but that I now even mattered to prepubescent boys who should be off playing football or cricket. "So what did they want?" I asked my dinner companion, who had gone over to see if they were expecting an autograph. "They thought you were Vivienne Westwood," he said.

Fifty years prior to this ego-crushing moment found me finally moving out of my first London rental in fractious Notting Hill and relocating to the relative calm of Battersea, just across the river from Chelsea. There, along with three Chinese actresses, I shared a flat on Prince of Wales Drive overlooking the rolling green acres, fun fair, and rhododendron bushes of Battersea Park. I then moved house about another hundred times before eventually settling in Royal Avenue in the center of Chelsea, which was very cool.

I knew just about everyone on the street. To me it was totally like a little village and had no connection with anywhere else. I hung out at all the Kings Road hot spots, which were full of experimental young artists, writers, people working in advertising agencies, fashion, and film, and I found it all madly existential. I saw many movies around this time because a lot of my friends appeared in them. I particularly loved the gritty new-wave British films from that period: *A Taste of Honey, A Kind of Loving, Saturday Night and Sunday Morning, Whistle Down the Wind.* I was even offered a part in one. The English director Tony Richardson, who was for a time married to the actress Vanessa Redgrave, picked me up one day as I strolled barefoot (I was being offbeat) along the Kings Road and asked me to be in his film version of John Osborne's stage play *The Entertainer,* starring Sir Laurence Olivier. It was a fun party scene full of modern-day debutantes, and I was required to tumble off a low roof into a rose bed, land on top of Vanessa's brother, the actor Corin Redgrave, and kiss him, which I did—although my bit was cut out of the film.

I also spent many hours decorating my various apartments, painting the walls plummy purple or dark blue, buying brightly patterned rugs and chunky Spanish/Mexican pottery from a shop called Casa Pupo in Pimlico, and seeking out must-have items like stripped pine tables and Welsh dressers from the parade of secondhand furniture shops along the New Kings Road. This was very much a thing of the time, applauded as a sign of one's ineffable taste by the color supplements that had started to accompany the Sunday newspapers. Later, when I traveled abroad on my magazine trips, I would shop in Africa, picking up tin plates in Nairobi, or return home with lots of colorful objects from Russia or linen from China. In Sri Lanka, I even became obsessed with the circular mosquito nets, which I found soft and romantic. Everywhere I went, I bought something else and invariably had to buy extra suitcases to carry my haul back home.

The artistic Chelsea people I usually ran around with congregated each evening at the Markham Arms, a rowdy pub next door to Bazaar, Mary Quant's Kings Road boutique, where I became a serious shopper—there and at Kiki Byrne, farther down the Kings Road. These were two of the first clothes shops in England to be called "boutiques," and two of my favorites. The fresh designs that changed every week were strictly for younger customers and nothing at all like the items for "young grown-ups" carried by the bigger stores that were simply clothes for mature women scaled down for teenagers.

Mary Quant's clothes were extremely popular. She was very advanced, ushering in the swinging sixties with her modern looks. I bought a sleeveless striped Quant dress with a low-slung belt and a short skirt that you could wear either over a skinny sweater or by itself. It had the kind of versatility that led me to wear it time and again, accessorized with extremely pointy shoes with kitten heels. As the "Mary Quant Look" spread and skirts rose higher and higher until they were little more than skimpy pelmets of fabric, there was a big problem with going upstairs on double-decker buses without showing your knickers or—even more disgracefully—your stocking tops and garter belt. So Mary began making little shorts to wear under her dresses. And then she revolutionized fashion once more by fostering the tights industry.

As it went on to become the very hub of London hipness, the Kings

Road became crowded with achingly smart Italian restaurants, as well as the groovy and popular coffee bars the Sa Tortuga and the Fantasie, and impossibly bright boutiques with trendy names like Top Gear and Countdown. These were co-owned by Pat Booth, a brash blond model from the East End of London who cleverly sank her earnings into the boutique business along with her boyfriend, James Wedge, a gifted milliner.

Despite its supremacy being challenged for a while by the West End's Carnaby Street, in the period when it buzzed with mod boutiques and mod teenagers on fancy scooters, the Kings Road remained the more natural haunt of rock aristocrats, international jet setters, and long-haired movie stars—and stayed that way for approximately the next thirty years.

Fashion became of even greater significance to me at the height of the sixties, when I began regularly flying to Paris for work. By then my eye was pretty much healed and I was back to working full-time. I had become fairly well known in British modeling circles, always included on top ten lists—but inevitably creeping in at number nine because I was considered avant-garde and fashionable rather than pretty. My nickname of "The Cod" had caught on. "Cold as a codfish but hot as a four-bar fire," trilled the headline of a personal profile in a now-defunct tabloid called *The Daily Sketch,* which I must say I kind of loved as it made me out to be sizzling and sexy, whereas I was more often viewed as kind of the opposite.

I started appearing in French *Elle,* which was then enjoying a reputation as a really good fashion magazine, and stayed in either a cheap little hotel decorated with chintzy wallpaper just off the Place de la Madeleine, or another, called the France et Choiseul in the rue St.-Honoré, that has evolved into the trendy and extremely noisy Hôtel Costes.

Since I was a new girl in town, my French agency, Paris Planning, sent me off on endless go-sees, where I was frequently pushed to the end of a long line of chattering and snooty French models, most of whom wouldn't give me the time of day. And when I did find work—such as at Elle Studios, which employed a number of photographers who could each use you for a couple of hours—the girls would disappear at lunchtime without saying where they were going. I would sit there, cold-shouldered and starving in the dressing room, wondering where they were until they returned, replenished and refreshed. It turned out that Elle Studios had a cafeteria, but they failed to tell me about it. It was a bit like being in one of those blackly humorous Jacques Tati films, so popular at the time, full of social misfortune resulting from snotty French bloody-mindedness.

I soon discovered that the Bar des Théâtres in the avenue Montaigne was the absolute meeting place for career-hungry models and eager photographers. By now I could afford more than "le sandwich." My budget would even stretch to "le hamburger" and a glass of the new Beaujolais or "vin ordinaire." Along the way I also managed to acquire a devilishly handsome new boyfriend. Albert Koski was a photographers' agent with long, dark romantic hair. He was a Polish Jew who dressed beautifully in tailored white Mao-style suits made by Farouche, and was often mistaken for Warren Beatty. I found him deeply seductive and quickly became crazy about him. I went to live with him in a beautiful house in rue Dufrenoy, just off the avenue Victor Hugo, with a small beautiful garden and a large beautiful cat, a great big tabby called Titov.

Parisians can be mean-spirited. Although we had a maid, I sometimes looked forward to stepping out of the house to buy provisions myself—only to find that the shop owners were (and still are) so rude and dismissive, particularly in our exclusive corner of the sixteenth arrondissement, that if you didn't speak perfect French they would just walk off, not bothering to listen or help you, saying things like "Bah!" or "Pah!" And whenever I took a cab, in the end, rather than trying to speak the language, I resorted to writing my destination down on a piece of paper as if I were living in Japan, although, of course, Albert would simply shrug dismissively and say, "If you can't take the French, don't try living here."

Twice a year, in January and July, my photo sessions were mainly taken up with French couture, which was traditionally shot through the night. Well-heeled clients needed to view the clothes at the couturiers' salons during the day, making them entirely unavailable any earlier for photographs. Even when modeling in the wee small hours of the morning, I was expected to show an appropriately haughty attitude. As the inimitable American fashion oracle and editor Diana Vreeland would say, "A little more languor in the lips."

But with the arrival of cheaper, mass-produced clothes—later known as "ready to wear"—we models had the freedom to express ourselves and behave in a more dynamically modern fashion. The clothes were younger and had more ease, allowing for movement rather than the ladylike restriction of couture. Makeup evolved in many eye-catching ways, too. An intense focus on the eyes was now the absolute thing: They had to be more expressive and dramatic and were known as "panda" eyes. The thin line across the top of the lid that in the fifties flicked up at the corners in a little comma became thick and smudged, curving down instead.

Each girl had her own individual style when it came to piling on the eye makeup. My particular thing was to draw an extra-wide stroke emphasizing the crease of the eye socket and add extravagantly long, spidery lines below the eye, a little like doll's lashes, then paint a dot toward the inner corner of the eye for reasons I can't exactly articulate except that it looked nice and "now." Later I discovered my crazy new eyelash look being called "twiglets" and credited to the young British model Twiggy. Well, they were very much mine. I was probably doing them before she was born!

Clothes were sporty, zippy, sensationally short. The modern look in fashion photographs was to be either wide-eyed, hyper-energetic, and in a hysterical rush, or floppy and passive, with knees together and feet turned in like a rag doll with badly stitched legs.

It was a wildly gregarious time for me, unlike today, when I prefer a quieter life and rarely go out to dinner with more than one other person. Albert and I never went to Maxim's or most places on the Right Bank because even back then they were considered "old" and "stuffy." Instead we liked to be seen at the Café Flore in St.-Germain, which was smokily packed with exciting young artists. We ate just across the road from the Flore at traditional bistros like Brasserie Lipp, with its Germanic, meat-heavy cuisine. Sometimes I would be taken as an extravagance to Caviar Kaspia, admittedly on the Right Bank in the Place de la Madeleine, but where the caviar is the best in Paris—and which remains completely unchanged. It has the same low-lit, old-fashioned, wood-paneled decor with glittering chandeliers and oil paintings of Russian sleigh rides and, to my mind, pretty much the same waiters, except that today it's far more a place where the noisy, screeching fashion crowd gathers at collection times. Back then it was totally hushed and suffocatingly bourgeois, a hideaway for many an elderly French businessman or right-wing politician to indulge a mistress as a treat.

The other place the fashion crowd flocked to back then was La Coupole, a massive art deco brasserie in the middle of Montparnasse that had been open since the 1920s. I first went with Max Maxwell, the art director of *Queen* magazine, and we joined a group that included Albert Koski, which is how we first met. I loved La Coupole. I could satisfy my weakness for *crevettes grises,* my favorite dish, prominently displayed among mountains of mussels, oysters, and crayfish on the extravagantly ice-packed *fruits de mer* counter in the entrance. There was a section on the right where all the fashion people sat, and where Albert and I would eat with the photographers he represented—Jeanloup Sieff, Marc Hispard, Art Kane, James Moore, Ronald Traeger, and Just Jaeckin (who later made the original *Emmanuelle* soft-porn film).

Dotted about La Coupole you could really see Paris in the raw, including shaky old parchment-faced French patrons who obviously hadn't missed a day of eating there since it first opened. Sometimes, if they were particularly impressed or amused by how you looked or what you wore, they would clap as you passed their tables. The most exotic, exceptional people entering through the swing doors—like the statuesque German model Veruschka and her Italian photographer companion Franco Rubartelli, or swinging London's Jean Shrimpton and David Bailey—would garner extra applause. Paris was crawling with models and their relatives, boyfriends, and hangers-on, because at that time the fashion scene wasn't just concentrated around collections time; it was fashion central all year round.

I had taken driving lessons at an early age in Wales, learning to zoom around one of the old abandoned airfields when I was about sixteen. And later—quite soon after my accident, strangely enough—I had passed my test in Central London driving barefoot, which I'm told is illegal in some countries. But even though I constantly raced through

London in my souped-up Mini, in Paris I didn't dare drive. The French, and the Parisians in particular, seem to me to have a suicidal disregard for road rules. I felt I would be taking my life into my hands if I even sat behind the wheel. I tried once, and managed to get halfway round the Arc de Triomphe before stopping the car and jumping out, screaming, "I can't go on!" Oh my God, it was terrifying—like being in the bumper cars at a fun fair, but far more hair-raising and dangerous.

Albert and I would aim to be at Le Drugstore in the Champs Elysées on a Saturday around midnight to buy the early editions of the English Sunday newspapers. Every other night, we could be found dancing (to a twitchy form of early French pop music called yé-yé) until dawn in the fashionable club New Jimmy's, before rushing off to work the next morning. I wore extra-small children's sweaters in Shetland wool purchased at Scott Adie in London that were all the rage among the French fashion elite, and very, very tight Newman jeans (you had to lie on the floor and energetically wriggle your way into them) that were made of paper-thin cotton velvet or needlecord and came in a huge range of wonderful colors. At the time they could be bought only from one little shop in a back street off the boulevard St.-Germain that was regularly packed with fans. I also shopped at the *Elle* boutique, which was new and completely cool. *Elle* magazine photographed select outfits, then put them into their boutique for one week to stimulate demand. My penchant for wearing super-modern, very short miniskirts was much tut-tutted by the easily disapproving French, whose fashionable and what they considered far more tasteful "mini-kilts" fell discreetly to the knee.

My idol was a French model, Nicole de Lamargé, who was very chic and also wore "le mini-kilt." She was the girlfriend of the photographer and *Elle* art director Peter Knapp and was known as the models' model. She was an extraordinary chameleon who could seem absolutely nondescript until she put on her makeup, and always ended up looking a dream. When it came to creating her own look, she was very sure of herself. And her personal style really typified *Elle*. It was modern, breezy, and approachable, introducing a fresh, positive, and upbeat note to the pages of the magazine. Nicole was the Linda Evangelista of her day but unfortunately died young in a car accident.

I derived a completely different, far more sophisticated sense of clothes from living among the Parisiennes and working for magazines like *Elle* and French *Vogue*—which was the one we models secretly longed to appear in, since Europe's two best-known fashion photographers, Helmut Newton and Guy Bourdin, worked for it. I was also soon made aware of the way fashion dictates style and how rapidly trends can come and go. Albert had an E-Type Jag that we drove down to Saint-Tropez every weekend; or we would put it on the train. We stayed just above the port in a small *pension* called La Ponche, took our *café complet* on the narrow balcony outside our room each morning, and rode our VeloSolex (a basic kind of moped) to the most fashionable beaches, either Pampelonne or Club 55 but more often Moorea, owned by Félix, man about Saint-Tropez and the proprietor of its chicest restaurant, L'Escale, in the port.

I sunbathed in the latest Eres swimwear made from a recently developed feather-light Lycra, but I refused to go topless even though it was the fashion of the day, thanks to Brigitte Bardot and the entirely relaxed attitude of the Saint-Tropez beaches. However, you needed to sunbathe and get at least a little bit brown, otherwise you couldn't compete with anyone. So I suppose I thought I was getting a tan when I was actually going bright red, peeling, and burnt!

Saint-Tropez was super-social. We cruised around in our smart gray E-type, meeting up with friends like the film actress Catherine Deneuve and her new husband, David Bailey; Lord and Lady Rendlesham; and Ali MacGraw (before she started acting) and her boyfriend Jordan Kalfus, manager of the well-known American photographer Jerry Schatzberg. At other times we headed over to the house of the English photographer David Hamilton, the same one that appears in all his erotic pictures of very young girls.

I was astonished by how fashion could change so fast in a few days. You would go to the South of France one weekend and denim was in. The next weekend when you returned, everything was about little English florals. I used to get so worried that I hadn't got it right. Catherine Deneuve and her sister Françoise Dorléac were the only ones I ever saw actually wearing the hard-edged space-age clothes of Courrèges and Paco Rabanne and looking completely at ease and relaxed. Except perhaps the evening when Catherine was sitting enjoying herself with Bailey, Albert, and me in the club Régine's and the waiter spilled an entire bottle of red wine over her new white sculpted Courrèges couture shift that must have cost thousands of francs.

If you went to L'Esquinade wearing the wrong thing, it was critical. You would be laughed at. They could be pretty bitchy, those fashion-mad French girls. I would never dare talk back to them about clothes or food. For me, the French were always so superior in matters of style. England was cool but never chic.

During this particular moment I was very into the angular designs of Pierre Cardin, so my dressmaker would run me up copies of Cardin couture. Emmanuelle Khanh, Dorothée Bis, V de V, and Christiane Bailly were among the absolute leaders of the new French ready-to-wear designers. Their clothes were accessible, short, and of the moment, in highly technological new fabrics like PVC and printed stretch jersey, which turned up a lot as hooded catsuits.

Throughout much of my Paris period, I commuted back and forth to London for work. At home, a major women's lib movement was under way. Everything was connected to the Pill. And everyone without exception was listening to the Beatles' *Sgt. Pepper's Lonely Hearts Club Band*. Words like "far out" and "heavy" were in common currency. I would run around each night in my fashionable French gear to seriously trendy clubs like the Ad Lib, off Leicester Square, with a fast crowd that included the actors Michael Caine and Terence Stamp, the photographers Duffy, Donovan, and Bailey, and people in vogue like Jane Birkin, Pattie Boyd, Rudolf Nureyev, Marianne Faithfull, Roman Polanski, the Beatles, the Rolling Stones, and various other rock groups who came and, equally suddenly, went. I don't remember ever getting completely blotto, though. It scares me to be that much out of control. So in situations involving a great deal of alcohol, I somehow managed to simply stop drinking and go home. After one wild night, I remember accepting a lift from Polanski. He stopped short at his house and tried dragging me inside. I escaped but had to walk the rest of the way back to my place.

The other thing that never hooked me was drugs. Some years later, in the early days of New York's decadent Studio 54, I was on the dance floor when a famous American film actor tried shoving poppers up my nose. That was horrible. Uppers and downers seemed stupid, too. And even though I don't mind being a bit relaxed, joints never did it for me either.

I kept my small rented apartment in West London Studios to use when I was not with Albert in Paris. The old brick building was popular with a number of successful young photographers, one of whom, Eric Swayne, was a particular friend who made a habit of dating the most eligible girls in London, such as the leggy model Pattie Boyd before she married the Beatle George Harrison, and Jane Birkin before she got together with the French singer Serge Gainsbourg. Eric was equally friendly with cool, newly famous folk like Keith Richards and Mick Jagger of the Rolling Stones. They sometimes came over and hung out in my studio. One afternoon not long after I had moved in, Mick had come over and started making out with me. But just as it was about to get interesting and I began thinking, "Here I am, kissing THE Mick Jagger," the telephone rang—it was Albert, whom I had not yet started dating, inviting me to Paris for the weekend—and the moment passed. A quick fling with Mick Jagger would have been one thing, but Albert was someone I felt I could really have a future with.

The studios were next to the grounds of Chelsea football club. The team usually played at home on Tuesday and Saturday afternoons, so on those days my entire neighborhood became overrun with charged-up fans. Chelsea was a notoriously aggressive team with a hard core of supporters, something I hadn't factored in as a potential problem when I took the apartment, although the seething roar of the crowds in the stadium next door might have provided a clue. I therefore shouldn't have been surprised when, driving home one afternoon on a visit to London from Paris, I ran into an especially nasty bunch milling about outside my door. The police were attempting to close off the road. Crash barriers were being erected. No matter how gently I tried inching my car through the mob, they grew more and more incensed until all of a sudden my little Mini, with me inside, was lifted off the ground and thrown heavily on its side. Although I wasn't injured, I was seven months pregnant by Albert at the time, and the next day I suffered a miscarriage. This turned out to be the only time in my life that I was able to conceive. The incident was one of the most traumatic of my life.

Although the late sixties were predominantly about Paris for me, there were events that frequently brought Albert—who had an office in Mount

Street, Mayfair—and me back to England. By then we had also acquired a London pied-à-terre together, a modern penthouse apartment in Ennismore Gardens, Kensington. It had a spacious terrace and large French windows with acres of glass. (This I will never forget because we owned a ginger tom who would run at them and bash his head, thinking he could get out onto the balcony. Then one day the window was left open when the cat ran at it and . . .)

The apartment was beautiful, but it never felt like a home to me. And though we were engaged for a while, Albert ended up spending most of his time in France, while I began to realize how much I preferred London.

My Paris moment had lasted four, maybe five years, during which time I had gone from having fairly long hair to a daringly short, drastic pixie cut—very much a copy of Mia Farrow's in Roman Polanski's hit film *Rosemary's Baby*. Now the time had arrived for me to bid a final adieu. I was to leave France considerably wiser about clothes, and not a little bitter about false relationships and infidelities.

I soon learned that Albert, my handsome fiancé—the ring, appropriately enough, was in the shape of a snake—had been conducting a lengthy affair directly under my nose with Catherine Deneuve's sister Françoise Dorléac. This continued right up until her untimely death, when her car burst into flames on the road to Nice airport. She was rumored to have been on her way back to Paris to beg him to marry her when she was killed.

I was in bed with Albert the morning the phone call came through, telling him that she had died. So he didn't lose just her at that moment. He lost me, too.

I was heading toward twenty-seven or twenty-eight years old, and though I was still a model, I knew, upon my return to living in Britain, that I wanted something more. I recognized I would have to turn away from modeling before long. It was not so enjoyable anyway, the peripatetic lifestyle, the constant jumping on and off planes, the odd working and eating hours. Also, younger and younger girls were coming into fashion, like the slightly androgynous, fresh-faced teenager Lesley Hornby, who was given a short bobbed haircut by my friend and Sassoon protégé Leonard, and launched on the world as Twiggy. I thought I had a couple more seasons left in front of the camera, but then, while I was being photographed in a London studio for *Queen* magazine, the formidably outspoken Lady Clare Rendlesham, a recent defector from *Vogue,* regarded me closely and said, "Grace, you should be a fashion editor. You're too old to be a model." Of course she was right. She asked me if I would like to join her at *Queen,* an idea that had never crossed my mind before and wouldn't have if it weren't suggested by someone of Clare's stature. She may have had a reputation for being a bit of a dragon, but the woman was very clued up about fashion. She was, in fact, the first editor in England to embrace the groundbreaking modernist designers of Paris such as Courrèges and Paco Rabanne.

Though I didn't accept, I realized Clare was completely correct about my instinct for

With the chefs from Mr Chow Restaurant.

styling. I was opinionated and always thought I knew better than most of the people whose job it was. And now, after living in Paris and with my newly acquired French assuredness, it was truer than ever. In photo sessions, I increasingly found myself reaching into my model bag and saying things like "I just bought these Charles Jourdan shoes. Maybe they would work better with this outfit" or "I think these Paco Rabanne earrings could help a bit."

Meanwhile, my personal life in London was looking good. After my breakup with Albert, I was about to enter into a serious relationship with Michael Chow, the soon-to-be-famous restaurateur.

Michael was charming, dapper, and very attractive. We had first met many years earlier when I was sharing the flat in Prince of Wales Drive, Battersea, with three Chinese actresses, one of whom was his sister, Tsai Chin. She and Michael were born in Shanghai and came from a large, highly cultured family. Their father was a legendary grand master of the Peking Opera, and in 1952 his parents sent Michael and Tsai to be educated in England. All three flatmates were in the stage production of *The World of Suzie Wong,* and Michael had a small part in it, too.

I was walking along the Kings Road when I bumped into him again. He had come from having lunch with Alvaro, who at that moment was the most celebrated restaurateur in town. "Do you want to see my new project?" Michael asked.

He took me to a building site in Knightsbridge. Everything was under construction. He explained that the concept was a Chinese restaurant with Italian waiters, because traditionally, they were much friendlier than the Chinese. He was also going to make the decor cleaner and much more modern, because most Chinese restaurants in London's East End and Soho at that time were far from glamorous; more like cheap canteens with tables crammed together to accommodate the large Chinese families who were their primary patrons. And he opted for Pekingese cuisine, not Cantonese. In short, he wanted an attractive environment where he could eat his own food. He took Sandro, a waiter from Alvaro's, to be his headwaiter, went to Hong Kong to seek out his chefs, and housed them in glamorous lodgings off Cadogan Square, not far from the new premises.

It was a sunny day. Michael is very impulsive. We had dinner, spent the night, and pretty much right away I moved into his apartment above a bank in Chiswick High Road. He shared it with the pop singer turned filmmaker Mike Sarne, who directed the legendarily awful *Myra Breckinridge,* starring Raquel Welch.

Michael was the first person I ever met who could genuinely be called a multitasker: actor, restaurateur, painter. He also studied architecture. Before I came along, he was dating a hairdresser with a salon in Sloane Avenue on the cusp of South Kensington and Knightsbridge. He had redesigned her space quite beautifully, but then she left him.

Living with Michael opened my eyes to a new kind of lifestyle: total minimalism. His apartment was as stark as an igloo, with none of the clutter and memorabilia that I, as a typical British girl, was used to living with. I remember seeing that there was hardly a knife or fork in the place, it was that extreme. But in the end the lack of possessions was beguiling, and I began to appreciate how cleansing it was to live this simply. Almost as if to cement our relationship, Michael and I had by this time also traded in both our cars and bought a Rolls-Royce Silver Cloud in beige and cream. It was very serious, and very fun.

Despite Clare Rendlesham's offer for me to join *Queen,* my sights were firmly set on my longtime favorite, *Vogue.* Marit Allen was the cool, in-the-know editor of British *Vogue*'s Young Idea section and the wife of Sandy Lieberson, who produced the extraordinary film *Performance,* starring Mick Jagger and James Fox. She set up a job interview for me with Beatrix (Bea) Miller, British *Vogue*'s new editor in chief, who had recently been poached from *Queen*. The two of us talked over lunch at Trattoria Terrazza in Soho. Bea touched lightly on many fashion subjects. She was also curious to know what my academic credentials were, and she seemed far more interested in what I was reading than in what I was wearing. Was I, for example, familiar with anything by her friend the famous author Lesley Blanch? "No," I said, because truthfully I had never heard of him. "Her, you fool," said Bea testily. I could sense myself being mentally marked down as a dimwit. Nevertheless, by the end of the meal I was recruited and would begin the New Year as a junior fashion editor on a salary of eleven hundred pounds per annum plus luncheon vouchers.

My nascent fashion-editing career was destined to coincide with the opening of Mr Chow, a starry affair that Michael combined with the birthday of the waifish Geneviève Waïte, a baby-voiced starlet of the day whose birthday cake arrived on the stroke of midnight.

Soon the restaurant was attracting a galaxy of celebrities and, even more significantly, the leading artists of the time. It was Michael's brilliant idea to provide them with free meals on the understanding that they would donate some of their art to the restaurant, which would make a perfect showcase for it. In fact, my contribution to opening night was to make sure the most famous artists delivered their finished works in time for the party. The American Jim Dine created a series of drawn hearts. The English pop artist Peter Blake produced a graphic image of two turn-of-the-century wrestlers, with Michael as their manager. Claes Oldenburg and Patrick Procktor supplied prints. Clive Barker made

Michael Chow and me – not quite on top of the world but on top of a soup can.

bronze casts of three Peking ducks, which still hang from the ceiling of the downstairs dining room. David Hockney's portrait of Michael ended up as the cover of the Mr Chow matchbox (I had attended Michael's initial sitting for this Hockney portrait, but I managed somehow to irritate the artist so much that he angrily tore up his original and insisted Michael return alone). Later the painters Ed Ruscha, Julian Schnabel, and Jean-Michel Basquiat would contribute to subsequent incarnations of Mr Chow in Los Angeles and New York, adding to what, at today's prices, must be a fabulous art collection worth a not so small fortune.

By this time Michael and I had moved house and were pursuing our new life in a quirky, Dickensian-looking gray brick terrace on the unfashionable outskirts of Fulham. I think he was keen to show off his prowess as an architect because he quite simply gutted the place and made it up to the minute with an interior full of white space, spiral staircases, and giant "pop" artworks. (Later, for his next marriage, he added a downstairs swimming pool, one end of which started in the kitchen.) Naturally, we were forever being photographed at home, draped among our symbols of "with it–ness" as one of London's most happening couples: him, the cool young restaurateur, nonchalantly swinging in a hammock hung from the minstrel's gallery; and me, the sophisticated style-maker, perkily sitting cross-legged atop a giant pop-art version of a Campbell's soup can.

Meanwhile, during all these demanding new changes of circumstance, my hair had gone from chicly gamine to weirdly bushy. In retrospect, I think it must have been a silent cry for help.

IV

ON BRITISH VOGUE

In which
Grace takes a
pay cut, goes
vintage-crazy,
grows her hair,
and tries
married life.

E ntering Vogue House at One Hanover Square on a cold London morning in January 1968, and moving through that unremarkable wood-paneled lobby at the fashionably late hour of 9:45 a.m., I realized with a sudden shock that this would be my first ever day job.

The building wasn't unfamiliar to me because, as a model, I had been there many times, taking the lift to the sixth floor to be photographed in the *Vogue* studios. Now everything would be different. Exiting on the fifth floor, I would be stepping into the brave new world of *Vogue* fashion editorial, one I knew existed, but only as a mystery behind the scenes of my favorite glossy.

The lift doors parted—and what a disappointment it was! Stretched out in a messy open-plan jumble before me was a sea of cheap, mismatched wooden furniture, cluttered desks that looked as though they

" I've had this GREAT idea Bea "

my Vintage look

had been salvaged from the streets, and rack upon rack of clothes squeezed tightly together. The old cork flooring was stained, there were endless rows of antiquated filing cabinets, and the fashion cupboard was literally that, rather than the huge streamlined hangar I am used to these days at American *Vogue*. Such a mess! And so shockingly different from the starkly minimalist life I was leading with Michael. Then there was the fashion staff—fewer of them than you might expect, and all in some strange way as mismatched as the furniture.

Senior fashion editor Sheila Wetton stepped forward, charged with showing me around. A tall straight-backed woman with waist-length iron-gray hair scraped severely back into a chignon, she looked more like a ballet teacher than a fashion person but was in fact an extremely stylish ex-model from Molyneux, the chic couture house responsible for dressing Princess Marina, Duchess of Kent, before the war. Then came the fashion editor Melanie Miller. Small, smart, and American, she seemed very foreign, loudly calling everybody "darling!" Mandy Clapperton was even smaller but quieter and more elfin, in vivid contrast to the editor of the social pages, Veronica Hindley, who was a big-boned, sexy blonde with a wayward, falling-apart Brigitte Bardot beehive. Helen Robinson, yet another fashion editor with prematurely graying hair, specialized in the more sporty clothes and rainwear; and right at the back in her floral Foale & Tuffin minidress and granny glasses, exuding cleverness, sat the petite and owlish Marit Allen, the person directly responsible for my being there. Oh, and Sandy Boler. This editor was one I'd had a bit of a falling-out with just before joining the magazine because she'd booked me as the model for a *Vogue* photo session but failed to mention I would be wearing only bras and knickers. Usually, models would be told if the job concerned underwear. Some girls refused because "underwear models," who specialized in this sort of photography, weren't thought of as being very "nice." So I was naturally a bit snippy with her.

After I'd been shown the ropes and allocated a half share in a cluttered desk, I was introduced to Di James, my warmhearted, highly capable assistant who has remained a lifelong friend. (Assistants are a crucial lifeline for a fashion editor, and I always become attached to mine.) I was obliged to share her with Mandy and Veronica. I was then shown the tearoom, which, of course, was pretty important, and fussed over some more by Sheila and Melanie, Sheila in particular because I had worked with her quite a bit as a model, and she was very nurturing (although she had one of the foulest mouths in fashion, and swore every second word). She looked on all the other women in the department as her daughters—even though in group photos, I was always as tall and alien as a giraffe. Eventually, it was lunchtime. Scampi and chips with a bottle of wine or two! As we walked around the corner to the *Vogue* team's regular little lunch venue, Buon Appetito, pushing through crowds of shoppers because our offices were sandwiched between the busy retail thoroughfares of Regent Street and Bond Street, I thought how odd it was that from now on my life would take place in two diametrically opposed environments, both concerned with style: shabby chic Hanover Square by day and super-slick Mr Chow's after dark.

Even though I was working from the first for a fraction of what I could be paid as a model, my time at English *Vogue* was absolutely fantastic. It may have been a little like being back at school at times, but I could realize all my fantasies. Which was why I ended up hoping my years there (all nineteen of them) would never end. I couldn't see why they should. Making money has never been a great concern of mine (I have never asked for a raise in my life), and at British *Vogue* no one had much money to do anything, which almost made it better.

My first photo session was a bit of a disaster, however. It was a kind of unisex idea modeled by the well-upholstered pop artist Peter Blake and his artist wife, Jann Haworth, dressed in matching polo shirts. Thinking back, I don't know what possessed me to come up with the idea other than that I knew them both quite well, having dealt with Peter and his paintings for Michael's restaurant. Anyway, the clothes would undoubtedly have looked better on models.

I spent a lot of time researching ideas in the Chelsea Antique Market on the Kings Road, a ramshackle tourist attraction where a jumble of stalls was busily selling off England's past—World War I army great-coats, chrome-plated thirties cocktail shakers, flapper dresses, steam radios, West End theater programs, posters from the 1920s, that kind of thing. I would comb through racks of vintage clothing, seeking inspiration for fashion shoots. In these early days a photographer like Helmut Newton or Guy Bourdin was very strong and came up with all the ideas for a *Vogue* photo shoot. I merely brought along the clothes to dress their pictures. But then I started having things made. Whole outfits. I mean, how else can you do what no one else is doing? However, one of my earliest and most unlikely assignments had nothing to do with fashion at all.

In 1969 the whole country was obsessed with Prince Charles's impending investiture as the Prince of Wales, to be held at Caernarvon Castle in an ancient Welsh ceremony reserved for the elder son of the reigning British monarch. The press had made much of the new crown, created for the occasion by Lord Snowdon and designed in such a way as to deemphasize the prince's jug ears. Although Snowdon was also a

Good Lord Anne, who are these people following you? ...

famous royal photographer—and indeed, part of the family—it was Norman Parkinson, in the end, who was selected to take His Royal Highness's official portrait at Windsor Castle, and he asked me to come along and help. "Bring some makeup," he said. "We might need it in case he comes in flushed from the polo field."

Naturally, I was nervous. It's one thing to make yourself up but quite another to apply makeup to the future King of England. And yes, when he walked into the room, he was red as a beetroot. "You're going to have to work on him," whispered Parks, while I noticed how the hot lights were turning the prince even redder and he was already sweating into his official ermine-lined robes. Meanwhile, I was trying to stick to protocol and keep my composure. My Cherry Marshall training came in handy at last as I curtsied—even if the attempt was rather ungainly. He, on the other hand, charmingly tried to put us both at ease. "I bet you do this all the time," the prince said as I blotted him with some face powder. "No, actually I've never done it before," I admitted embarrassedly. Parks then took some pictures, and while I leaned forward to give another little touch-up to the prince's face, he took a Polaroid. "If you stole that picture, I bet you would make yourself a fortune," the prince suggested conspiratorially.

Next came a series of action shots of Princess Anne riding her horse across the castle grounds. As we raced alongside her in Parks's open-top Mini, with Parks standing on the passenger seat in order to poke up through the roof taking pictures, and me driving carefully so that he and his camera wouldn't fly out, we almost collided with the Queen, who, along with a crowd of yapping corgis and a tray-bearing manservant, was on her way to take tea on the lawn.

When I first arrived at British *Vogue* it was fun going to the fashion shows—a different kind of fun from how it is now. We weren't there to be seen or to be fabulous. Everybody was kind of anonymous, there to look at the clothes.

The London equivalents of a Paris couture show were usually held in Mayfair, at heavily mirrored, slightly oppressive, marble-clad establishments such as Hardy Amies and Norman Hartnell. We called them *couturiers* but these people—with names like John Cavanagh, Victor Stiebel, Mattli, Worth, Digby Morton, and Michael—were more like highly accomplished dressmakers to the rich, titled, and famous, using beautiful materials for personally fitted clothes. A number of them were "by appointment to the Queen," and the outfits were all stiff and rather unmemorable, like those the Queen wore, and were shown on stately, older-looking models who bore a passing resemblance to the Queen, too. They stepped out onto a long, low catwalk installed in the salon, heads erect and shoulders back, holding a card which had the number of the outfit on it—so much easier for me, because I didn't have to draw it in order to remember it; I just wrote down the figure. They then continued walking very, very slowly, leaving enough time halfway to execute plenty of twirls so the audience could absorb all the details. And that's how the whole show went. There was no music, no scenario, and no drama to distract you from examining the clothes.

The couture in Paris was much more exuberant and exciting, but still one hundred percent about the clothes. Scores of dedicated *petits mains* and hundreds of man-hours combined to give us these uniquely fresh creations. Designers like Patou, Scherrer, Givenchy, Ungaro, and Nina Ricci debuted collections that were lighter and younger than those in London and shown on models who conveyed a cosmopolitan and insouciant attitude. These were the looks that dictated the direction of fashion across the world.

During a typical week of shows, the magazine teams were expected to supervise the shooting of the couture all night and attend the shows during the day. In order not to exhaust myself, I was a bit exclusive and didn't try to see every collection after having so little sleep.

Yves Saint Laurent was one I never skipped. He was modern. He proposed an entirely different couture, one that reflected the influences of youth, popular music, and what was happening in and around the streets of Paris's Left Bank. It was not at all for little old ladies. Cardin and Courrèges were modern too back then, but theirs was a different kind of modernity: It was futuristic, and I don't usually "get" futuristic, because I think it's just an effect. Dior I found a bit shocking. There was always one point in the show where they sent out three exotic fur coats together in a group for *les petites bourgeoises* and they were usually made from some extremely endangered species like snow leopard. I considered it rather disgraceful and didn't care for Dior at that time.

Sometimes, while we editors were discreetly elbowing to enter a show, there would be a ripple through the crowd and a low whisper, "It's Mrs. Vreeland!" It would be like the sea parting as she swept in, an imposing, angular figure who marched rather than walked, her entourage from American *Vogue* following behind in a long trailing line as in a scene from *Funny Face.* The British *Vogue* contingent, meanwhile, was decidedly more low-key. I think our representatives consisted solely of Bea Miller and me. We had no entourage and there was no British *Vogue* office in Paris to look after us, although Susan Train, American *Vogue*'s point person there, did help out a great deal. But until the eighties, when Anna Wintour came along as editor, we mainly worked out of our hotel rooms.

At the shows, the team from American *Vogue,* with Vreeland in the center, usually sat in comfort on a deep sofa, and American *Harper's Bazaar* sat on another. Lowly British *Vogue* didn't qualify for a sofa. I sat on my tiny gilt chair behind Bea and surreptitiously drew the clothes, my sketchbook shielded in my lap. Many women in the front row wore gloves. There were certainly smokers; ashtrays on tall stands stood next to some of the chairs. There was always a particular reverential kind of hush about the couture. The ready-to-wear, on the other hand, was much more relaxed and abuzz.

I always sketch at fashion shows. Drawings jog my memory more than any photograph. At the time I began attending the Paris haute couture, there was much secrecy surrounding the collections. The clothes were always hidden away in the designers' ateliers beforehand beneath large, concealing dust sheets, and there was a strict embargo on releasing any photographs until an agreed-upon publishing date. If this embargo was broken, you were banned from all future presentations for life. While you watched the show you were absolutely forbidden to draw the outfits, although I always did. If any hawk-eyed employee of the salon caught you, both you and your notebook were immediately confiscated and you were ignominiously ejected from the *maison* on suspicion of stealing: of selling the ideas to manufacturers who would copy them. Those were also the days when you couldn't turn up one minute late for a show because the door would be slammed in your face.

In between the fashion obligations of my new life at British *Vogue,* I married Michael Chow in September 1969. In the months beforehand, we briefly separated but got back together, and when we did, he was eager to marry straightaway. I was a bit apprehensive, but invitations were suddenly on their way while I was at the collections in Paris. Di, my assistant, rang me out of the blue and said, "Did you know Michael is drawing up the guest list right now?" Later, I realized that this could only be the action of someone strongly accustomed to making decisions for other people.

The ceremony was to be at Chelsea Registry Office. We arrived in our Rolls-Royce and promptly received a parking ticket. Only two other people were present, the South African photographer Barry Lategan and his girlfriend, Mary (she was also his assistant), who acted as witnesses. I wore a green crushed-velvet dress with trumpet sleeves by Laura Jamieson from the Sweet Shop. Michael wore a velvet suit by Piero de Monzi and handmade two-tone shoes. For the wedding photographs taken afterward by Lategan in his little Chelsea studio barely five minutes away, I gazed lovingly into my husband's eyes while he, being somewhat shorter than I, stood on a box.

At the wedding reception, held in Michael's brand-new Knightsbridge restaurant, I was rather intimidated by all the celebrity invitees, so I hovered on the edge of the party all evening. Michael's sister Tsai Chin took the opportunity to berate me for having walked out on her brother some months before. She said, "Now that you've married into our family, you had better behave yourself," or words to that effect. Michael, meanwhile, wanted to leave early. An expression my mother used came floating back to me: "East is East and West is West and ne'er the twain shall meet." She, however, completely missed the wedding, having not wished to leave her little dog at home in Wales because he had grown too old to travel.

After spending our wedding night at the Carlton Towers hotel just around the corner from the restaurant, Michael and I took off for Capri, arriving by helicopter on the tiny island for our glamorous honeymoon, whereupon I immediately came down with chicken pox. The spots appeared the moment we got to our hotel. I spent five days in a darkened room recuperating before flying back home.

During my first twelve months at British *Vogue,* I acquired a reputation for being impressively eccentric because I was never seen in public without a hat or a tightly wound headscarf. I owned tons and tons of these long twenties scarves, most of them printed with art deco patterns and each similar to the ones that pop stars like Mick Jagger were draping around their fashionable necks at the time. I experimented by wrapping them around my head, then twisting and tying the long ends to make a tight, concealing turban, which, apart from an alternate hat or two, I wore every single day. The sole reason for this was the terrible state of my hair. I had been trying to grow it out, yet hairdressers wouldn't stop snipping away at it, making it look even more dreadful than before.

By now Michael was going into the restaurant every single night. And I, as what now would be considered an early example of the "trophy wife," accompanied him, even though I was exhausted from a long day at *Vogue*. As you might imagine, I didn't really take to playing the social hostess, sidling up to customers to ask if they were enjoying their meal or listening patiently to a litany of their complaints. So in the end I opted to stay isolated in the booth downstairs and play hat-check girl instead. It was peaceful and the tips were very good. But being the owner's wife, I naturally felt obliged to add my earnings to the pool of cash shared out among the general staff.

Whenever we were not in the new restaurant, at Sunday lunchtime, for instance, Michael and I entertained at home. I cooked Peking duck in our bright red Aga after it had been prepared by the chefs at the restaurant. (To make the meat more tender, the birds for some reason had to be inflated with a bicycle pump.) Lunch was served on a full-size billiards table, which cleverly transformed into an extremely generous dining table.

It was all highly contemporary, exquisitely photogenic, utterly enviable domestic bliss . . . until I fell in love with someone else.

V

ON
TAKING PICTURES

In which
Grace peers
through the
lens of her new
world of
happy snappers.

T rips were a real luxury at fashion magazines in the seventies. I loved them. There had never been an opportunity for long-distance travel when I lived in Wales, where our glimpse of the outside world came from such publications as *National Geographic* and *Picture Post*. I didn't travel far at all until I was eighteen, and then I left home for good.

Unlike today, when an average location shoot—complete with photographer, models, hairdresser, makeup artist, production people, scouts, prop stylist, and numerous assistants for everybody (although I have only ever had one)—can be concluded in two or three hectic days, back then we might take off for anything up to three leisurely weeks. We absorbed the atmosphere, waited as long as necessary for the best light, and took time off for the models to get suitably tanned. Things would always turn out fine as long as our pictures included a good publicity

My shoot in Hyde Park makes the wrong thing look so right.

shot of the airplane—or even just the tail of the plane—because the flights and accommodation were normally given for free.

My first fashion trip as a *Vogue* editor was to Jamaica in 1970 with my old friend Norman Parkinson, who built his dream house in neighboring Tobago. I can still recall the first moment of incredible warmth that enveloped me as I stepped off the plane in Montego Bay, the sudden awareness of the friendly people all around, and the perfection of the white sand. In Wales I had not come across any black people at all, so to discover a whole island of them was overwhelming. It was the beginning of a lifelong love affair with the West Indies.

My take on traveling had very much to do with Parks. He educated me, making me see that you need to get involved with a place, not just take a bunch of clothes on a plane and photograph them on a beach. Nowadays, there are fashion teams who can go to the same locations I have been to and come back with photographs showing just a tiny bit of blue sky. How modern! And they think they have done a fabulous job! But what's the point?

Parks taught me such a lot about how to work when you are in foreign lands, about always keeping your eyes open, as you never know when you might find something inspirational to enhance the photographs. For instance, he and I were on a shoot in the Seychelles in 1971 with the model Apollonia van Ravenstein, standing on miles and miles of virgin white sand. Suddenly a dog appeared out of nowhere. Apollonia stretched out her arms to call it, and at that moment, the picture sprang to life. Parks became a kind of mentor, a father figure during my early *Vogue* years. And I would work so hard to learn about the location before we went away. Sometimes I failed, as when our trip to the Seychelles took us to a remote island bird sanctuary. After a nightmare ten-hour ride on a tiny fishing boat, during which we all threw up most of the way, the sanctuary turned out to be little more than a stinking dung heap of bird droppings—although we did manage to get some of our most memorable pictures there.

It is always so difficult to capture fashion combined with a sense of place, so I would throw myself into research. Whenever these trips were in the planning stage, there were books piled high all over my office. Bea Miller would put her head around the door and stare in shock. "But Grace, you never read!"

Apart from Parkinson, the stable of photographers I worked with during my early years of fashion editing included Bailey, Donovan, Barry Lategan, and Clive Arrowsmith, with occasional guest appearances by Snowdon, Sarah Moon, Sacha, Duc, Cecil Beaton, Peter Knapp, and Guy Bourdin and Helmut Newton, the great stars of French *Vogue*. But the one photographer I would dearly have loved to work with was the legendary American perfectionist Irving Penn. I had to wait another twenty years for the opportunity.

Rumors circulating at *Vogue* soon after I joined had it that Mr. Penn was in England to take pictures of flowers—a certain rose, to be exact—for his latest book. Having always wanted to meet this world-renowned figure, I went up to the *Vogue* studios on the sixth floor to hang about in hopes of bumping into my idol. There I discovered that he hadn't been given a studio at all but a corner of the tearoom, where he set up his composition on a little table near the window. As he didn't want to upset the rose with an electric lightbulb, he was augmenting the natural light with a candle. I looked around, searching him out and dying to cross paths with him. But in my youthful ignorance, I somehow expected to see someone cool, like David Bailey. So I didn't notice the slight, unassuming figure in the pressed shirt and trousers who walked by me in the corridor until someone said that if I was looking for Mr. Penn, I had just passed him.

Toward the end of my time at British *Vogue,* in the early eighties, I had a second chance to meet my hero on one of my many trips to New York, where I both attended the collections and worked freelance on Calvin Klein's advertising shoots. One day I confessed to Calvin, with whom I was now very friendly, that one of my dreams was to finally meet Irving Penn. Because he was involved with Penn, who was shooting the pin-sharp still-life advertising shots of the company's products at the time, Calvin said, "I'll set it up for you." And so I went to the great man's studio on Fifth Avenue. It was absolutely tiny. He came out of his office and we sat at a small Formica-topped table where we talked for hours, chatting away like two old friends about photography then and in the past, and about what made a great fashion image, a subject on which he set a very high bar. It was amazing to have a conversation with such an astonishing master. He was so passionate about his work, yet so diffident and self-deprecating about his towering achievements.

David Bailey, whom I had previously worked with as a model, was tough. The most important person on any of his shoots was, without doubt, the photographer. Followed by the model. He used the same girl again and again, and that girl was usually his current girlfriend.

Bailey liked making fashion editors run. He would tease us a lot and never show the shoes, cropping in really tight on all the photographs because he liked to make them fill the frame. As I have always been known as an editor who likes to show the shoes, you can appreciate that this upset me more than most.

However, I did go on a great many very enjoyable trips with him—Peru, Africa, Australia, Corsica, the Côte d'Azur—and he didn't crop those pictures so much. Although he was a great traveling companion, for one trip to South America he came up with the concept—a particularly bad one, in my opinion—of going there by himself to shoot all the backgrounds, then returning to a London studio, where he wanted to project the images and photograph a model standing in front of them. I offered a favorite model of mine at the time, a Hawaiian/Japanese beauty named Marie Helvin, who was exotic, with a bit of a tan—which was convenient, since she wasn't going to acquire one in the studio. Bailey's reaction was "I don't want to work with any fuckin' girl you suggest," or something equally polite, but I insisted. The next second Marie and Bailey were madly in love, he married her, and they were living together in an enormous dark house filled with screeching parrots in North London that also served as his studio, looked after by his Brazilian manservant, Cesar.

Another frequent collaborator was South Africa–born Barry Lategan, known for his softly lit studio pictures and poetically misty location work. His images epitomized the fashion mood in London, when makeup was very painterly and fashion was rather ethereal, something Bea Miller allowed me to indulge in with him, even for numerous covers.

Because she had a journalistic background and was pretty smart, Bea insisted that fashion should have something to say, or at least deliver a lively point of view. "I had this idea in my bath this morning" was something she regularly said to us.

One of my favorite Bea ideas was a shoot in 1971 with the photographer Peter Knapp. It took ten (I think) long-held rules governing ladylike behavior in public, as determined by Emily Post in her books on etiquette, then demolished them by showing ten photographs of models doing the exact opposite. For example, in contrast to a caption ruling,

"A lady never applies her makeup in public," model Cathee Dahmen was seen at a table at Mr Chow looking glamorously self-absorbed, in high-voltage 1930s style, as she applied her lipstick in the mirror of an art deco compact. Another showed a typical group of middle-aged, traditional English nannies pushing prams through Hyde Park while the flame-haired model Gala Mitchell, in vibrant satin hot pants, pushed her pram past them in the opposite direction. The caption this time read something like "A lady never dresses to stand out in a crowd." This eagerness to flout stuffy old rules gave British *Vogue* relevance again after it had languished for years in the wake of its more forward-thinking rival, *Queen,* and enabled readers liberated by the swinging sixties to relate to it.

Meanwhile, avant-garde young fashion designers as accomplished as any in Italy or France were on the rise. London's Royal College of Art and various other seed beds of British talent produced names like Ossie Clark, Foale & Tuffin, Zandra Rhodes, and Bill Gibb, a talented group joined by newcomers Sheridan Barnett, Katharine Hamnett, and Adrian Cartmell. The thirties style of Barbara Hulanicki's Biba was proving seriously influential. British icons of glam rock such as David Bowie and Marc Bolan were delivering androgyny and men's makeup to the mainstream. Glitter and a peculiar tinselly glamour filled the air.

The Welshman Clive Arrowsmith was a wild photographer who fitted well with these crazy times. He was a bit of a rock and roller, never far from one of his collection of guitars, occasionally breaking out in extremely loud jam sessions with his assistant Willie and a few friends. I knew Clive throughout his blissed-out Hare Krishna seventies phase. He produced beautifully lit, somewhat hallucinogenic photographs, very much of their era, mostly shot in the studio. Somehow, we did manage to go on one disastrous trip to New York (he had a terrible fear of flying and needed to get roaring drunk to board a plane, ably supported by Willie), where he became totally paranoid and refused to go outside. Our intention was to photograph all along the eastern seaboard of America, but he was interested only in places he could get to and immediately return from the same day—the Statue of Liberty, Central Park, Chinatown, New York's St. Regis Hotel, Connecticut, Yale University, etc. He was a really good photographer, just unbelievably off-the-wall.

It was on this same trip that I went to Madison Avenue and paid an early visit to American *Vogue* (which I was in awe of), escorted around the building by Bill Rayner, the Condé Nast financial director. Bea Miller had persuaded him to look after me. Walking down a corridor, we bumped into fashion editor Polly Mellen, who mistook me for an assistant, thrust a bag of clothing into my hands, and instructed me to return it to the designer Oscar de la Renta. Then we ran into Leo Lerman, the witty and urbane features editor (as well as a familiar face at Bea Miller's London parties), who seemed to know everyone who was anyone and arranged for me and my team to visit Andy Warhol's Factory and photograph all the extraordinary-looking people there. I was fated not to meet with American *Vogue*'s legendary editor Diana Vreeland, though. Looking me up and down as I stood outside her office, knees knocking under my miniskirt, while all around us whirled the chic and dynamic *Vogue* staff, Bill Rayner thought better of it. "Maybe I won't take you in there today," he said.

VI

ON
BEGINNINGS AND ENDS

In which
our heroine
recognizes
that life
is often a
long series
of losses.

H aving shared both a desk and an assistant for a while at British *Vogue,* I graduated to having Di James to myself, but then she departed. Thankfully, my next assistant, Patricia McRoberts, was exclusively mine from the start.

An English girl of independent means who went on to marry a world-class polo player, Patricia was flamboyant. She always drove her Mercedes dangerously fast until the day she crashed and wrote it off, only to replace it immediately with an Alfa Romeo. Meanwhile, I moved gingerly around town in the Rolls-Royce I shared with Michael. By some means I even managed to win a rare parking space in the *Vogue* garage—although it unfortunately turned out to be unsuitable for anything bigger than a Mini.

Patricia and I took off on frequent shopping sprees to YSL. She dyed her hair magenta and, with my friend Polly Hamilton, who before com-

me with Rosie, Tristan & Finn

ing to *Vogue* had worked for the British teenage fashion magazine *19,* we formed a formidable little trio. We sat together at fashion shows in a tight-lipped line, along with friends like Caroline Baker, fashion editor of *Nova,* and Norma Moriceau, fashion editor of *19,* extremely aloof and wearing severe 1930s felt hats or the latest thing from Yves. Or facsimiles of Yves, depending upon our individual circumstances.

By then I too, having gone from a little to a lot of hair hidden under my hats and scarves, decided, with the hairdresser Leonard, his colorist, Daniel, and the photographer Barry Lategan, to create a radical new look. My hair was to be dyed with henna, which is messy but great for the condition, and I would be given a perm, a big frizz rather like the ones my mother gave me when I was a little girl. We planned to unveil it to melodramatic effect in a set of photographs taken by Barry as a major

my YSL zouave pants

pre-Raphaelite or Renaissance moment. Apart from cutting it short and going radically blond after my second divorce, then trimming it down again in my early days at American *Vogue* when Anna Wintour—much taken by the cute-looking short hair of Linda Evangelista—pressured me into doing so, nothing has changed much over the past forty years.

In the seventies and eighties we were usually waiting to see what Saint Laurent had done simply to know in which direction fashion was going. The power of the dresses! The grandeur! The girls so tall and imperious! I loved the beginnings of his fashion shows, which started with looks that were mannish and strict, then progressed to the amazing colors of the dresses. If

you went to Morocco, where he kept one of
his most beautiful homes, La Majorelle, set
in an intricate perfumed garden that, once
seen, was never forgotten, you would understand. *Le smoking,* his version of a man's
tuxedo for women, so chic and flattering;
the indulgence and voluptuousness of the
Ballets Russes collection; the Braque collection; Cocteau; Picasso; Russian peasants;
Spanish toreadors; Porgy and Bess—so
much creativity and such prolific talent that
just sitting and watching it was exhausting. I
feel very fortunate to have seen those shows;
to me, they were like a series of art exhibits. I
did faint a couple of times in the early days
but I'm not sure if that didn't come from

my favorite YSL coat

missing breakfast rather than being overcome by emotion. Whatever it was,
Bea Miller would revive me with the barley sugar sweets she kept in her
handbag expressly for that purpose.

Yves and I were never very close personally. We didn't go out to dinner or anything like that. But I was good friends with the people around
him—his muse, Loulou de la Falaise, who designed the extravagant YSL
costume jewelery; her husband, Thadée, son of the painter Balthus; and
Clara Saint, who handled the international press. It was Clara who always rang me after the show to see what I thought of the collection because Yves, flatteringly, "wanted to know."

When he began to show from his own little salon in the rue Spontini
after quitting as the chief designer at Dior in the sixties, many of the
world's press who could not get in stood huddled outside in the street,

pleading, "How was it?" as we all filed out. But I shall never forget the terrible sight of him in the late eighties after his *défilé* had moved to the Grand Salon in the Hotel Intercontinental. He was so hopelessly bloated and out of it. Pierre Bergé, the president of Saint Laurent, on one side and a bodyguard on the other had to grab him by the elbows and literally drag him along the catwalk, under that huge chandelier and beautifully painted ceiling, to take his bow. The newspapers that morning had reported that the great couturier was on his deathbed, so I presume this was their way of showing it simply wasn't true. And I remember the ghastly grandeur of his final couture show held at the Centre Pompidou in 2002, just six years before he died, with its cold industrial hardness contrasting with the sweepingly operatic clothes, and with the great and the good and every model and face he was ever associated with there—but looking much, much sadder and older.

In the seventies I dressed almost exclusively in Saint Laurent. Save for one disastrous evening, that is, when I turned up for dinner at the home of Clare Rendlesham. By now this crushingly intimidating woman had quit the world of glossy magazines and become the directrice of the newly opened London branch of Saint Laurent Rive Gauche. Legendary for terrorizing her contemporaries in her magazine days, she added to her notorious reputation for rudeness by chasing customers from the shop if she decided that whatever they were buying didn't suit them. And if she considered their image to be one not worthy of wearing the Saint Laurent label, she even accosted them in the street. Which makes me wonder why, as I pressed her front doorbell, I didn't see my unfortunate mistake. "What is that terrible thing you've got on?" Clare demanded through gritted teeth, blocking my way through the entrance. It was a perfectly beautiful vintage dress from the antiques market. "You have to go back and change, because you're not wearing Saint Laurent," she sniffed, closing the door sharply in my face. And so back home I went.

Once again I was spending a lot of time in Paris, not just as a *Vogue* editor but because I had started seeing the young Vietnamese photographer Duc, for whom I left Michael Chow. My assistant, Patricia, who had generously lent me the deposit on the St. John's Wood flat I had moved to, helped me out again by occasionally lending me the travel money to pop over to France and see him.

At the beginning of our relationship, Duc assisted the photographer Guy Bourdin, which is how I first met him. He was tall and skinny, with beautiful shoulder-length hair, and he always looked immaculate, even in worn jeans and a jean jacket. There was something otherworldly and innocent about Duc. One of the cameras he used was shaped like Mickey Mouse, and I loved the way people reacted to it by making the funniest faces whenever he took their picture.

There was a sort of cabal in Paris back then, made up of a great many of Duc's Vietnamese cousins, many of whom at one time or another also worked as assistants to Bourdin. Whenever it was convenient, these relatives would use each other's papers to travel, because the French authorities were rarely able to tell them apart. Sometimes, when he had misplaced his, Duc would visit me in London using his cousin Hyacinth's passport, even though they didn't resemble each other at all.

He lived in a tiny, rented room on the Left Bank's quai des Grands Augustins above Lapérouse, a dark and cavernous eighteenth-century restaurant riddled with secret passageways. Here he slept on a foldaway bed and played Doors albums on an old gramophone. We ate at Vietnamese restaurants such as Long Hiep around the corner in Saint-Germain's rue de la Montagne Sainte-Geneviève, newly fashionable because of the fad for Vietnamese cuisine that had just hit Paris. We also went to many lower-profile restaurants serving authentic Vietnamese food that Duc knew about but were totally off the fashion track. He had no money (Bourdin seldom paid Duc's or anybody else's wages on time), but he was idealistic and loyal and, like many of his peers, considered it an honor to work for Bourdin.

It was an exceptionally romantic, bohemian period in my life. Duc and I would wander along the banks of the Seine for hours, hand in hand, like all those lovers you see in old black-and-white French photos. He was penniless, and I wasn't much better off. But we were always chicly dressed.

We stayed together on and off for almost five years, until late 1972. He gave up his tiny room soon after I met him, so after that, whenever I arrived in Paris—which was most weekends—I never quite knew where I would be staying because he moved around from friend to friend, cousin to cousin, often sleeping on the floor. We spent our days together scouring the flea markets for bargains. Or we would drive out to Deauville, stay in cheap hotels, and gorge ourselves on shellfish. It was a fun time for shopping. Yves Saint Laurent was at the peak of his fame, and Duc gave me his illustrated children's book, *La Vilaine Lulu*. In return, I gave him some Yves Saint Laurent trousers to go with a vintage satin baseball jacket sent to him from New York.

Whereas I knew most of the clique around Yves Saint Laurent, Duc knew many of the people around Kenzo, my other favorite designer of the time. These included the models Wallis Franken and Louise Despointes; the press officer Barbara Schlager and her photographer boyfriend, Uli Rose; and another up-and-coming young photographer, Arthur Elgort, whose first ever job with me was photographing Kenzo's startlingly bright clothes on a group of girls and boys running through the Jardin des Tuileries. Personally, I started having a big Kenzo moment, too. I loved wearing his pretty, peasanty clothes. There was a particular long, ethnic-looking, wraparound skirt with multiple pleats that I wore constantly back then. It fastened low on the hips with strings that wrapped round and round and held it in place. But those strings could also come unfastened in a second, and you would occasionally find yourself standing in your underwear. Then there were his huge oversize blazers and rugby-striped knits. Everything Kenzo did was so joyously colorful and naive—a bit like his spectacular fashion shows, which had models dressed as toy soldiers and ballerinas, firework displays, and on one unforgettable occasion, a snow-white horse trotting down the catwalk carrying a girl dressed as a fairy princess.

my Kenzo moment

Eventually, Duc went out on his own as a photographer. When he came to London, he stayed with me in my little basement flat in St. John's Wood. It had a beautiful stretch of garden, which pleased him greatly because he loved gardening. He was also a wonderful cook, teaching me Vietnamese cuisine and, most important, how to make my favorite Vietnamese soup, a seriously complicated dish consisting of chicken—with extra chicken feet—pork, noodles, bean sprouts, dried shrimp, Chinese pickles, spring onions, and lots of fresh mint and coriander, that took an entire day to prepare but was inexpensive and lasted us a week. He was unbelievably strict about neatness. I smoked at the time, and if so much as a tiny piece of ash spilled on a table, he would pounce. It seemed odd to me that someone who didn't have a house of his own could be so intensely house-proud.

The other strange thing about Duc was that, unlike any other photographer I worked with, he preferred to shoot very few pages. No wonder he had no money. Two were ideal for him because he could envisage an entire story in a single spread. He also had the most terrible temper, especially after a drink or two. On a *Vogue* shoot in Kensington Gardens, he lost it dramatically while posing the individual-looking American model Wallis Franken, who was dressed in a sailor suit, in the middle of Round Pond. When I happened to mention that her top was looking a little wrinkled, he snarled, "Why don't you fix it, then?" As he turned on me, his camera flew straight from his hand into the water and sank like a stone. He was forced to finish the session using the tiny quarter-frame Canon Dial camera he had bought me as a present and which I carried around with me all the time.

Gradually, Duc and I saw less and less of each other due to circumstances pulling us in different directions. Our final break came when I spoke to him long-distance after my sister, Rosemary, died. He seemed so detached, unable to comprehend how deeply sad I felt—possibly because in Asian culture, death is perceived so differently.

I had taken on the heavy responsibility of my sister's welfare several troubled years before I arrived at British *Vogue*. Having divorced her husband, John, in 1962, Rosemary came down from the Midlands to live with me in London, bringing her large ginger cat, first to my temporary flat in Pond Place off the Fulham Road, then to one in Beaufort Street, Chelsea. I had been looking forward to moving there because it was supposed to be my first big apartment to myself after many years of sharing.

Cooking a Vietnamese soup with Duc

Every attempt to find Rosemary employment didn't work. I did get her a job waitressing at the Soup Kitchen, an offshoot of the Stockpot, but she lasted only a day. She wasn't entirely sure what she wanted to do. She loved art and applied herself by staying at home painting small watercolors that, with their orange skies and purple grass, were all pretty trippy. But mostly, she spent her days wandering around London's various museums—a country girl who never really found her place in society after her separation.

At first my sister's marriage had gone well. She created the most beautiful, romantic environment near Stratford-upon-Avon for herself and John. Ivy Bank was a tiny thatched cottage with one of those perfectly typical English gardens, tangled and overgrown with flowers and vegetables that she then set about filling with local children, to whom she gave painting lessons. It was a dream life. Except for one thing—the lack of children of her own.

Had Rosemary been brought up in London, she might have become a debutante and attracted the perfect suitor. Or maybe she could have become a model and traveled, like me. But despite having taken a secretarial course in typing and shorthand (which, incidentally, most young girls did in those days as a matter of course), she was never cut out to be a serious working woman. She had married young and been a country housewife, gardening and painting and preparing for children that didn't arrive, which was all a far cry from pursuing a career path in the city. When she came to stay with me, she was more than a bit lost. She fell into the habit of chatting with complete strangers, druggie types and serious addicts whom she ran across outside the museums she visited. One of them (who easily could have been a homeless person) she married in a registry office almost as soon as she met him, while I was out of the country.

Modeling assignments for catalogs and magazines regularly took me to Germany now, and this was great because they paid me in cash. I kept all the money in a chest of drawers in my bedroom. But one day when I returned to England, the cash was gone, and Rosemary's highly suspect new husband was gone with it.

Shortly afterward, Rosemary suffered some kind of nervous breakdown. After collapsing in the street, she was taken to Cane Hill Hospital, a grim, Victorian-looking institution in the London suburb of Croydon, full of gibbering patients cowering in corners. They strapped her to a bed and gave her electric shock treatment. She was there for three weeks or so, and then she was back on the streets. And yes, it was the same old, same old.

Then my sister met a pavement artist, Kevin Rigby, who was working in Trafalgar Square outside the National Portrait Gallery. He was twenty-two. She was around thirty. Kevin was sweet-natured, idealistic, and gentle, with long red hair down to his elbows. He came from a good army family up north but had since become a bit of a rebel.

Kevin and Rosemary embarked on an affair that quickly led to my sister becoming pregnant, although they never lived together. She took a room off the Kings Road in Markham Square in a house where, once upon a time, I had rented a room. Nine months later, Tristan, my nephew, was born down the road in a hospital in Parsons Green. Soon after, Kevin drifted to Nepal and became a Buddhist monk, illustrating books about his religion. In 1974 he would be found dead under mysterious circumstances on the border with Afghanistan.

During the pregnancy, Rosemary had contracted jaundice and from then on remained terribly sickly. Our mother was unable to deal with the situation. She wanted nothing to do with Rosie, pretending to anyone who asked that the baby was the fruit of a brief reunion between my sister and her ex-husband.

After four years of living in London with Tristan, Rosemary moved back to Wales and a house in Holyhead provided by her ex-husband, John, who thought she would be better off in close proximity to my mother. Of course, as soon as my mother saw her cute little red-headed grandson, she was transformed into the typically doting grandmother.

During all this time many of Rosemary's druggie friends followed her down to Wales and were supplying her with certain substances. She eventually acquired a new boyfriend, a local shipyard worker who lived at home with his mother, and she became pregnant again, giving birth to her second son, Finn, in 1970. The details are a little sketchy after that. She was suffering from bronchitis, skinny, ill, and had an argument with her boyfriend. Afterward, she supposedly took an overdose of Valium and fell asleep. The boyfriend called an ambulance that took her to a medical center. Somehow a stomach pump was wrongly used. Her lungs collapsed. She died two days later, on Christmas Day 1972. I paid my last visit to find her on life support, unconscious.

It was horribly tragic seeing Rosie hooked up to all those tubes. After her funeral, Finn, who was eighteen months old, was taken into care by the boyfriend's mother. Tristan was taken off to be fostered by Karen Alderson, a friend of Rosemary's who lived nearby in Tre-Arddur Bay and whose children he was already friendly with. Because he eventually boarded at the boys' prep school next door to our hotel, my mother was able to see him all the time.

One thing I shall never forget was the incredible kindness of the shoe designer Manolo Blahnik. He came to my flat when I returned home from my sister's funeral, consoled me, and kept me company all night so that I wouldn't be alone. He really helped my peace of mind. It's remarkable how someone with such a flighty reputation, from the upper reaches of fashion, which are often so heartless and cold, could in reality be so thoughtful and caring.

A few months after my sister's death, I attempted to adopt Tristan. I had been helping out his foster parents up until then, paying for his schooling, among other things, and having him stay with me during part of his school holidays. But because I was unmarried, the authorities suddenly turned nasty and threatening. They told me I was an entirely unsuitable person, and if I continued to push with adoption proceedings, Tristan would be taken away and placed in a children's home. So he remained with the Aldersons awhile longer, and it wasn't until I finally remarried that he came to live with me and went on to further his education at Normansal, a prep school in Eastbourne, and the public school (English for private school) Milton Abbey.

I last saw Tristan's half brother, Finn, who I believe is quite mathematically bright, at my mother's funeral. He was fourteen years old. I understand he still lives somewhere in Wales. In the meantime, Tristan, who has pursued numerous careers—from tending to the hounds on an English country estate to selling property in the Dominican Republic—set about the task of learning more about his father via the simple recent expedient of Google. My nephew has now followed his trail to Nepal, fallen in love with the country, and started to learn about Tibetan art.

VII

ON
CAFÉ SOCIETY

Wherein
seventies chic
meets fashionable
freaks in
the smartest
of cliques.

B ea Miller had a way of coaxing the best out of everyone. She also had an instinct for recognizing special talent. It was she who first introduced me to Karl Lagerfeld. It was 1971, the beginning of his ponytail period. To me he was an idiosyncratically handsome man, with a bushy black fin de siècle beard that he scented with the last drops of a discontinued perfume, Black Narcissus by Caron, of which he had secured all the remaining stock. He wore a monocle, shirts with stiff, old-fashioned celluloid collars, and carried a fan. Usually, he was accompanied by Anna Piaggi, his muse, a latter-day Marchesa Casati who was powerful at Italian *Vogue,* and her companion, Verne Lambert, an eccentric Australian who carried a silver-topped cane and collected and sold antique clothing.

In Paris we might on occasion go for lunch at the Closerie des Lilas

My Seventies Set

Manolo   Anna   Pat   Antonio   Donna   Karl
Blahnik   Piaggi   Cleveland Lopez   Jordan   Lagerfeld

along with Karl's boyfriend, Jacques de Bascher de Beaumarchais, who invariably arrived impeccably dressed in the style of a turn-of-the-century dandy; the illustrator Antonio Lopez and his friend Juan; the live-wire American models Pat Cleveland and Donna Jordan, fresh out of Andy Warhol's Factory in New York; and the remarkable Polish model Aya, who was discovered selling secondhand clothes in London's Kensington Market. She based her everyday look on 1950s fashion photographs and would stand about, her face a mask of fifties cosmetics (beneath it she had rather bad skin), striking angular period poses even when no camera was trained on her. She was always flawless in Antonio's drawings, which made her look stunningly sculptural.

Karl was working as designer for Chloé—a seasoned French label that previously specialized in pretty blouses—as well as freelancing for a number of Italian brands where his name never appeared. He was always perfectly satisfied to play the "gun for hire" in the fashion world and, until Chanel hired him in 1982, preferred not to be associated with just one thing. In that respect, among others, he was very much the antithesis of Saint Laurent. Perhaps this is why he never tried to build his own line into something so important. But he did a great many extraordinary things for Chloé, calling on his vast knowledge of historical movements in art and design to inspire their collections.

Everyone in those days had to attend a Chloé show. A key moment in any season was when enthusiasts surged backstage afterward to congratulate Karl and he would pick out one of the must-have accessories for next season and insist that you wear it straightaway, six months before it was available. These trinkets were like priceless trophies and sometimes—as with an exquisite feather-light lamé scarf he gave me that epitomized the art deco–mad seventies—became the object of everlasting envy among friends and colleagues.

In the evenings we all congregated at the Club Sept, which was the new generation's version of Régine's, the traditional hangout for play-boys and socialites, except this was ninety-nine percent fashion and gay. I remember dark banquettes and little tables tightly positioned around the walls of a crammed dining area skirting a postage-stamp square of dance floor where a great deal of bumping and grinding went on. Paloma Picasso was often there, looking striking with two male escorts.

We had tiny budgets in those days, and Karl generously lent us his impressively grand apartment in the Place Saint-Sulpice for our photo shoots. It was beautiful and spacious, an opulent shrine to art deco, al-though I had the distinct impression that the mercurial Karl was grow-ing tired of it and would soon be moving on.

I shot Anjelica Huston and Marie Helvin there with Bailey; Pat Cleve-land with Bourdin; and a model named Kathy Quirk with Helmut New-ton. The Helmut shoot—a typical "rich woman living the pampered life" scenario—featured my assistant Julie Kavanagh, who went on to become the London editor of *Women's Wear Daily* and the author of acclaimed biographies of Rudolph Nureyev and the British ballet cho-reographer Frederick Ashton. On this occasion she was obliged to dress up as a stereotypical little French maid, complete with starched apron and hair band. Cathy was shot lounging on Karl's pristine ivory silk-covered sofa, being given a manicure by the real-life manicurist of Helmut's wife, June.

With Bourdin, we had Pat Cleveland leaning against an exquisitely lacquered 1920s cabinet of enormous value. While the hot lights grew hotter (Bourdin used high-strength tungsten lamps for his blindingly clear lighting effects), I noticed the lacquer on a nearby door start to bubble. I shouted for the assistants to shut off the power. Thankfully, the blister receded and a major incident was averted.

Art deco was the revival of the hour. Fashion had gone entirely retro. Makeup and clothes were relentlessly thirties. Lipstick was plum, prune, or aubergine. Hair was waved or pin-curled. The ranunculus was the flower of choice. People flocked to the giant new Biba emporium in Kensington, housed in the formerly stuffy department store of Derry & Toms, to revel in the whole reproduction thirties lifestyle. Houses were filled with Clarice Cliff's distinctive orange and black period pottery. By now I had amassed a wardrobe overflowing with beautiful vintage dresses and a huge collection of art deco bangles and pins from the Chelsea Antique Market and the Marché aux Puces (flea market) in the Clignancourt district of Paris. They were made of Bakelite, an unstable early form of plastic reputed to explode under extreme temperature conditions.

my Walter Albini suit

The other most fashionable designer of the day, the Italian Walter Albini, in a wildly extravagant display of largesse had the international press flown to Venice to attend his latest fashion show, which was meticulously thirties-inspired. We arrived on the lagoon just before sunset, traveling by motor launch to the Hotel Danieli, where the rich, varnished interior was as filled with period detail as Luchino Visconti's *The Damned,* to discover our rooms drowning in heavily scented gardenias. Later that evening we all boarded gondolas for St. Mark's Square, where we were ushered into the fashion show at the Caffè Florian by brilliantined, thirties-looking waiters to the sounds of a string quartet. I was escorted by David Bailey and dressed all in white—a big white coat over a vintage silk 1920s tennis dress.

Helmut Newton and I had worked together as model and photographer during my career in the sixties, and it was as an unexpectedly guest-appearing model that I now worked with him for British *Vogue* on one of our most memorable fashion shoots. It was 1973, in the midst of his "swimming pool period," and he had the idea of creating a shoot that looked like a slightly decadent cocktail party held around a pool. As he was spending his regular summer vacation at his little house in Ramatuelle, a village in the hills above Saint-Tropez, and he didn't like to travel far to a location, we were to take the photographs at a hotel pool in town. Models arrived early to take a couple of days' tanning time, and the evening clothes I had brought, which weren't very inspiring, were discussed. The hairdresser on the shoot, Jean Louis David, whose wife, Danielle Poe, was one of our models, occupied himself cutting June Newton's hair.

During all this, Helmut kept eyeing me beadily as I hung out by the pool in my purple Eres two-piece, fifties sunglasses, and brand-new shocking-pink vinyl Yves Saint Laurent high heels. Finally, he said, "This story is boring. I think we'll put you in the pictures to make it more interesting." And that's exactly what he did. The odd juxtaposition of me floating about in the pool or standing there in my bikini drinking cocktails alongside models dressed to the nines in shiny evening gowns and dinner jackets gave the whole shoot a documentary feeling that is still imitated today.

Helmut and I had a fairly easygoing relationship, although he could be notoriously mean to other fashion editors and models. And he was never less than direct. Over twenty years he regularly asked me, "When can I do a nude picture of you?" As time went on and because I kept repeatedly putting him off, he would never fail to add, "Before it's too late." Then one day he turned to me and said, "You remember how I always wanted to do that nude before it was too late? Well, now it is."

My assistants (I never failed to choose beautiful ones) were given strict instructions to always wear sexy high heels, never sneakers, when working with him because that would put him in a much better mood.

In all the years we worked and socialized together, the only time we ever had a major falling-out was when I wanted to include one of his more controversial photographs in the book Karl Lagerfeld was publishing of my work. Helmut and I had collaborated at one time on a series of fashion photos for American *Vogue* featuring the German platinum-blond Amazon Nadja Auermann wearing little black dresses. While we mapped out the session he said, "I am going to do one picture like the story of Leda and the Swan. I will need a stuffed swan, and it's going to be raping Nadja." Well, I just nodded, thinking, "There's no way this will ever happen when Anna gets to hear of it." But the next second Helmut is telling this story to Anna on the phone and she is saying something like, "Oh, Helmut darling, what a great idea!" So a stuffed swan is eventually tracked down from a shop in Paris specializing in taxidermy and shipped at great expense to Monte Carlo, with Anna now saying, "Oh well, you know, I just wanted to humor him." Anyhow, we did the picture with a view that it would probably never appear. But incredibly, it did. And he absolutely refused to let me reprint it. In the end, however, the picture I would dearly love to have used—unfortunately never taken—was the one where Helmut was lying spread-eagled on the

How's this Helmut, do we look like "Leda and swan" now . . . . ?

bed with the stuffed swan between his legs, showing Nadja exactly how it should be done.

A money-making sideline at British *Vogue* in the seventies was Vogue Promotions, which inhabited a place vaguely positioned between editorial and advertising. I did very little of these, being far too busy with my single bona fide editorial shoot a month. But there was one concerning the photographer Guy Bourdin and a very French blue bubble bath product called Obao that I agreed to do and shall never forget.

Guy was a tiny and very, very mischievous photographer, like a naughty little boy. He spoke only French, and though I had forgotten most of my convent-taught knowledge of that language, we always managed somehow to communicate. He worked most of the time with Heidi Morawetz, an Austrian makeup artist who was so much more than that: She was his right hand, completely responsible for realizing many of his wilder projects, finding huge (real) fishtails for mermaid shoots and tracking down a great number of the crazy things he sketched to convey his ideas. You have to remember, there was no retouching or digital trickery in those early days, so if Guy wanted a model to fly or be a mermaid with a fishtail sticking out of the sand, he would have to find a way to create the illusion out of reality.

The pictures for the bath product were scheduled to take place near his country house at La Chapelle on the Normandy coast one dull April day when the weather was freezing and overcast and the sea had turned an unappetizingly murky gray. The idea was to have the model look as though she were flying naked over the sea, then swim through bright blue water and drip it along the beach. But Guy wanted the ocean to be startlingly blue, an eye-popping blue, and the water wasn't blue enough. In fact, it wasn't blue at all. So Heidi managed to assemble various blue dyes and test them out in the bath of the hotel where we were staying (I wonder if the walls are still splashed today). Finally, at the hour of the shoot, we all trudged down to the water's edge and began tipping bucket after bucket of this blue dye into the sea. And of course it all got washed away. We tipped in more. And it all just washed out to sea again. Then we tipped in some more. And . . .

So we gave up on this idea to concentrate instead on the girl flying across the waves. A submerged wooden platform was built at low tide to hide the fact that she would be supported. The tide rolled in. The platform collapsed. It was rebuilt. The tide rolled in again. The whole thing collapsed again. Eventually, Guy settled for the simple idea of a girl running out of the sea leaving a trail of bright blue (paint) drips in her wake. It was surreal and beautiful. But in the end the clients didn't like it. They wanted something more conventional and luxurious to sell their bath product.

A tall, handsome young photographer with an English pallor, Willie Christie escorted me to a Zandra Rhodes ball at the Berkeley Hotel in 1973, for which I borrowed a Cinderella-style floaty chiffon Rhodes ball gown, the kind of thing I usually love in fairy-tale photographs but not so much on me. I chose Willie, who was once Clive Arrowsmith's assistant, to be my escort on the recommendation of my ex-assistant Patricia. They had dated at one stage but had broken up by then, and for once I didn't have a boyfriend around. "He's really eligible. He has his own black tie, and he can afford to buy his own ticket," she enthused, referring to Willie's aristocratic background (he is the grandson of the Marquess of Zetland).

We danced the night away until all the guests were gone and we were the last couple standing. Then, at the tail end of the party, he and I

crammed ourselves into his little green Mini and drove back to my basement flat in St. John's Wood, where he stayed the night. Within a short
span of time I had moved out of my place and into his house in Gunter
Grove, Fulham, which he shared with the manager of the pop singer
Bryan Ferry, who remained for a while, then discreetly moved out.

Willie was obsessed with glamorous old Hollywood photographs of
movie stars. He would copy the sets inexpensively and take great pains
to study their dramatic black-and-white, shadow-filled lighting. A year
later I was to work with him on his first shoot for *Vogue*—a moodily lit
fashion story inspired by the classic Bogart movie *Casablanca,* with the
model Marie Helvin crooning into an old microphone while a man in a
white suit sat behind her playing the piano.

Lady Jean Christie, Willie's mother, was a splendid woman, hilari-
ously funny and outspoken. Every weekend we went off to stay with her
in her roomy old country house near Newbury, deep in the horse-racing
depths of the English countryside, and each Sunday her many friends
hurried over for "drinkypoos." She liked "a little tipple" for dinner,
starting with sherry and ending with port. She also worried quietly
about Willie running through his inheritance because his attitude to life
was so devil-may-care.

Willie was a really kind person. He enjoyed life—maybe a little too
much. The period before our marriage had us frequently heading down
to Devon, taking my nephew Tristan with us, and staying with my
friend Polly Hamilton (another new face at *Vogue*), her husband, Peter,
and their young son, Jake, in their rambling old West Country farmhouse. While Polly and I busied ourselves cooking, gardening, and
doing rustic things like shelling peas and feeding the geese and the pigs,
Willie and Peter would hare noisily along the narrow, winding English
country lanes on their gigantic Harley-Davidsons, sending the locals

scurrying into the hedgerows. The first time Willie took me down to Devon was, in fact, on the back of his Harley. This was moments before a strict English law came into force making it mandatory to wear a crash helmet. I remember my long red hair flowing in the wind as I pressed, shivering, against Willie's back, even though I had exchanged my fashionable denim miniskirt for the relative warmth of blue jeans— probably the first and last time I ever wore a pair because I was absolutely never the blue jeans type.

One weekend a short while later, Polly and I visited a nearby cattery, and we decided to buy some beautiful kittens. They were a species called British Blue. Polly chose George, and I took his brothers, Brian and Stanley. Owning cats again made me extremely happy. They seemed a sign of a settled life with Willie.

A subject occupying the country during this period was self-sufficiency, the money-saving premise of growing your own food products by utilizing solar energy and preserving water by sharing a bath. Britain was at that moment gripped by endless power cuts and huge unemployment. There was even a British TV comedy, *The Good Life,* highly popular at the time, that made light of people trying to live in this fashion. It now became the inspiration behind a fashion shoot masterminded by me and photographed by Arthur Elgort at Polly's Devon farmhouse. It starred the French actress Aurore Clément modeling an assortment of tweedy coats, vintage dresses, and gumboots while pegging out the washing with Polly's new baby boy, Harry, tucked under her arm. In the photographs, Aurore looks the epitome of British pluck. Her determined expression as she marches between rows of homegrown cauliflowers and cabbages convincingly suggests that she could solve Britain's energy crisis single-handed.

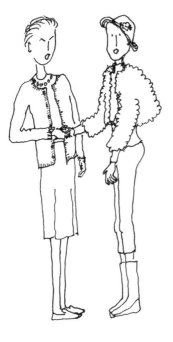

meeting Tina

As Karl Lagerfeld moved on to another grand apartment and a new inspiration in decor later in 1973, I heard once again from Michael, from whom I was officially divorced, though we remained on friendly terms. I was working in Paris and he was there, too, staying at the Hotel Lotti while bidding at auction for several key pieces from Karl's impressive collection of art deco furniture, including an enormous lacquered dining table he coveted that originally came from the old French luxury liner the *Normandie*. He called to say, "I want you to come and meet my next wife."

I had already heard from several sources that Michael's bride-to-be, Tina, was a very pretty, cool, and avant-garde young model of Japanese-American extraction. So, to make an impression, I rushed over to the Yves Saint Laurent salon to borrow something cool and avant-garde to wear. The outfit they lent me was from Yves's notorious forties couture collection, the one that scandalized all of Paris and included a green box-shouldered fox-fur coat called a "chubby" that came with leggings and wedge shoes. I then put on my makeup and my little blue velvet hat and went over to the hotel. Meanwhile, Tina had apparently heard that I was a very well-dressed person, too, which to her way of thinking translated as very classic, so she was dressed to meet me in a super-traditional English twinset and pearls. Thus, in a strange way, when we did meet, we were wearing each other's clothes. Nevertheless, right from the start we got on incredibly well.

The more I saw of Tina, the more convinced I was that she was the best-dressed woman I had ever met. Her tastes were subtle, minimalist, and utterly refined, yet alleviated by the most charming touches of humor. She could wear an eccentric accessory like the fresh flower corsages she put together herself and pinned to her traditional cashmere N. Peal cardigans, but she never crossed the line into the vulgar. She bought the most ravishing examples of Balenciaga couture at auction and owned a unique collection of vintage silk cut-velvet cheongsams as well as several museum-worthy Fortunys. Yet she could wear the simplest outfit—one of the beautiful little cotton T-shirts made for her in China, a pair of the gray flannel Kenzo trousers she endlessly had copied in Japan, and some plain brown leather loafers—and still be the chicest woman in the room.

A little while later, when the opportunity arose for me to arrange a photograph of her for *Vogue,* to be taken by the legendary Cecil Beaton, I imagined one of those classic Beaton images from the thirties with their glamorous, highly stylized settings and Tina lounging in her antique cheongsam like the film actress Anna May Wong. But, as with many other maestros, the living legend was less interested in his yesterdays and far more concerned with looking relevant and "modern." He wanted her leaping in midair. Hoping he would change his mind, I filled the studio with flowers and Japanese paper parasols, then waited for him to arrive for the sitting. We waited and waited. In the meantime Tina, who was an expert in flower arranging, having studied it in Japan, whiled away the hours by taking the undistinguished selection of lilies I had brought and creating a beautifully photogenic display. Finally, Beaton arrived. He looked around. "My God. This is terrible!" he said, staring at the flowers, whereupon he pulled them all out and totally rearranged them himself. I had completely forgotten that he, too, considered himself an authority on the subject.

Despite all the drama, the photograph he took of Tina lounging on the sofa surrounded by parasols was not modern at all. He had created theatrical pools of light, which gave the portrait an incredibly sad and haunting quality. The next year, a severe stroke left Beaton semiparalyzed until he died in 1980. It was probably his last great picture.

Tina died in 1992 from AIDS complications. She was the first woman I knew of who succumbed to the terrible disease. In fact, I had no idea up until then that it was even possible for women to contract AIDS.

In 1975 I paid my second visit to Jamaica with Norman Parkinson. Our models this time around were to be the illustrator Antonio Lopez and the Texan model Jerry Hall, who went on to become the girlfriend of the singer Bryan Ferry, and later to marry Mick Jagger. Antonio and Jerry were officially engaged at the time—very much a couple, albeit a fairly unlikely one—staying in their own "honeymoon" bungalow at the Jamaica Inn in Ochos Rios, around which we planned to base our shoot.

Antonio was a great New York fashion artist who famously took models with potential and turned them into glamazons or larger-than-life Warholian supermodels, advising them on how to look and pose. Jerry was his newest protegée, a towering cowgirl who stepped off the plane in Jamaica in one-hundred-degree heat wearing her first major modeling purchase—a floor-length fur coat. Because the couple shut themselves away from us in their room every evening, after a time I casually inquired how things were going. I was a little taken aback when Jerry told me that, although they slept together in the same bed, they spent their nights discussing the finer points of her makeup. Antonio would work on stylized drawings of her, and she was expected to adopt the look, paying particular attention to her hair and the enhanced contours of her face, which would turn her into the living vision of his sketches.

Years later, thanks to my frequent, enlightening trips to New York a decade before Antonio's sad death from AIDS in 1987, I would come to appreciate the powerful relationship between the gay world and the fantasy world of fashion.

That same year I was to work with Jerry Hall and Parks once again on a *Vogue* trip to Russia—the first time a magazine was allowed to go there and take fashion photographs. At the planning stage back in London, we came across very few pictures confirming any of the sights we might see on our two-and-a-half-week journey across what was then the Soviet Union. All we knew was that we planned to start shooting in Moscow and hoped to finish in Leningrad, formerly St. Petersburg, after traveling through Tajikistan, Turkmenistan, Azerbaijan, Armenia, and the Caucasus. And all we could be sure of was that there were many heroic statues standing from the time of the Russian Revolution.

Parks hoped to include several of these monuments in his photos, but just in case there was a problem, he said, "We are going to bring our own." So I organized a polystyrene plinth and had it constructed and painted to resemble a slab of gray stone with "Jerry Hall, *Vogue* Magazine in the USSR, 1975" inscribed on it in Cyrillic letters. This we carried around with us virtually everywhere. One of our photographs shows Jerry in Red Square sitting atop it, reading a newspaper. In another she is using it like a diving board, poised as if about to plunge into Armenia's Lake Sevan.

We were an extremely tight little group: Jerry, Parks, his wife, Wenda, who was to write the *Vogue* travel piece, his assistant, Tim, and me. I took suitcases filled with red clothes—a lot of which, due to a lack of color pages, were thanklessly published in black and white—and I brought neither assistant, hairstylist, nor makeup artist. Jerry had to rely on all those tips from Antonio to look the part.

The Russian authorities made it a full and binding condition of the trip that all the rolls of film had to be processed and printed before we returned home, and there would be guides to indicate where we could and could not point our cameras. Before we left England, someone told me it was likely our rooms would be bugged too, and that the top two floors of any of the country's tourist hotels would be taken up by eavesdropping devices. We didn't take this so seriously and, after checking into my hotel room the first night, we moved about loudly, joking, "Hey, Big Brother, are you listening?"

When the job was completed and it was time to leave for home, Parks, who was to stay behind waiting for the final film to be developed, walked up to me and murmured, "Grace, I'm really quite worried about how they will process the photographs, because when I told them what type of film I'd used, they had never heard of it. Can you smuggle one roll from each setup back with you just to be safe?" "No," I said, "sorry, I can't. I love *Vogue,* but I'm not sure I want to spend the rest of my days a political prisoner in a Russian jail."

"I can take them," Jerry piped up. "The authorities never, ever search me. I'll put them in my makeup bag."

"On your own head be it," I said, crossly.

We arrived at the airport, where, sure enough, the customs officers were soon going through every single bag, turning them inside out and upside down and being incredibly thorough. I became highly suspicious and asked a young official what was going on. "We have been tipped off that you are carrying unexposed films and anti-Russian propaganda," he said, in broken English. I tried to explain that we were guests of the tourist board, but they carried on regardless.

Jerry's new boyfriend, Bryan Ferry, had given her several of his recordings, which she listened to throughout the trip on her portable tape machine. These were confiscated and taken away to be played at half-speed in case they contained any secret messages. It was obviously only a matter of time before the officials uncovered the rolls of film in Jerry's makeup bag and fished them out.

The film came in professional rolls of the type that, when used, are secured with a paper sticker stamped with the word "Exposed" in large letters. I quickly pointed this out to the authorities. "See," I said, "you are looking for unexposed film, and this says 'Exposed.'" Thankfully, the Russian officials managed to somehow confuse the words "exposed" and "unexposed." Now all I needed was to keep them confused enough to let us go. Our plane was leaving. The steps were being removed, and it was about to pull away along the runway for takeoff. But we made it just in time, and escaped with our contraband!

When Parks returned to England, however, he carried with him the rest of our pictures, and all of them were perfectly processed. In fact, they were much better done than those we had so nervously smuggled back to London.

Willie and I were married at Chelsea Registry Office in November 1976. I wore a black jacket,

my YSL red satin blazer
a Liberty print skirt

a royal blue silk blouse with a tie neck, and a purple-printed peasant skirt, all by Yves Saint Laurent Rive Gauche. Willie wore an Yves Saint Laurent suit. The witnesses were Willie's mother, Lady Jean; Willie's sister, Carolyne; and Carolyne's rock-star husband, Roger Waters of Pink Floyd. My former assistant Di James and my then-assistant Antonia Kirwan-Taylor prepared the food back at our place in Gunter Grove, and all the *Vogue* girls, along with Bea Miller and the diffident Chinese art director, Barney Wan, arrived to celebrate. (There are two things I always required of my assistants. They had to look good and be able to cook, because in the early days there was no such thing as catering at any *Vogue* photo session).

Later that day Willie and I took the car—a Land Rover we had recently used on a photo shoot up in Scotland—and sped off to Paris to photograph the collections. We had arranged beforehand to combine our honeymoon road trip with a short French gastronomic tour, stopping off at a couple of places on the way. But our first stop was an unscheduled layover in Brighton on our wedding night after missing the last boat across the Channel. We arrived at the Grand Hotel covered in confetti. Back then, the place was crumbling and miserable, with one mournful light shining in the dining room. I remember seeing a little mouse run across the floor.

Not too long after our wedding, I journeyed to Paris again, this time with Barney Wan for a collections shoot at Studio Pinup in the rue Daguerre with the Swiss photographer Lothar Schmid; his statuesque model girlfriend, Carrie Nygren; and another girl called Marcie Hunt. The clothes were all by Yves Saint Laurent, Chinese-inspired, sumptuous, golden, and lavishly trimmed with sable. Dinner was delivered to the studio by Barney's friend Davé, soon to open his own Chinese restaurant on Paris's Right Bank and destined to become a firm favorite of the fashion pack. Davé had a famous habit of taking out his tarot cards at soirees and predicting the future. He had already performed for a whole bunch of celebrated jet-setters, including Yves Saint Laurent and Princess Grace of Monaco. It was the shock of seeing in the cards a few years later the car accident causing the princess's death that led him to give up holding readings altogether. But in those days it was normal practice as a kind of party piece for him to take out the pack and foretell the future for pretty much everyone working on a shoot. "I see a suit-case. Someone is leaving," he said when he came to me. Well, I thought, this prediction wasn't so uncanny after all, because I was indeed leaving after the shoot to return to London.

Arriving back in Fulham the next day, I put my key in the door. And there was Willie, sitting on the sofa with a suitcase by his side, saying, "I need some time on my own." Then he walked out on me. All of which was kind of shocking.

Later I discovered that he had left to go on holiday with a model friend of mine, and that for some time, they had been conducting a tem-pestuous affair behind my back. So it wasn't so sudden after all. And even when they both came back with suntans, I hadn't a clue until Wil-lie's mother told me her son had been seeing a girl called Shirley. Then everything fell into place.

We divorced after barely six months of marriage. I kept the cats and moved into a new apartment close to my former one near the Chelsea football grounds. The toughest thing about the whole situation was that Willie and I had reopened adoption proceedings and been due to pick up my nephew Tristan and have him come live with us full-time on the day after Willie walked out. Now I would be collecting him on my own—obviously not the best of circumstances for Tristan or me.

VIII

ON STATES OF GRACE

America
calls, Grace
answers,
and then
has a cow.

H ard as it was, I threw myself back into my work. With Tristan returned to boarding school, I took off for New York for the first time since my fateful trip with Clive Arrowsmith seven years earlier. British *Vogue*, I discovered, had a very good name over there—which came as some surprise to me, because up until then I thought our reputation stopped at Dover. It was 1978. I stayed at the Algonquin, which subsequently became my hotel of choice whenever I returned. Accompanied once again by *Vogue* art director Barney Wan, I set out to conquer Manhattan.

New York—"the Big Apple," as they were calling it—was unbelievably exciting. The energy, pace, and scale were in such sharp contrast to London. And the American collections were so refreshingly pared down. I could relate to the designer Perry Ellis, whom all the young

"Tell me Azzedine, does my butt look big in this?"

people loved. Zoran made minimal and clever clothes, and the quality of his cashmere was fantastic. Oscar de la Renta was so handsome and charming—I remember him doing a lot of sexy black lace Spanish-style dresses. Ralph Lauren made everything look so dashingly western. But it was Calvin Klein who really took me in another direction. I discovered that simple and understated didn't necessarily mean boring; it could mean minimalist and chic. And comfortable! You could move in these clothes.

Soon I was traveling back and forth doing frequent photo sessions for British *Vogue,* always on standby to save money, which is very nerve-wracking when you carry endless customs forms and are accompanied by a load of trunks filled with designer clothes but have no assistant for support.

Only later, when I worked freelance on advertising for Calvin, was I flown to America and back by Concorde. He was very generous. (If anyone expressed jealousy, I told them I had earned it because, until I was forty-five, I nearly always traveled standby.) The money was also a great surprise. When he mentioned he must pay me and how much did I want, I said something like, "Oh, it's no big deal. Give me whatever you like." I'd had a very nice time, and after all, they did pay my airfare and hotel. It was a little unexpected, then, when he said he would be giving me a check and sending his bodyguard to accompany me to the bank to cash it. But when I looked, what I really couldn't believe was the amount. It was more than I made at *Vogue* in an entire year. Finally, I was able to pay all of Tristan's school fees without having to worry. Going back to London, I stuffed the cash down my underwear for fear it would be taken away by the customs officials.

Among the photographers I worked with most often now were Peter Lindbergh, a German who lived in Paris and liked to do most of his shoots on the beach at Deauville; and Paolo Roversi, an Italian in Paris who never left the studio. Handsome, with a very sexy voice, Paolo did beautiful, poetic work shooting only in large-format Polaroid on a plate camera, in either black and white or in very saturated colors. I found this technique, where you immediately saw and judged the results, a little unnerving, like digital photography is now, but Paolo's pictures were truly romantic, and I loved them.

I also collaborated frequently with Arthur Elgort, Bruce Weber, Alex Chatelain, Albert Watson, and Patrick Demarchelier. Patrick was among the band of what the American photojournalist Bill Cunningham used to call "The Frenchies," a peripatetic group of good-looking young Frenchmen jetting between Paris, London, and New York that also included the photographers Pierre Houles, André Carrara, Gilles Bensimon, and Mike Reinhardt, and the hairstylist Didier Malige. This distinctly continental *bande des mecs* attracted swathes of pretty girlfriends with their seductive Gallic mumbling. Patrick, I think, spoke more clearly then than he does now, but since he repeats everything several times, you eventually begin to understand. He is a great photographer who is very good at lighting and equally at home in the studio or the open air. This is rare. He also excels at celebrity portraits—those of Princess Diana being especially well remembered—and spotting pretty girls. When we visited Barbados in 1983, for example, we took the model Bonnie Berman, freshly "discovered" working as the coat-check girl at Mr Chow NYC, and Patrick transformed her into one of the most memorable British *Vogue* covers ever.

By this time I had grown close to the people from Browns, the little London shop that was the first to endorse the new wave of American designers. Together with its owner, Joan Burstein—affectionately known as just "the Mrs."—and her team of assistants, we would try out the lat-

my disco look

est New York restaurants while they were visiting on buying trips. There was Odeon, where the cast of *Saturday Night Live* hung out; Hatsuhana, which introduced me to Japanese food and went on to become my favorite; Da Silvano, where the fashion crowd had just begun to gather; Un Deux Trois, popular among theatergoing folk, with its cute canister of crayons on every table (they are still there) so you could doodle on the paper tablecloths. And afterward, Studio 54 or one of those crazy alternative clubs such as the Gilded Grape, where trapeze artists hung overhead by their heels and which was truly like going to a freak show or some over-the-top circus with drag queens dressed as Grace Jones. I also remember all the straight boys around this time being mad for the husky-voiced disco diva Amanda Lear, whose sexual origins were shrouded in mystery. They were dying to go to bed with her just to find out what lay beneath.

Robert Forrest, the indefatigably social fashion director of Browns, took me to all these gay clubs along with his friend the Australian hairstylist Kerry Warn. They were always warm and chatty, although it sometimes seemed as if I were eavesdropping on some secret, impenetrable language based on gender change. "Ooh, she's a butch woman!" they would say to each other, for example, ogling the straightest-looking waiter in a restaurant, or President Gerald Ford would metamorphose into "Miss Geraldine Ford." Robert was inexhaustible, always seeking out the newest this or the latest that. It was he who brought back home from his trips the latest American chart-toppers such as "Native New

Yorker" or disco hits like "Le Freak." He and Mrs. Burstein spent their free American weekends at a little place she rented in the notoriously gay enclave of Fire Island. Kerry was also a veteran of my photo sessions with Albert Watson, a bustling Scot living and working in Manhattan whose photographs—hard-edged, energetic, and disco-bright—most accurately captured the spirit of the day.

I think I first heard of AIDS when I was out and about with Kerry and Robert. All the talk up until then had been about herpes, with herpes jokes becoming hugely popular in a vulgar kind of way. Now AIDS came along, and this was serious—and deadly. There was so much fear and rumor connected to it, like that if you shook hands with a gay person, you were going to catch the disease: People were that naive. Everyone didn't suddenly pull out their condoms, though, and in England, AIDS and its dreadful consequences were hardly ever mentioned at all.

That same year I went to a wildly different part of America—Tucson, Arizona—for a shoot with Alex Chatelain. By now our team for trips had been extended. Didier Malige came to style the hair, and Bonnie Maller would do the makeup. The model was Kelly Emberg, a breezy American ex-cheerleader who later moved in with the singer Rod Stewart and had a daughter with him. The location manager was, I remember, intense about the search for enlightenment (so fashionable at the time) and tried introducing us to the world of EST. She even suggested we all sit around in a hot tub holding hands and telling the truth. I always find that kind of thing, as well as health fads like colonic irrigation, more hokey than meaningful.

The clothes we took with us for this shoot were mostly made of leather. One Zoran wrap was practically a whole cowhide. We shot in the kind of rugged cowboy country where spiritual cults are rarely embraced and where men are men and not easily confused with the Village People.

Breaking for lunch at some dusty diner or other, I scanned the menu looking for something recognizable to eat. Ribs, I thought in my very English way. Wouldn't that be something like a dear little lamb chop with mint sauce? A carcass arrived. Not only did it not fit onto the plate, but it was the size of an entire herd. I nibbled away politely for a while, then offered it to the huge cowhands sitting and salivating at the next table. It was gone in a minute.

In 1979 British *Vogue* traveled to China on what was to be the first fashion trip to that country undertaken by a Western glossy magazine (that is, if you didn't count Arthur Elgort going there for American *Vogue* some months before to follow Nancy Kissinger around). Again my photographer was Alex Chatelain and the hairdresser Kerry Warn, and the model was Esmé, the latest American "it" girl, who had strikingly boyish features, thick eyebrows, and short, cropped hair. The negotiations had been complicated, political, and long, and resulted in two photo shoots that had to be carried out at the same time, mine and a commercially driven *Vogue* promotion styled by my colleague Liz Tilberis and supervised by a smooth-talking South American fashion Mr. Fixit named Roberto Devorik, who was paying for the entire historical venture.

For my photographs I chose a wardrobe of fanciful, brocaded chinoiserie-inspired clothes, which, on arrival, I immediately abandoned. Stepping off the plane, I had been surrounded by hundreds of people: men, women, and children all wearing plain, functional Mao suits in either khaki or blue. Everyone, no exception. Little babies might have been allowed to wear clothes with a duckling or some such embroidered on them, but after the age of three, everyone looked exactly the same. (This was a far cry from my subsequent trip to China some twenty years later, when the uniforms had been jettisoned in favor of sequins and a rather garish notion of Western dress.) Completely inspired, I rushed off to buy these suits to put on my model (and, I have to admit, acquire a whole new wardrobe for myself). After all, we were there to make pictures of modern-day China. Thankfully, we didn't need to worry about clothing credits so much back then.

We took trains everywhere: sleepers. It was amazing. We stayed in huge hotels with vast bedrooms—many bigger than my present apartment—that were normally occupied by important Chinese delegations. We took pictures of Esmé drinking tea in a railway carriage, sitting in a station waiting room on a huge white sofa with our guide, and standing by a lake in her utilitarian cotton suit in homage to a famous lakeside propaganda picture of Chairman Mao, whose inescapable image was everywhere. Our guide, Mr. Ko, was wonderful. He was well read, spoke very good English, and on our final night, sang "Edelweiss" to us dreamily over the dinner table.

Later, I received the most beautiful letter of thanks from him, saying how his time spent with us had changed his life and expressing how much he wished he could visit us in England—although regulations were so strict in those days that he never would have been allowed out of China.

Returning to London, I felt completely exhilarated by my trip. It left me appreciating minimalism in new ways, which was ironic, seeing as I arrived back overloaded to the maximum with Chinese badges, sheets, bedcovers, starched white cotton slipcovers, and antimacassars. These last were on every chair I saw in China, in every school, hotel, airport, station, and on every train seat. Maybe it's because the men put so much grease in their hair. Now, filled with a new desire for plain, unfussy functionalism, I draped them over all the furniture in my London apartment, exchanging my chintzy covers for plain white.

Throughout the seventies, Bea Miller regularly held the most amazing dinner parties. Guests would include Tony Snowdon and his wife, Princess Margaret, alongside Peter Sellers and Britt Ekland, Paul and Linda McCartney, Liza Minnelli, the author Antonia Fraser, journalists Mark Boxer and Kenneth Allsop, fashion designer Geoffrey Beene, the actor Michael York (who was a fixture, as was I), and George Harrison and Pattie Boyd. The dinners were always catered, and the hired waiters were often more than a little drunk and incapable before the end of the evening.

Bea was a wonderful hostess who managed to cram so many famous people into her tiny basement flat in a small gray brick house off the lower end of the Kings Road that it was like one of those competitions to see how many students can be stuffed into a telephone box. Afterward Barney Wan and I would stay behind to do the washing up in the minuscule kitchen because by then the waiters were completely out of it.

Many of Bea's famous friends would also drift in and out of *Vogue*'s offices to see her. Despite being intensely private personally, she seemed to operate a very relaxed open-door policy as far as hip Londoners were concerned. I, on the other hand, rarely received visitors other than the photographers who came to discuss or show their work. So the day the punk designer Vivienne Westwood came calling, I was completely flummoxed.

She marched directly into the fashion room totally unannounced (a far easier thing to do in the days before security guards sat in the lobby) with a bag full of bondage trousers and a ring through every orifice, saying, "I should be on the cover of *Vogue* wearing things like these." She had a very aggressive manner. Everyone in the office shrank from her challenging demeanor. But in the end, I stood my ground, talked her down, and she eventually left, while startled people went back to looking through their clothes rails, saying, "What was that?"

As we entered the eighties, the designer whom the entire fashion community gossiped about was Azzedine Alaïa. Small and Tunisian, with a short temper to match, he had the chicest French girls lining up for his clothes. He operated out of a town house in Paris on the rue de Bellechasse but never held full-blown fashion shows, only hush-hush in-house presentations for buyers, friends, and clients. I heard about him through the Browns network of Robert Forrest and Mrs. Burstein, and I was persistent and intrigued enough to wangle a viewing even though he was rumored to harbor a distinct aversion to the press.

We arrived at Alaïa's Left Bank salon at the appointed time and were asked to wait. And wait. And wait. Finally, we were allowed back to where the buyers had gathered to watch a solitary girl wearing his intriguingly cut black clothes wander through the little suite of interlocking rooms that made up the floor, followed, after a long pause, by another. Onlookers, studded about on little poufs or sitting at the buyers' tiny tables, were focused with laserlike intensity on the way the designer's fluid seams and zips shaped the clothes across the lines of the body. People looked as if they had unearthed the Holy Grail.

When it was over, Alaïa came out, a tiny figure dressed head to foot in black with an even tinier dog under his arm. We were introduced and I gathered, despite my limited French vocabulary, that he was seriously saying *Vogue* should put him on the cover along with Patapouf, his little Yorkshire terrier. It took a while to sink in that he was joking because his sense of humor is so wickedly deadpan. But finally, he chuckled.

Azzedine came on the scene at a time when Yves Saint Laurent, Kenzo, and Karl Lagerfeld were at the pinnacle of Paris fashion. Yet he astonished everyone with such a different way of looking at the body. His clothes were flattering and sensual and made you look so curvy. You couldn't help but marvel at all those darts shaped to give you a very small waist, which I've always found attractive. I thought it was great, too, that such a small operation created things so beautifully. There was so much artistry and couture cutting—and it wasn't even couture. Nothing was hidden away beneath embroidery or layers; they were just very feminine clothes contouring the body perfectly. You could see fashion turn a corner at that moment, and the eighties became defined by his look—no doubt about it.

I loved Azzedine's clothes and began wearing them exclusively. From then on he was in every story, and if it wasn't an Azzedine story, it looked like an Azzedine story.

The marriage of Lady Diana Spencer to Prince Charles in 1981 turned the whole country—and British *Vogue*—upside down with the endless rumors that Diana was in close consultation with the magazine about her trousseau and royal wardrobe. While some paparazzi and journalists skulked around the Mayfair salon of David and Elizabeth Emanuel, the young couple chosen to design and make the wedding dress, and even stooped low enough to raid their outside dustbins for telltale scraps of likely material, others hung about *Vogue*'s doorstep just up the road in Hanover Square, hoping to run across the bride-to-be. At one stage Diana's sister Sarah did work for Bea Miller, and the princess did indeed come into Vogue House several times to discuss clothes with Anna Harvey, a discreet senior fashion editor who was the best person to advise her; she was also called upon to visit Kensington Palace, help Diana make clothing decisions, steer her through the heaps of craziness coming from the English designers, and keep her choices on the straight and narrow. If I, on the other hand, had been consulted, I probably would have suggested a few of my favorites and put her into Yves Saint Laurent, Azzedine Alaïa, or something by Karl Lagerfeld, which would have been entirely out of order because she was supposed to dress patriotically in British designs. But I wasn't remotely interested. I was also the last to know whenever she was visiting, although I do recall the offices becoming spectacularly quiet when she was rumored to be on the premises.

Much of my time between 1980 and 1984 was dedicated to creating photo stories in the great outdoors with Bruce Weber. Not only did we refine the narrative style of shooting that he and I became most associated with at British *Vogue,* but we also collaborated on several campaigns for Calvin Klein.

Calvin was one of the first to take out huge wedges of promotional material in the international fashion press. So I wasn't surprised when the phone rang one day while I was sitting at my desk at *Vogue* and I picked it up to find him on the line. "Grace, who do I have to contact about advertising?" he asked. "I want to do twenty-five pages in British *Vogue.*" I almost fell off my chair. "Richard Hill," I said, giving him the name of our affable, laid-back publisher. Assuring Calvin that I would put them in touch with each other as soon as possible, I immediately raced off along the corridor to find Richard, and arrived at his office just as he was putting on his coat. "I have Calvin Klein on the line, and he wants to buy twenty-five pages of advertising," I gushed trium-phantly, feeling not a little overexcited and, I must say, pleased with myself for having played some small part in this immensely lucrative moment. Richard, on the other hand, looked rather put out. "But I'm just going to lunch," he said, continuing to slip into his coat. "Can't you tell him to call back in a couple of hours?" I couldn't believe it. Here was British *Vogue,* which usually dropped to its knees pleading for a mere single page from a designer, being handed twenty-five, and this guy was going out for lunch! It was, as they say, the limit.

By now I had forged a steady relationship with the French hairstylist Didier Malige. We became closer and closer because he was working with Bruce constantly, as was I, so we were always being thrown to-gether. We didn't really start dating seriously until 1983. I remember this because in 1982 we had been working in Barbados with the photogra-pher Patrick Demarchelier, and Didier was always lighting my cigarette in a romantic, chivalrous way. A year later, he had become my steady boyfriend and was always ripping the cigarette out of my mouth. (Now I no longer smoke, having given it up when I came to America.)

Back in Wales, following Uncle Ted's death in the sixties (and long after I had departed for London), my cousin Michael had inherited all his father's interests, including our hotel. But because his heart wasn't in being a property owner, he bought a caravan and took to the open road instead. Then, after discussions with other family members, he decided to sell off our hotel to a large brewery, but he built my mother a house adjacent to the annex, which enabled her to retain use, in retirement, of her beloved little garden. She had remained quite active, giving rides to children on a couple of ponies and a donkey she kept specifically for that purpose. The house was not terribly well built, but it did have four bedrooms, where she could house all the local stray cats and dogs she had begun to take in. At a certain point, it seemed to me that whenever I visited, hundreds of animals were lodged there, on every chair, with some of them climbing onto the mantelpiece. And on particularly bitter nights she even brought the donkey inside to shelter in the kitchen.

All that caretaking had to be given up when she herself was encouraged, in her eighties, to move out of her place and enter an old people's home, situated a short distance away in another part of our village. Completely on her own after losing a husband, a daughter, a brother, and a sister, she was increasingly opposed to anyone helping out and couldn't countenance the prospect of welfare people visiting her because she was certain they had come to steal from her. She also imagined herself being constantly spied on.

In the home, which was more of a large house, there were no more than six or seven other elderly people. A Yorkshire terrier was also living there and as she no longer had a dog of her own (she had kept Yorkshire terriers all her life), my mother was happy to adopt this one as her new canine companion. She loved it dearly, often saying, "I hope I die before this dog." Then one day, after accompanying it for a walk around the garden, she came in and sat down on a big comfy sofa, it jumped in her lap, and she died. So she got her wish. She was eighty-two.

I was on a photo shoot in Hawaii with the photographer Hans Feurer when the news reached me in a late-night call from Liz Tilberis, my close friend at British *Vogue,* but I told no one—except for Didier, who was with me when the call came through. I have always had a strong aversion to thoughts of death and showy demonstrations of grief, far preferring silence and grieving inwardly. Besides, it was impossible to get off the island where we were staying. We were forced to remain and had two more days to finish the job. I know many people might find my way of thinking about work at a time of tragedy somewhat callous—but to me it was form of consolation. I somehow managed to get the funeral delayed, then went back home. On my return, Willie, my ex-husband, was kindly waiting back in London to rush me straight there.

That same year, 1985, I was, somewhat belatedly, made fashion director. My first act was to redecorate the *Vogue* fashion room with the help and guidance of Michael Chow. Basically, I had all the tatty old flooring ripped up and chic blond wood laid down. Modern plate glass and tubular steel Le Corbusier tables were installed, replacing the rickety old wooden desks that seemed to have been salvaged from the Great Fire of

my Calvin Klein
check suit

London. The whole fashion staff was given natural wicker and chrome Breuer chairs, and the walls were painted white. Michael thought there should be a strict rule that no one was to be allowed to attach more than one photograph of a child, boyfriend, or animal to a pinboard (an implausible notion in sentimental old England). A corner of the room was partitioned off with plate-glass walls, and this was to become my office. Liz Tilberis called it "the fishbowl."

My assistant was now a girl named Lucinda Chambers, who before coming to me had worked for the editor. She would arrive each morning looking like a flower in outfits she made herself, and sat at her desk outside Bea's office sprouting petals of organza. I have never known anyone more passionate about clothes. Nor more blissfully scatty. Once we had to go off together for a New York fashion shoot. She was supposed to pass by my flat in the taxi and pick me up on the way to Heathrow Airport. But she hadn't written down the street address. And although she urgently needed to call me, she couldn't find my phone number, as I was unlisted. She stopped at a public telephone and rang the operator in floods of tears, but they wouldn't give out any information. "But you don't understand. I am her assistant," she wailed. Finally, the operator relented and phoned me. "I've got this madwoman on the phone who says she is your assistant," she said.

On that same trip—the first time a fashion editor at British *Vogue* was actually allowed to take an assistant abroad—we checked into the Algonquin in Manhattan, and I warned the two friendly doormen, Mike and Tony, that Lucinda was a little absentminded, whereupon they tied a label to her wrist that read, "If found, please return to the Algonquin."

Despite that, the girl was just so cute to have around. She had tons of friends who would pop in to visit her at the *Vogue* office. One of them was a young Peruvian photographer named Mario Testino, who was always hanging around. In the end I couldn't help myself. "Who is that annoying boy?" I asked exasperatedly. "You have to get him out of here." But it never really deterred him. Mario kept right on coming.

After Lucinda—who has since gone on to my old job as fashion director of British *Vogue*—my assistant was Sophie Hicks. Everything about Sophie had to do with being a boy. No makeup, hair cut like a boy's. She even wore men's underwear. Her idea of evening dress was the thirties lounge-lizard Noël Coward look of a man's silk dressing gown worn over a pair of tuxedo trousers with men's patent lace-up dress shoes. Sophie went on to become an architect, married, and had three kids, including two beautiful daughters whom everyone is now dying to photograph.

When Bea Miller retired from editing British *Vogue* after twenty-two years, she told me I should try for her job. I did go for an interview with Bernie Leser, the managing director of British Condé Nast, but deep down I knew I wasn't suited for it. When the high-ups at *Vogue* asked me for my honest opinion, I said, "Anna Wintour should get the job," not knowing that Anna, then the creative director of American *Vogue,* whom I knew from the fashion world on both sides of the Atlantic, had already been asked. What the pro-Anna power brokers at American *Vogue* probably said to her was "Go over to England for a few years, get some experience, and when you come back, we'll make you editor in chief of American *Vogue*."

The first time Anna came to the British collections made a telling impression. She hadn't officially started at British *Vogue* quite yet, but she wanted to work out exactly who was important. We, the editorial staff, were all used to hanging about together, being chummy and chitty-chatty, but she wasn't. She was far too busy running off to important meetings. And the fact that she turned up at the British shows accompanied by her friend André (Leon Talley, fashion news editor of American *Vogue*) didn't go down too well either. For a time it almost seemed he was running the whole show because Anna kept deferring to him, telling us things like, "André thinks we should be doing a story on so-and-so" or "André feels such-and-such is really important."

Anna made it clear from the first day that although she liked me and was very supportive, work was work, she was the boss, and that was that. No contest. In an employee/employer situation, it was never going to be like sitting down with a mate. Two days into her editorship, she said to me, "Oh, I'm going to a screening, and I want you to come with me." The film, a French production titled *Betty Blue,* starred a new sexy actress called Béatrice Dalle, whom everyone was talking about and whom Anna thought of having photographed for the magazine. So we sat down in anticipation as the lights dimmed. Now, anyone who has ever seen this film knows that the opening scene, which goes on and on in dead silence for well over five long, embarrassing minutes, shows a naked couple screwing on a bed—very vividly and very realistically—while the camera pans in closer and closer. As we watched, I became more and more fidgety, sinking lower in my seat and feeling extremely uncomfortable while Anna was rigid and unmoving. No sign of any emotion at all. I then realized how much significance Anna places on willpower trumping feelings.

During the preparations for her first issue of British *Vogue,* I was expected to oversee the shooting of the collections and was summoned to a meeting at the rented apartment Anna was living in with her then-husband David Shaffer, which was rather beautiful and overlooked a pretty square in Kensington. She was sitting cross-legged on the sofa looking very skinny in her eighties Azzedine Alaïa leggings and a huge orange sweater, despite the fact that only a few weeks earlier she had given birth to Charlie, her first child. She had a thing about the coltish young English film actress Amanda Pays, whom she wished to have photographed for the cover of her first British collections issue wearing a traffic-stoppingly bright orange coat by the designer Jean Muir. I can't tell you how many cover tries of that coat we shot and reshot until we arrived at the ultra-simple image on a stark white background that she wanted.

It was such a different way of working for me. Anna's mission, com-

A new hair cut
& Calvin Klein dress

ing as she did from the commanding heights of American *Vogue,* seemed to be to take its whimsical little cousin by the scruff of the neck and propel it forward into a brave new world. I didn't want to have a battle over this or give her a hard time. So I began thinking seriously about the conversations Calvin Klein and I had been having in which he urged me to come and work for him in America.

It was 1987, two years since my mother had died. Tristan was through school by now and living in Oxford, cramming for further exams and intent on taking a business and computer course in London, which basically meant I could leave. Before, it would have seemed so final and far away, but with Tristan becoming more psychologically independent and Didier encouraging me by saying, "I'm sure you will move to New York one day," I was on my way.

There was such a buzz about New York. A self-confidence. Working girls wearing snowy-white trainers and clutching polystyrene cups of coffee elbowed determinedly past you in the mornings on their mission to climb the corporate ladder. Times Square glittered dangerously. Tabloid headlines screamed about Central Park killers and cocaine busts. Fashion designers like Bill Blass, Diane von Furstenberg, Ralph Lauren, Halston, Donna Karan, and Calvin were fast becoming mass-media celebrities. Money appeared to be no object, even though everyone talked about New York living on the edge of bankruptcy.

I stayed on at British *Vogue* for another nine months, during which time I went from wearing everything Azzedine Alaïa to wearing everything Calvin Klein. Meanwhile, our daily work ethic changed considerably along the way.

Gabé Doppelt, Anna's new assistant, who came from the British society magazine *Tatler,* was sent to New York on a crash course to learn how things were done over there and brought back, among other things, "run-throughs," the practice of trying on a stand-in model, before a shoot, all the clothes you intended to use. We had to go through so many hours of run-throughs, it was awful. In my opinion, it simply isn't possible to simulate the mood one hopes to achieve in a beautiful photograph taken on location by putting the same clothes on the wrong girl in a grimly lit office. Besides, no decent-looking model ever wanted to come in and try on the clothes just so we could see how they looked, because how far was that going to advance her career? Neither did we have the same extensive and efficient messenger service to pick up and return all the clothes as they do in New York. We often dragged them around ourselves. Or we had a nice young chap called Alistair ferry all the clothes back and forth in his secondhand rattletrap, and probably stop a few times along the way.

I honestly don't know how Anna survived. There was no spirited atmosphere, no determination, everything was deemed "impossible" or "Ooh, I don't think so," and the solution to most problems was "Mmmm, let's have a nice cup of tea."

I must say, the way the English press attacked Anna all the time was pretty stupid, with stories calling her Nuclear Wintour or headlined "The Wintour of Our Discontent." She made news because of what she was doing to old British *Vogue,* where everyone was used to getting in late and not working terribly hard. If Anna ever saw anyone sitting around, she would immediately give her ten shoots to do. She didn't like the English tweedy and Wellington boot thing I was fond of because she considered it frumpy. The Italian designer Romeo Gigli was hugely influential at the time—skirts worn close to the ankles with flat shoes. She didn't care for this, either. Anna's *Vogue* was all about chopping down the skirts and modern girls running through the streets in very high heels.

I flew to New York to do a great many of these shoots for the new cleaned-up *Vogue,* especially covers. On strict instructions from Anna, my mission each day was to take the film over to Alexander Liberman so he could cast his critical eye over it and tell her what he thought. Mr. Liberman, a dapper magazine gentleman of the old school secretly known around the Condé Nast building as the Silver Fox, was the right-hand man to Condé Nast's owner, S. I. Newhouse. He oversaw every publication. A white Russian who, quite early on in his career, became American *Vogue*'s art director, he was also a well-known modern artist and a sculptor of enormous painted metal constructions destined for public and corporate spaces. I found him an elegant man, with his trimmed gray mustache, tailored gray suits, and overpoweringly quiet voice. He never thumped a hand on the desk to make his point and was very spare and direct. I had met him several times previously: Every five years or so he had flown over to see British *Vogue,* comment, and dispense advice to Bea Miller. She was not a complete fan, though. She thought everything he told her to do was appropriate for American rather than British *Vogue.*

I'm a person who usually likes an ordered, straightforward home life. I don't leave a house or a job often. But when Calvin offered me the position as his design director, he made it easy for me to move. I thought, "If I don't go now, I'll be here for the rest of my life." I was loving all things American at the time, and I suppose I was also being a little bit daring.

After all, it's not so adventurous to make this kind of move when you're young, but a bit more so when you're forty-eight or forty-nine. Most important, I was in love with Didier, and he lived in New York—I thought he would take me more seriously if I went to live there.

I gave my notice while I was away on a fashion shoot in America. Someone told me that the story broke in *Women's Wear Daily,* but I never saw it because I never read it. Anna coolly accepted my resignation on the day she turned thirty-eight. "I would have preferred a different birthday present," she was rumored to have said.

At Calvin I learned to think fast, act fast, move fast. Anna had taught me that nothing is forever. "Let's just move on, shall we?" she will invariably say, because she knows you can't dwell on things you unfortunately cannot change. In their way, Anna and Calvin are very similar. Their birthdays are only days apart.

With Albert Koski in New York for Harper's Bazaar. *Photo:*
Louis Faurer, 1966. Courtesy of Harper's Bazaar

*Test-driving Mary Quant's
minidress and shorts with the designer,
London. Photo: Eric Swayne, 1966*

*Going head to head with Vidal Sassoon
in his Mayfair flat, London, 1964. Photo
courtesy of Vidal Sassoon archives*

Eating shrimp in Normandy. Photo: Duc, 1971.

Powdering Prince Charles for his official investiture photograph, Windsor Castle. Photo: Norman Parkinson, 1969. © Norman Parkinson Limited / Courtesy Norman Parkinson Archive

My marriage to Michael Chow, London. Photo: Barry Lategan, 1969

*With Helmut Newton, Manolo Blahnik, Anjelica Huston, and David
Bailey in the South of France. Photo: David Bailey, 1974*

My boyfriend, Duc, left, playing dress-up with Guy Bourdin, 1971

With Karl Lagerfeld, Paris. Photo: Julie Kavanagh, 1974

At my wedding party with Willie Christie in Gunter Grove, London, 1976

Tristan plays model, Shelter Island, N.Y. Photo: Bruce Weber, 1980

IX

ON
BRUCE

In which
Grace goes to
the dogs, and to
Australia, New
Mexico, and
Maine, then ends
up in England
with a garden on
the head.

B ruce Weber's pictures and his life are one. His photographs are all about relationships, and the people he works with become his extended family. And when those people bring in more people, the family grows bigger and bigger until it includes their outer circle, too. It's a bit like Bruce and his dogs. He loves golden retrievers and keeps acquiring more and more. He can never be done with one of anything. It's always about a crowd.

I first met him in the disco-crazy New York of the late seventies. Naturally, I knew about him because he and the British *Vogue* fashion editor Liz Tilberis had worked together earlier on. She loved him because he was "real and earthy." Also the photographer Barry Lategan, whose LaGuardia Place apartment I sometimes stayed in, told me, "You must meet my agent's boyfriend, Bruce. He's a wonderful young photographer."

down Tao, down Billy, River, Dream .... Kodi down ..!

So we set up an appointment, and he and his agent, Nan Bush, came to see me, she with Bruce's portfolio tucked under her arm. Bruce handed me the book, and I started leafing through it. All I could see was page after page of photographs of his dog, a beautiful golden retriever called Rowdy, but a dog nevertheless. This was followed by some pictures of his cats, followed by pictures of his station wagon and his 1965 Chevy. Finally, on the very last page, there was one photograph of a girl. "Oh, it's just pictures of things I love," said Bruce with a shrug. But the moment he started his storytelling, I felt an immediate connection, and we both sensed that we would enjoy working together.

Bruce really is a hopeless romantic. When I returned to London, we would talk on the phone at night for hours—long, late, very costly transatlantic conversations—about our ideas and stories for British *Vogue*. He particularly fantasized about casting, and talked about putting disparate people together, or which boy and girl would make a couple with great chemistry like Spencer Tracy and Katharine Hepburn. I'm convinced Bruce fantasized about Elizabeth Taylor when he was a child and then began a lifelong unrequited love affair with her in his imagination—although in her later years they did finally meet and become close friends. And he would come up with a lot of visual concepts involving American painting, photography, and writing. In a way, he is responsible for my love of America and its culture. I mean, I'm hardly a reader, and in those days the States seemed such a long way away from me back home in England. But he would tell me about artists like Alfred Stieglitz, Edward Weston, Edward Steichen, Georgia O'Keeffe, Paul Strand, Imogen Cunningham, and Ansel Adams. Bruce knew all their stories so well that he could make them come vividly alive.

Our first trip together—which, strangely enough, was to Australia, not America—came out of a story Bruce saw in *National Geographic* about a girl who traveled across the outback by camel. Initially, we wanted to use the same girl for our photographs—she seemed rather pretty—but we could never track her down because she was always off riding her camel. So we used the model Nancy DeWeir instead.

Bruce and his crew from New York, the model, her boyfriend, who was Bruce's assistant, and the hairdresser Kerry Warn flew to Australia one way around the globe, while the *Vogue* travel editor, Martin O'Brien, and I flew from London the other, with me dragging heavy suitcase after suitcase of army surplus clothes and enough paraphernalia to furnish a campsite.

Twenty-two hours later, we finally reached Perth, where the customs officials decided to go through every bag. Out came each pot, pan, can of beans, gas ring, sleeping bag, and mosquito net. "What's this?" they asked, roaring with laughter after fishing out a bush hat with hundreds of dangling corks that I had sewn on for what, back in England, we thought was an authentically Australian outback look. Luckily, it put them in such good humor that they allowed us to pass, even though I hadn't been particularly careful with the customs forms.

Our next shoot, in 1981, was a story set in Santa Fe, New Mexico, and inspired by the painter Georgia O'Keeffe. We happened upon an old tepee standing right there on the trail and used it in the pictures, but our main props were the extraordinary church in Taos and various adobe buildings. Our models were a very pretty and preppy American girl named Sloane Condren and a boy, Jon Wiedemann, who went on to marry the actress Isabella Rossellini and whose father started the Outward Bound School in Albuquerque. We took mostly black clothes and silver and turquoise jewelry in homage to O'Keeffe, and frothy white cotton Victorian nightdresses worn under rough knits and plainswoman jackets, which in turn seemed to provide strong inspiration for the next collection—"The Santa Fe Look"—by designer Ralph Lauren. The tousled hair and bare scrubbed faces of the models in the story also heralded a whole new look in beauty. Up until then, the fashion had been for heavy makeup and tough-looking hairstyles. Bruce's vision brought a completely new, natural aesthetic to fashion photography.

Bruce was really hoping, while we were there, for an opportunity to take a portrait of the rawboned O'Keeffe, but he was completely rebuffed by the reclusive artist right up to the last minute. Then Barney Wan, who was holidaying in San Francisco, flew in to help. Dressed from head to foot in red, O'Keeffe's favorite color (he really did his homework), he spontaneously knocked on her front door to ask if he could cook her a Chinese dinner. She, equally spontaneously, said yes and, after mellowing significantly, agreed to be photographed by Bruce.

That same year I stayed with Bruce in his house on Shelter Island. I had been invited there, along with my nephew Tristan, to spend the summer holiday. It was a small place, completely charming (all the buildings on the island were charming in that "gingerbread house" kind of way), and the lawn sloped gently down to a small dock where a little wooden motorboat was tethered. I probably compared it to the island of my Welsh childhood—except the weather was so much better.

Bruce with his new puppy Hud

Bruce was always surrounded by such attractive people. There was something so appealing about this large extended family and the easygoing summer-camp atmosphere he created. It wasn't fancy, like going to stay with the Duke and Duchess of Whatever. You would sit with a bottle of wine or two and talk until the early hours. And he would engineer his photo shoots to take place around the house and include all the people who were hanging out there. He generally worked every day, even when everyone else was on vacation. That summer his major shoot was a story for *GQ* with a fishing boat and "clam diggers" dressed up in big knits, big aprons, and even bigger waders. Bruce put Tristan in the photographs, and they are some of my favorites ever taken of him. I have prints of them all over my home. And Nan was always there, calmly in control and ready to cook for everyone. "Dinner for twenty-three? No problem." Nothing fazed her.

Bruce was always incredibly generous when you stayed with him. His car would suddenly become your car. He would invite me to borrow his station wagon and go for a spin. Or he would accompany me to the local antique shops, where he often tried to persuade me to buy more than I could ever afford. "Oh, come on Grace, you know you deserve it," he would say with a laugh whenever I hesitated over yet another purchase. And, inevitably, if I didn't get it, I would find out later that he had bought it for me.

I'd like to say I adopted Bruce and Nan's lifestyle (though not the large groups), but I guess I copied it—certainly their aesthetic and their decorating style, which is always so comfortable. I definitely copied Bruce's way of propping up hundreds of photographs on shelves and having piles of books dotted about everywhere.

Bruce and I have many friends in common. One is the Scottish stylist Joe McKenna. Previously a jobbing actor with nothing whatsoever to

Hud

do with fashion, Joe got his early break when he was cast in *Coronation Street,* a popular British television soap opera, in which he played the son of some leading characters.

He and I first met because he regularly turned up at British *Vogue* during the eighties to borrow slides from the fashion shows while he worked at *Tatler* magazine, which was one floor below us at Vogue House. From then on, we became firm friends, and he has always supplied a shoulder for me to lean on through all the highs and lows in my life.

Joe loves magazines and occasionally accepts a job on them. But he is also incredibly mischievous, a practical joker in the worst possible sense in that he is so good at it—which doesn't suit an office environment. So he has carved a niche for himself styling freelance for photographers such as David Sims, Inez van Lamsweerde and Vinoodh Matadin, and Bruce, with whom his working relationship dates back to the eighties. Joe also works a great deal in Paris with Azzedine Alaïa, another great practical joker, and when they get together . . .

At the height of the supermodel craze, they rang Linda Evangelista from Azzedine's workroom very late one night, disguising their voices, and convinced her she was needed urgently for a fitting with Karl Lagerfeld at the Chanel premises on rue Cambon. And so off she went—despite it being the early hours of the morning—to find the whole place shuttered and dark. More recently, when I was having a tortured time trying to finalize the deal on my present Manhattan apartment, Joe called up pretending to be the realtor and made me believe that the deal had fallen through, whereupon I broke down in tears. No amount of apologizing helped there at the time, but he is someone you just can't be angry at for long.

In 1982 Bruce suggested that he and I pay homage to the legendary pioneering photographer Edward Weston. A cast of thousands was assembled in Bellport, Long Island, where Bruce had now moved. He always had a working team in place that included Didier for hair, Bonnie Maller for makeup, and John Ryman, a local artist, to build all the props. Canvas backdrops were erected to imitate Weston's makeshift portable studios. A lithe and sloe-eyed young dance student named Nathalie (the real-life girlfriend of the boy playing Weston for us), who had never modeled before, was co-opted to play a version of Tina Modotti. The seventeen-year-old Puerto Rican model Talisa Soto was brought in to portray the equivalent of Weston's partner, Charis. Sundry other characters included a young girl named Shelly; an older woman named Joli, who owned an antique shop on Bleecker Street; another, larger, more masculine-looking local woman called Betty, who was Shelly's aunt; and a whole group of boys.

To me this was the most powerful story we ever did together. Bruce says that one reason Weston came to mind as a mythical character who deserved to have a story built around him—albeit a fashion story—was that he was so totally dedicated to photography that his fingers turned black from forever being immersed in the chemical fixative.

It was also the first time I had ever styled a male nude—if you can call it styling. The darkly good-looking American model Bruce Hulse, who was our Weston, was asked to

Hud

climb a tree for a portrait, and as I stood beneath it, all I could hear was Bruce saying things like, "Oh, gee, you look so handsome. Could you take off your shirt?" And the shirt would flutter down. Then it was, "Wow, that's so great. Now can you take off the trousers?" And down would come the trousers. Finally, it was "And the underpants?" This was where I averted my eyes, just as the Y-fronts came tumbling down about my head.

As a memento, Bruce made me a beautiful scrapbook of photographs from the shoot. It is probably my most treasured possession.

"You know," Bruce said to me one day in 1983, "there's this painter Andrew Wyeth, and I really love him, and he lives in Maine. His paintings are all in these pale, washed-out colors. So wouldn't it be great to do some pictures using clothes in the same colors?" He went on to tell me that there were three generations of Wyeth painters—Andrew, his son Jamie, who lived nearby on Monhegan Island, and Andrew's father, N. C. Wyeth, who did the original illustrations for *Treasure Island*. Bruce spent a great deal of time working on the shoot in Andrew's house in order to re-create precisely the diffused light in his work. We all felt so privileged to be invited into the lighthouse he sometimes escaped to. Stepping inside was like stepping into one of his paintings: Chalk-white, sparse, curtains blowing.

Just as we were about to leave, Andrew turned to me and said, "I would love to paint you. How long are you staying in Maine?" I could sense Bruce beside me, almost about to faint. "It would be so great, Grace," he whispered. "You should stay on." I, being the fool that I am, heard myself saying in my English way that, while I was honored to be asked, I was "expected back in the office by Monday."

This page and overleaf: Homage to Edward Weston, with Talisa Soto and Bruce Hulse, Bellport. Photo: Bruce Weber, 1982

"Dear old Brett Boy –
– you write well – you
spell badly – you're a dear
old fellow and I love you
heaps – Dad."

Edward Weston, in a letter to
his son, Brett

the family

"Do what thy manhood bids thee do –
from none but self expect applause" is a
dangerous precept and only to be used by
those with a stiff backbone – a willingness
to suffer and a sense of humor. I realize
I have written over your head."
– Edward Weston in a letter to his family

Jeff

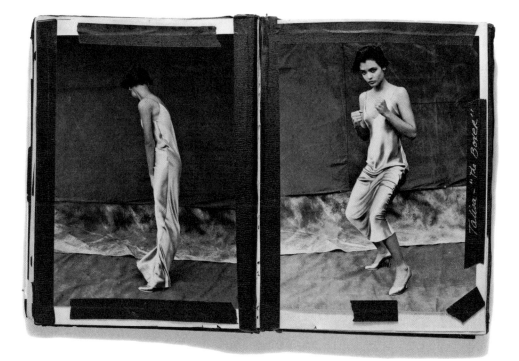

Talisa – "The Boxer"

In 1984 Bea Miller wanted to dedicate the December issue to "the Englishwoman." Bruce and I were inspired to do a story with a Cecil Beaton mood in the country gardens belonging to the great-aunt of British *Vogue*'s features editor, Patrick Kinmonth. We were also influenced by a magical shoot we had done earlier that year at Karl Lagerfeld's French country estate. It was conceived as the publicity campaign for Lagerfeld's first collection in his own name, and the photographs were taken in the fairy-tale forest surrounding his chateau in Brittany.

The models, Linda Spierings and Lynne Koester, were both tall, willowy, and spritelike, with dark hair. The clothes were beautiful and chic, though not perhaps very Bruce. He, of course, wanted to do woodland nudes. Meanwhile, the women representing Lagerfeld's company had become more and more agitated throughout the day as they saw the high heels and jewelry that accompanied the clothes on the catwalk not being used in any of the photographs. To tactfully remove them from the scene, Bruce suggested they go off and find some men to put in our pictures. Meanwhile, Didier, who had been wandering around the forest, discovered a huge tree stump covered with moss and ivy that he thought might be useful as a hat, and he promptly put it on a model's head.

Everything had started to look surreal and mysterious. The company women then returned, having picked up a choice of two hitchhikers, one

Hud

a French soldier with a shaved head, the other an unremarkable local lad. The men seemed taken aback by the scene. I really think they were expecting an orgy. "Can you make them outfits out of ivy?" Bruce asked me eagerly. And so I did—dressing them up over their underwear, I hasten to add. Sadly, the resulting pictures were never used, despite their being close to my heart and loved by Karl. They were replaced in the campaign by some rather boring catwalk photographs.

While we were preparing for the *Vogue* shoot in the English country-side, Didier and I had been watching Patrick's great-aunt prepare some exquisitely hued dried flowers from the garden—she preserved them with glycerin—and we were determined to use some in the pictures. The resulting story, with the faded, dusty-colored flowers pinned to slightly old-fashioned, English-looking clothes, or arranged in the hair with yards and yards of tulle, was ravishingly romantic. I even forgot the heart-stopping panic I felt as the girls were being photographed hurdling over the great-aunt's precious rose beds.

Back at *Vogue*, I waited expectantly for the pictures to turn up. But Bruce had done a layout of his own and made them into a crazy scrapbook. So what eventually arrived were collages with the photographs of the models cut out and stuck down, and no sign at all of the incredibly atmospheric gardens. "This was not what I envisaged," Bea Miller said evenly when she saw them. In the end, Bruce did hand over the sublime, unadulterated images, but because he felt artistically betrayed, he was rather upset with me.

Later we made up, and one of the first bouquets I received when embarking on my short career at Calvin Klein after leaving British *Vogue* was from Bruce and Nan.

X

ON
DIDIER

In which
Grace learns that
love means
never having
to run out of
hair spray.

Things with Didier were becoming more serious. I wasn't pushing for marriage, though. I haven't got such a great track record in that department. Besides, the state of marriage seems to bother him, too. If Didier wants to be somewhere, it is because he really wants to be there and not because he is being forced.

In a relationship you have to give a lot. You can't be too selfish. You can't have everything your own way, and you do give up a certain independence. Living with someone all the time is great if you keep it surprising and don't allow yourself to become too complacent. It's also highly risky doing a job with someone you are living with, so I'm always nervous whenever Didier and I are slated to work together on a shoot. First, he is a problematic traveler because he is very susceptible to sound,

"Zis is 'ow we do ze kitty comb-out"

and if the room we get is too noisy, we may have to move several times. On a recent shoot in England, we stayed at Brighton's Grand Hotel, which was famously targeted in a bomb blast when Margaret Thatcher and the delegates for the Conservative Party conference were grouped there in 1984. Here, we moved rooms six times before we found one to his liking. Second, because Didier likes a touch of intrigue and game-playing, you have to be prepared to be tweaked around when he's working on a shoot. "Am I doing a catalog?" is a favorite sarcastic remark if he is ever so gently reminded to get a move on with the subject's hair. On the other hand, he is very, very romantic. Since the first days of our friendship, whenever we worked together, he always wrote me wonderfully flattering notes afterward in formal, old-fashioned English. They said things like "Thank you very much for inviting me" or "It gives me great pleasure to be in your company." Or he would send me bunches of pretty flowers, usually roses, or a postcard of some beautiful painting from an exhibition he had seen.

Our first summer together, without my knowing, Didier went out and bought a sailing boat. He knew that, as a child, I had been slightly jealous when my father built a little wooden dinghy for my sister and me and named it *Rosie,* after her. As a further surprise, when we went to collect his boat from Shelter Island, where it had been shipped, I discovered Didier had named it *Grace.*

At the time he hadn't a clue how to sail, and going out with him became rather unnerving, as the waters around Long Island Sound can be quite choppy and the winds quite squally. Often the fog comes down with little or no notice and obliterates the coastline. These days I seem to have lost my pioneering spirit, and I feel rather guilty, as I refuse to sail with him unless there is absolutely no wind. Then of course we become becalmed, and that drives him really crazy, since we have to use the engine to return home.

As a child, Didier used to visit his mother at the veterinary clinic where she worked. There, it was his job to groom the cats and dogs. This is probably where his love of hairstyling began. The vet had some very important clients, the famous Carita sisters, who owned a hair salon in Paris. I think they agreed to take Didier on as an apprentice after seeing what a good job he had done on their poodle.

I faintly remember working with him as far back as 1972. I was still going out with Duc, and we were photographing in Paris for British *Vogue*. As well as being the fashion editor on that shoot, I was modeling. The photos had me standing in front of the Eiffel Tower with two other girls and wearing the same forties Yves Saint Laurent outfit I wore when I dressed to impress Tina Chow. Because my hair was enjoying one of its more unsightly in-between moments, I had a hat clamped tightly to my head and was the only one not to have my hair styled by Didier. Afterward I worked with him rather a lot with all the new young French photographers.

Didier likes telling people how much I ignored him back then and how I even acted in a snooty manner toward him. As if I would! He spoke no English, so I just couldn't understand a word he said. Besides, he was married then, so it was impossible to get together.

Years later I discovered he hadn't particularly liked me at first; in fact, when I modeled, he always thought I was terrible-looking and not pretty at all—at least not his idea of pretty. As it was, in his early days of working for British *Vogue*, he fancied my close friend and colleague Polly Hamilton much more than he did me, until they fell out thanks to their mutual stubbornness. But for some time he retained an eye for a pretty

Didier with
Barty Pumpkin

French girl, as I would discover on a rather tense shoot in Paris with the grand royal photographer Tony Snowdon.

During his heyday, Snowdon always gave fashion pictures a certain stature, rather like Annie Leibovitz does now, although he liked to play at being humble. "Call me Tony," he would say, but if you crossed the line and were overfamiliar, it was back to "Snowdon, actually." When we traveled to Paris to shoot the couture collections on the young French actress Isabelle Pasco, then the partner of the iconoclastic film director Jean-Jacques Beineix, the French press got wind of it and started chasing after us. But as I tried ushering the royal photographer back into our chauffeured car to keep him from being bothered, I realized he was getting terribly annoyed with me because he actually rather enjoyed it.

Our couture shoot was fairly hazardous. We worked in a very small studio with one of those very large Lipizzan dressage horses. Snowdon wanted the animal to rear up in front of Isabelle, who was improbably tiny and stood on a pile of telephone books so her long dress wouldn't concertina on the ground. Meanwhile, I grew more and more furious because Didier, who was semi-officially my boyfriend by then as well as the hairdresser on the shoot, had become rather taken with her. So every time I caught him being very French and flirting while he combed her hair, I rushed in on the pretext of adjusting her dress and stuck a pin in her behind. Yes, I can be a bitch, too, sometimes.

Apart from the flirtations, I was always struck by Didier's beautiful manners, but it wasn't until we moved in together that I came up against how deep-seated his old-fashioned reticence and sense of decorum really are. One day soon after I had moved to New York, he called me from a work trip in Japan and asked me to pick him up at the airport upon his return. I had not seen him in several months, and this was the first time he had been to my new residence. "Are you coming upstairs?" I asked as we arrived at my apartment. "Maybe. We'll see," he replied. And then, sometime later, "Will you be staying for dinner?" "Maybe. We'll see." "Are you staying the night?" "Maybe. We'll see." And then the next morning at breakfast, "Will I be seeing you later?" "Maybe. We'll see," he said once more.

This went on for several weeks in its considerably noncommittal, delicate way. It was only when hundreds of extra bags turned up containing can after can of aerosol hair lacquer, wigs, brushes, combs, tongs, and hair dryers that I knew our situation was permanent, and I settled into a life which, during its finest moments, balances home and work with a gentle equilibrium.

XI

ON CALVINISM

In which
our heroine
goes minimal,
makes a heap
of money,
and misses
magazines.

When I went to work for Calvin Klein, I felt like the new girl at school, hiding at my desk behind my welcoming four hundred vases of flowers. I was in the design room on New York's Thirty-ninth Street, in the heart of the Garment District. Though my title was design director, I wasn't exactly sure how that should be interpreted or what the parameters were. No one had told me beforehand, although I assumed I was there to direct the design team. But in a very real sense, I had the feeling the team hated me simply because I wasn't Calvin. From the start, Kelly (Klein), Calvin's new wife, couldn't quite figure out why I was there, either, and practically everyone was annoyed by my title. I was on a huge salary for one and a half years (which soared even more when I was offered a job by Ralph Lauren). I always assumed it didn't matter who was

"Now where did I put my collections ideas?"

the boss as long as you got the job done, but I guess that is easy to say if you are—sort of—the boss.

Anyway, I never thought of becoming a designer. It never even crossed my mind. So it wasn't as if I was trying to steal anyone's job.

After I had been in the position a few months, on an "inspiration" trip to Spain for the fall/winter '86 season, my colleague Steven Slowik, the head designer in my department, was prompted to create a stole in heavy duchesse satin decorated with motifs taken from the ceiling of the Alhambra Palace in Granada. The stole was then beaded in Paris by Lesage, the celebrated couture embroiderer who had worked with every grand fashion house from Yves Saint Laurent and Dior to Schiaparelli and Chanel. As you can imagine, it turned out to be probably the most expensive stole in the world, and if I had been more objective, I would have seen that it was not a suitable item to include in the collection of what, after all, is a sportswear company. Another time it was our idea to make everything in pale, pretty prints inspired by the flowers in an English country garden. I then asked my favorite English hat designer, Patricia Underwood, to make charming little straw boaters for the show—another big mistake, as it turned out. America's fashion bible, *Women's Wear Daily,* published a terrible write-up, strongly criticizing the collection for abandoning Calvin's modern identity. I was accused of trying to recast an American icon as an English one.

Well, in the end I have to agree that they were right. My ideas about clothes, which are inseparable from the aesthetics involved with presenting them in magazines, had proved completely wrongheaded and far too grandiose for Calvin's minimalist aesthetic. My efforts showed that I was not good at leading a design team, and certainly not one that worked on the basis of designing from the ground up. Eventually, I might even have led the company into deep trouble. Calvin, unfortunately, was in rehab at the time, but when he came out, he was furious. He fired Steven and hauled me over the coals. "This can never be allowed to happen again," he yelled. My million-dollar mortgage flashed before my eyes. "He's going to fire me too," I thought. But he didn't.

Calvin, you see, has always been concerned with image, the advertising image and the all-encompassing lifestyle it promotes. To him it was the most important thing, and at least this was something I was qualified to help with. I was immediately set to work on the first ever print advertisements for his new breakthrough fragrance, Eternity.

The location was Martha's Vineyard, the photographer Bruce Weber, the models Christy Turlington and a conventionally handsome French actor named Lambert Wilson. The bottle was, I think, a replica of an old one discovered by Kelly, and the perfume's name was inspired by the exquisite eternity ring Calvin gave her when they were first wed, purchased at auction from the estate of the late Duchess of Windsor.

Because Calvin built his enormous success on the back of overtly sexy advertising, and because his high-profile social life had not, up to this point, been that much associated with upholding family values, the Eternity campaign, with its sweet images of romantic love and the circle of life, came as a huge surprise. People observed the more than passing resemblance that Calvin bore to Lambert, and the certain similarity Kelly had to Christy, not to mention the idyllic family atmosphere complete with model children conjured by the ads, and wondered what was going on. My feeling is that it was Calvin's way of distancing himself from his wild past and the debauchery of the Studio 54 era, and of making a stand against the spread of AIDS. As always, his timing was perfect, the campaign succeeded, and his perfume sales went through the roof.

If I'd skipped Calvin Klein and headed straight to American *Vogue,* I never would have understood how American fashion works. The approach is very different here from how it is in England; it's very real and much more to do with business. Businesslike interactions extend to other aspects of everyday life. For instance, my assistant Carol at Calvin told me how to open a bank account and showed me how to use a bank card. In England we didn't have those. I banked at Coutts, the royal bankers, where everything was courtly, gracious, and "olde worlde," and the uniformed doorman would say "Good day, sir" or "Good day, madam." Suddenly, I was here in Citibank, New York, where everything was highly automated and there was barely a human being to be seen.

After a while, I must confess, I did begin thinking about a return to magazines. Working at Calvin, by this time, had become a little uncomfortable. My great friend Zack Carr, who had been head of design several years earlier before leaving the company to pursue other interests, had lately returned to replace Steven Slowik. Our once easygoing and very friendly relationship was under strain. Zack was extraordinarily talented. He had helped create the whole Calvin design aesthetic from day one. But mine was officially the higher position, which obviously irked him. So when conflicting instructions were issued a couple of times to the workrooms, it caused tension.

I adored Zack, who had played a major part in my love of American fashion when I first began to visit New York. He, on the other hand, loved talking about iconic European designers such as Balenciaga and Yves Saint Laurent. Before I joined Calvin, we spent long evenings together discussing them into the wee small hours of the morning. I had taken my holidays at Bruce Weber's house on Shelter Island with Zack, and had traveled to Morocco with him and his boyfriend, John Calcagno. I had treasured our friendship and didn't want it to end in bad feeling. So, since my first love was magazines, I decided a move would be no bad thing.

When it was announced that Anna Wintour had been appointed the new editor in chief of American *Vogue,* I immediately rang her office from my desk at Calvin Klein to offer my congratulations. I then found myself asking her assistant, Gabé Doppelt, whom I knew from London when we worked together at British *Vogue,* "Do you think she would have me back?" "Wait a minute," said Gabé, disappearing into muffled silence for a brief moment. Anna came on the line and said, "Meet me at Da Silvano at six." So I did, and that evening at the table, without missing a beat, she said, "I'm starting on Monday. Would you like to start with me?" I vaguely recollect her asking if I would like to have some dinner, but by then I was in a bit of a daze.

This was a Friday night, and I had somehow to reach Calvin before he read anything about it in *Women's Wear Daily* on Monday morning. Finally, I tracked him down, and he couldn't have been nicer. I love him for that. I think it was best for both of us, because I really wasn't suited for life on Seventh Avenue.

XII

ON
AMERICAN VOGUE

In which
Grace learns
the ropes,
taking care to
avoid the
knotty problem
of bling.

O n what was to be my first day as a fashion director at American *Vogue,* I called Anna's assistant, Gabé, and suggested that I go in with her
because I was too nervous to arrive at the magazine's offices alone.
Dressed in Calvin Klein's black pants and white shirt, with a fuchsia
Calvin Klein Resort double-ply cashmere cardigan tied around my waist
(I thought it would make me look less fat), I entered 350 Madison Avenue, Condé Nast's address before the company's headquarters uprooted
to the showier monolith of 4 Times Square. I also thought I was doing
a "power look," one we in England associated with American *Vogue,*
while we were all walking around in our drab but arty black.

Anna called everybody, and I do mean everybody, into a conference
room that same day to discuss where she intended to take her brave new
Vogue. She explained that she wanted it to be younger and more ap-

It's the bling thing — all together in Chanel jackets.

proachable and to have more energy. And then she had various staff members take the stand. Many questions were asked about the new regime, such as whether we would be photographing entire designer looks, and whether the basic structure of the magazine would change.

We were a mixed bunch. Some editors had been there for years, others were freshly arrived, but we all had one thing in common: We each considered ourselves the top of the class and had a strong personality to accompany it.

Unlike the almost Dickensian working conditions I had experienced at British *Vogue,* pleasant amounts of office space—with their own closets in which to store the clothes they were shooting—were allocated to the American *Vogue* fashion editors, or sittings editors, as they were then called. These were me; Carlyne Cerf de Dudzeele, the French former fashion editor of *Elle* and by far Anna's new favorite; Polly Mellen, whose tenure dated back as far as the great days of the former *Vogue* chief, Diana Vreeland; and Jenny Capitain, who was German and had modeled for several of Helmut Newton's naughtier photographs (one of which had her wearing little more than a neck brace). There was a huge accessories room, ruled with an iron hand by the new accessories editor, Candy Pratts. Candy had previously designed the windows at Bloomingdale's, which, under the inspired leadership of Kal Ruttenstein, promoted the younger designers. Phyllis Posnick was executive fashion editor, coordinating the fashion room so that things ran smoothly for the rest of us. She was not involved in photo shoots back then, but later she worked on beauty photographs and any special features requiring a telling image or two.

A girl called Laurie Schechter, whom Anna brought over from *New York* magazine, was responsible for the various shoots in the "front of the book," those newsy opening pages of the magazine. That was an idea Anna totally owned, and one she worked on extremely hard to make busily interesting with more reportage, backstage photographs, and exclusive pictures that no one else managed to get of pretty girls who dressed well and attended every party. Through *Vogue,* Anna was creating her own modern-day socialites, contemporary "it" girls.

My debut at American *Vogue* was a sitting featuring white shirts. I had only one and a half days to put it together instead of the usual month it might have taken me in England. "What are you going to do for your first story?" Anna had asked. Panicking a little, I said, "Erm, I'll do white shirts." (I hadn't seen any fashion up close other than Calvin's for over a year and a half.) In no time at all, the fashion department gathered together racks and racks of white shirts all looking pretty much the same. I accessorized them with hundreds of little crosses, very delicate and very me—something that, in these days of political correctness, would not be allowed, as all forms of religious symbolism are now strictly against the rules of *Vogue.*

Before each shoot, there would be a meeting in the planning room. You arrived with still-life snapshots or Polaroids of all your clothes, laid them out like unworthy offerings in front of Anna; the magazine supremo, Mr. Liberman; art director Derek Ungless; and sometimes the assigned photographer, before whom you made the case for what you proposed to do. In this instance I wanted to photograph my white shirts outdoors in the Hamptons using natural light, close to the house of the photographer Patrick Demarchelier, who would be taking the pictures. But Mr. Liberman had other ideas. He said, "I think you should do the photographs with six girls running in the studio. Then the lighting quality will be good." I was completely thrown. I couldn't think of any way to do the story other than my original idea. But afterward Anna said, "Just go and do it how you want. It'll be fine. Don't worry. We only needed to get Alex's opinion." So we photographed the story my way, and Anna absolutely loved it. As did Mr. Liberman.

I seemed to be busily shooting, shooting, shooting every day. Organizing my one story a month for British *Vogue* didn't, in retrospect, seem like such a busy scene. Then there were the run-throughs and the endless market editors. This was fascinating to me because I had never worked or consulted with a market editor—a person whose job was to know all the clothes in the collections and call them in for the editors, making sure to spread the credits as widely as possible. As the clothing industry in America is so huge, they were an essential element to getting the job done.

There was a great deal of pushing and pulling between me and my colleagues over clothes for our sittings. Transparencies of the latest international collections shot from the catwalks would circulate around the offices, and we had to put our initials against the outfits we wanted to shoot. When we were abroad, traveling from one set of shows to another, we would often stay up all night, Polaroiding selected looks from the shows or choosing them from contact sheets with the aid of a strong magnifying glass.

But wherever we were, Carlyne always got her choice in first. Every single time. Manolo Blahnik, for instance, would send over sample pairs of shoes from his latest collection for all the editors to use. They usually ended up squirreled away in Carlyne's closet. When we were at the collections, she would play tricks. Polly Mellen used to look across at everyone's notes, so Carlyne would make a big show of following something ugly on the catwalk, ostentatiously taking note of anything especially hideous, like a floral bathing cap. And Polly had to have it.

Polly had ruled the roost under Grace Mirabella, Anna's predecessor, and had begun her American *Vogue* career even earlier. She was respon-

sible in the sixties and seventies for many of the magazine's most memorable and influential sittings with the photographer Richard Avedon.
Now Carlyne was in favor, and poor Polly had a tough time as she strug-
gled to assert her relevance, trying to be supermodern and accessorizing
her models with about nineteen watches, as Carlyne famously did in a
sporty style she created early in her career at French *Elle*. And as I now
did, too, in a very Carlyne-style shoot featuring Naomi Campbell looking sexy in a car with some Dalmatians—because I thought it was the
way to get on. Gilles Dufour at Chanel kept giving me brightly colored
little Chanel jackets, like those championed by Anna and Carlyne, and
I must confess I wore these as well, even though they were far too brash
for me—because, like everyone else, I sought Anna's approval and
wanted to fit in.

Meanwhile, Jenny Capitain liked to be first. She was all about doing
everything before anyone else. Carlyne, on the other hand, couldn't care
less about being first; she just had to have it. If Azzedine's collection arrived from Paris, it promptly vanished straight into her closet. Carlyne
was very close—or not, depending on the day—to André Leon Talley,
whom Anna appointed creative director.

André is very tall, grand, and overwhelming, a black man of such im-
mense presence and style that you can't possibly imagine him waking
up, looking rough, and having a bad day. After working for Andy Warhol at *Interview* magazine, he made his name at *Women's Wear Daily* in
their Paris bureau, and as the personal assistant to Diana Vreeland when
she was in charge of the Metropolitan Museum's costume exhibits, before settling at *Vogue*. He would visit Vreeland's apartment in her later
years and read to her.

Equally strong-willed and opinionated, André and Carlyne were always either in cahoots and inseparable, or dramatically feuding, running

in and out of each other's offices talking secretively and theatrically shutting the doors: slam, slam, slam. They were often arguing or sulking or not speaking to each other at fashion shows. If you happened to be seated between them, it was dreadfully uncomfortable, like having a big dark cloud above your head.

André took his ambassadorial role at *Vogue* seriously. He dressed extravagantly and traveled imperially, often redecorating his room at the Paris Ritz when he arrived for the collections with personal items stored in the hotel's basement. As for shoots, André didn't do many, but they were usually the important ones featuring personalities. I remember him directing sessions with people like Madonna, and there was a cover for which he valiantly tried to turn Ivana Trump into Brigitte Bardot. He was always toweringly present at the collections in the power hierarchy of who was sitting next to Anna. (If you were badly placed, it meant you were a nobody.) I would often feed him ideas I liked and felt strongly about, and he would feed them to Anna. He, on the other hand, would determine how we dressed for special *Vogue* events or parties, and he didn't like the fact that I wore flat shoes all the time.

In those days he always appeared to carry lists with him of desperately important and urgent things he felt should go into the magazine. He would either tell Anna personally or, if he was away, fire off numerous dramatic faxes to her from wherever he was, all written in the hugest capital letters and punctuated with enormous exclamation marks.

Back then Anna hardly went anywhere without André. He was closer to her than any husband, and their relationship has lasted a lot longer than most marriages (especially mine!). It was he who, in a fashion meeting one day, came up with the idea of "red-carpet dressing," a notion I heard for the first time right there, which grew into such an intense mass-media reality that we seemed to be permanently rushing along that

Grace, you really can't go for dinner with Karl in flat shoes....

red carpet, chasing down celebrities. He was even the one called on to escort some of those celebrities—Sylvester Stallone, Sandra Bernhard, and Renée Zellweger, to name just three—around the Paris collections.

In 1995, I inherited André's title. (He was by then living in Paris and later came back to *Vogue* as editor at large.) The biggest difference between his time as creative director and mine was that I spoke directly to all the other editors, discussed their ideas from a fashion standpoint, and took them back to Anna. I was very much the go-between, listening to my colleagues' points of view and in some cases pacifying them. André didn't exactly come and talk to us about our sittings. He talked directly to Anna, and she would pass on his directions to all the relevant editors. They would also draw up the guest lists together for the parties Karl threw for her in Paris; then André took them round to Karl, whom he was extremely close to, for approval.

Sometimes both André and Anna made stopover trips in London to catch up on the latest Brit-art finds or to meet with fashion's new young talents like Alexander McQueen, introduced to them by Isabella Blow, Anna's onetime assistant at American *Vogue* and by then a major personality on the British fashion scene as well as McQueen's muse.

Anna adored André. I remember her fiftieth-birthday present arriving at his party in the restaurant Chez Georges in Paris, an American *Vogue* favorite. It was a huge, distinctive orange box fastened with brown ribbons, and it contained an Hermès bicycle. I don't think it was ever removed from the wrapping. Later it was packed up and shipped back to André's place in New York, where it sat in its box like a trophy for the longest time.

André's move to Paris coincided with his being given a substantial advance for writing what was widely expected to be the definitive biography of Yves Saint Laurent. Unfortunately, the designer was not at his best and had begun collecting some dire reviews. Some critics were outspoken enough to suggest he had entered a creative cul-de-sac. Suzy Menkes, in the *International Herald Tribune,* compared one collection to "a down-market travel brochure." At the same time, Anna, who had never been the hugest fan, started sidelining his clothes from *Vogue*'s collection reports.

For a legend of Paris fashion such as Yves, a standing ovation at the finale of his collection was a given, no matter how good or bad the show. But Anna now made a regular point of not stirring from her seat, and because she did not budge, neither did we. This line-up of obdurate American editors sitting in an ocean of standing celebrants scandalized the French press and infuriated Saint Laurent company president Pierre Bergé. American *Vogue* was banned from YSL for a while, leaving André to straddle a sharp fence. In the end the Saint Laurent book never reached completion, possibly because so much had been written about him already, or maybe the access simply dried up. In any case, people soon forgot about this feud, especially when the gossip moved on to Giorgio Armani and his displeasure with all of Condé Nast for not paying enough attention to his clothes, either.

Back at the magazine, boards of Polaroids were made up to show what clothes you would be photographing next, all approved by Anna. I once asked Gabé, "Why can't I just tell Anna what I want to shoot?" before realizing the answer. With everything documented, you couldn't smuggle something into a photo session without her knowing. Unless you were Carlyne. She handed in boards of Polaroids that had nothing whatsoever to do with what she was actually shooting. Or she would bypass the process altogether and have all the clothes she wanted delivered directly to the studio where she was working.

It was pointless complaining to Anna, saying things like "She stole my dress," because the reply would simply be "This is not a girls' boarding school. Deal with it yourself." However, despite outsiders' elevated view of *Vogue* as a temple of cool and sophistication, a girls' boarding school—with its sulky outbursts, tears, and schoolgirlish tantrums—was exactly what it occasionally resembled.

To mark the end of a season's shows, you would be summoned to a fashion ideas meeting. It was like a final exam, and we all dreaded it. Sometimes it would be in the evening, and there would be a dinner attached, especially during the Paris collections, and this would take place in the Salon d'Été, one of those grand and gilded private dining rooms at the back of the Ritz. Very nice food and wine were set out on a large oval table, and everything was elegantly arranged in customary fashion by Fiona DaRin, the eternally unflappable head of *Vogue*'s Paris bureau, who worked hard to placate our demands each season when we descended on her city. You had to stand up, sing for your supper, and offer your ideas—although you didn't really want to reveal your ideas for fear everyone else would poach them. Worse was when people had written down suggestions in advance, and you could see Anna with sheafs of paper in front of her with words like "stripes" or "spots" on them. With a pitying look, she would say, "I've read your ideas, and you all want to do the same thing: spots and stripes," before turning with relief to the more verbal people of the fashion features department to help her out.

Every other night there was a party. We were all expected to be wildly social and work hard at the same time. Anna threw numerous events in New York to promote the magazine at some much anticipated new restaurant—usually the latest venture of the fashionable restaurateur

Brian McNally, because in those days it was all about English Brian and his chic French wife, Anne, one of Anna's closest friends.

Anna looked to England for many of her staff, too, including James Truman, who, like me, was already ensconced in New York but had worked for *The Face* in London. He went on to be editor of *Details* magazine before moving up to become editorial director of Condé Nast when Mr. Liberman retired. Anna imported Hamish Bowles and Camilla Nickerson from *Harpers & Queen,* and Plum Sykes from British *Vogue,* giving the magazine a reputation for a certain kind of English snob appeal.

In 1989 I began working with Bruce Weber again, doing two stories with him that year. The first shoot was a fairly straightforward one featuring resort clothes in Miami on Talisa Soto, one of our favorite models, who had recently made the leap into cinema with a lead role in the latest James Bond film. Bruce cast her opposite Rickson Gracie, a Brazilian martial arts champion, to provide the necessary chemistry. The second, more complicated assignment was photographing the boxer Mike Tyson and Naomi Campbell, who were in the middle of a tempestuous on-again, off-again affair.

Bruce had been very supportive of my move to America. We had worked well together on the advertising at Calvin Klein, and we still saw each other a lot. Didier was working with him steadily, too. As we planned our story together, Bruce and I would have an ongoing conversation about the job. Which in this instance was not shaping up so well.

Naomi and Mike Tyson's dating began in Paris, where the French press was intrigued by his public wooing of her. But friends kept warning her that he could be trouble—dangerous, even. So it seemed to be blowing hot and cold.

During a dinner at the Brasserie Balzar in Saint-Michel with Linda Evangelista and the photographer Peter Lindbergh, Linda's cell phone rang, and a distraught Naomi came on the line, babbling about Tyson. "Come over here immediately," insisted Linda, forever the supermodels' head troubleshooter. Naomi dutifully arrived trussed up in a tight little Azzedine Alaïa dress, her hair totally disheveled, her tights shredded. She had apparently been with Tyson when he had spun alarmingly out of control. "So I 'ad to 'it 'im over the 'ead with me 'andbag," she memorably said (the bag in question was a fairly large, sturdily constructed model). And so it was off again. But not for long.

Back in New York, Bruce really wanted to photograph the boxer, who was at the height of his fame and in training for a championship fight with Evander Holyfield in Atlantic City. Didier was also dying to meet him, being a longtime fight fan. When he first arrived in New York, Didier became a member of Gleason's Gym, where many famous fighters, including Roberto Duran, did their training, and he would box there regularly. So *Vogue* tried organizing a photo session with Tyson and Naomi. But Tyson said no. Now Naomi stepped in to persuade him otherwise, and succeeded.

We arrived in Atlantic City to be told that Tyson was unavailable because he was having his head shaved. Bold shapes, like lightning bolts, were being meticulously clipped, street-style, into his hair by his personal hairdresser. We waited. And waited. Finally, he emerged, and I managed to talk him into wearing one of the outfits for the shoot made especially for him by Gianni Versace. Then out onto the public boardwalk we went, taking reportage pictures of the happy couple in the open air—and, of course, with literally thousands of rubberneckers pressing in on us. After a photo or two, Tyson suddenly walked off and disappeared. For a couple of hours. In the meantime Naomi had spotted his adversary, Holyfield, out on a training run and gone swanning over to say hello. "I hope Mike doesn't find out I did that," she said, giggling slyly, "because it's like talking to the enemy."

Eventually, Tyson returned for more photographs, having packed in a few meetings about tactics and training along the way, and at a certain point he whispered something to Naomi, who came over to us, giggling again. "Mike wants to do a nude with me," she said. "What? Where?" I asked, my jaw dropping. "Here." She indicated the boardwalk, which had been overrun by even more onlookers. Bruce was completely up for it, so in the next second, Naomi had brazenly whipped her top off, Tyson had peeled off his shirt, and she was lying facedown on the mountain range of muscle that was his chest, while Tyson's manager, Don King, held back the leering, hooting, goggle-eyed crowd. Afterward I flung around Naomi's shoulders the cashmere blanket I always take with me on a shoot to provide comfort and protection for the models. Bruce snapped away as they walked back to the location van. Tyson was gently holding her hand. Naomi looks young, fresh, and vulnerably pretty. It's my favorite picture in the story.

Nineteen ninety-two. It was the high point of bling. Colors were citric. Skirts were ridiculously short and figure-hugging, and makeup was unsubtle and harsh. South Beach in Miami, Florida, was the place to be for magazines photographing their lead fashion stories because it guaranteed appropriately loud, neon-lit backgrounds and remained seasonably fair, apart from the odd hurricane. It was possibly my least favorite place on earth.

Bruce Weber kept a house there, as did Gianni Versace and his sister, Donatella (the unbelievably garish, over-the-top Casa Casuarina on Ocean Drive, in front of which Versace would be shot dead five years later). Production and model agencies sprang up. Hair was big. The Miami-based hairstylist Oribe, always dressed in a half-unbuttoned Versace shirt and white jeans, was the master of this style. Accessories were larger-than-life, too. As were the girls.

The original supermodels were Christy Turlington, Linda Evangelista, Cindy Crawford, Claudia Schiffer, Naomi Campbell, Stephanie Seymour, Tatjana Patitz, Estelle Hallyday, Karen Mulder, Nadège, Bridget Hall, and Carla Bruni. They were considered a "must" in photographs and on the catwalk. Versace is generally credited with being the first to pay a fortune to put high-fashion photographic models on the runway—although way back when I started in the sixties, Mary Quant used photo models, too, as did Kenzo and Thierry Mugler in their shows in the seventies and eighties.

But by the nineties, fashion people definitely didn't want to just look at a clotheshorse anymore. It was all about charisma. And these girls showed more attitude and paraded their outsize personalities (as well as their outsize fees), whether it was on the catwalk, in a magazine, or in personal appearances. And they lasted—ten years or more. Then their replacements arrived, all saying they would never become as spoiled as the originals. But guess what? They were. They wouldn't do "doubles" (two girls in one shot), and they would never do group shots, either, except for Steven Meisel.

Steven is a major fashion photographer of our time. No one can dispute it. He has a very broad range and a very deep interest in fashion, not to mention the fact that he is technically brilliant. I first met him in the eighties, while I was still at British *Vogue*. He came into the office at a point when he hadn't been taking photographs for long. But from the moment he picked up a camera, he never looked back. Previously, he had worked as a professional illustrator for publications such as *Women's Wear Daily,* and he arrived—a skinny, black-clad figure wearing tons and tons of eye makeup—in the company of *Vogue* senior fashion editor Anna Harvey. I gave her such a look!

Steven and I eventually worked with each other on one of Anna Wintour's first British *Vogue* issues, which was all about dance and shape, and I soon discovered how exciting it is to work with someone who is much more knowledgeable about fashion than oneself, and Steven certainly is. Almost every evening these days he watches reality shows or goes online to look at gossip and fashion sites, and that is his pleasure: to find out who is making fashion, who has done the hair and makeup, and who the newest girls are. He still has endless incredible ideas for fashion stories. He's also interested in the style of older women. Steven's mother grew up in Hollywood and was very elegant. Give him an iconic figure like the sixties model Veruschka, or someone of that stature, and he is fascinated because they come from a time before he entered the fashion fray. But his paramount interest is in developing new models. If you drew a family tree, you would see that almost every top girl has started with him. Besides making Linda Evangelista into something exceptional, he established Christy Turlington, Kristen McMenamy, Karen Elson, and later, Daria Werbowy, Coco Rocha, and many others—all those girls with whom he has done remarkable defining stories in Italian *Vogue.* Whenever he falls in love with them, their careers are made.

"Supermodel." Such an ugly term. Back in the bling years, it gave many of them a reason for behaving bratty and spoiled. But it is important to remember that this was a moment when everything changed. So much was demanded of them: crisscrossing the Atlantic every few days to get off a plane and go straight to a studio without the time to take a

Going native in Africa with Arthur, Keira Knightley and Masai tribesmen shower, to look bright and fresh, to work, and to get back on a plane; going from campaign to catwalk to personal appearance with no chance to relax, and all-night fittings to attend. Is it any wonder that out came the champagne and drugs?

On the other hand, the old guard like Yves Saint Laurent still preferred regular models with catwalk training for their shows. But whereas in the seventies and eighties many of these *cabine* models were beautiful, professional black girls like Mounia, Amalia, and Katoucha, in the nineties he might field an occasional crowd-pleasing celebrity like Laetitia Casta, the French model turned film actress whose figure, more Renoir than Modigliani, always seemed to be bursting out of her outfits. Then there were "special bookings" girls like Carré Otis, who was never a favorite of mine, and Tyra Banks, who was a bit of a flash in the pan but became famous after Karl decided to put her in a Chanel show. With her big tits and incredibly thin ankles, she was never really cut out to be a high-fashion model, and you could see she would go on to do something else. She did, of course, host a television show about modeling and enjoyed huge popular success.

From the beginning of his time at Chanel, Karl was in love with the idea of taking a certain girl and making her the star of the season. At first it was women like Inès de la Fressange, who embodied a new kind of social gamine. Later, he was in favor of that girl being of a type not at all associated with Chanel's somewhat bourgeois chic, like Claudia Schiffer or Stella Tennant, the rebellious granddaughter of the Duchess of Devonshire who, in the early days, wore a punk ring through her nose.

Ah, the early nineties. Not very me. We always seemed to be shooting in Florida with slick photographers like Tiziano Magni and Sante D'Orazio. But I went with the flow—until my time came.

XIII

ON
THE BIGGER PICTURE

In which
our heroine
grows into
famous Grace,
with stories
galore and plenty
of space.

I n the late summer of 1992, while I was still pushing against the brashness and vulgarity of the entire era, I planned a photo session with Steven Meisel in the yellowing fields of upstate New York. For a long time I had wanted to use romantic, vintage-looking dresses in *Vogue* because I've always loved them and worn them myself. It's a very English thing. But whereas in England I might have styled them in a countrified way with Wellington boots, this time around I decided on the tougher look of Doc Martens, the kind of work boots favored by American road gangs, loggers, and construction workers. Steven, meanwhile, wanted to use boys in the pictures, so he suggested I dress them in big holey sweaters and kilts.

It was a look much inspired by his boyfriend, Benjamin, who was a devoted fan of Kurt Cobain of Nirvana and the whole slacker look of the Seattle scene. Steven had used this style for a recent set of photo-

Shooting a Prada special with Steven Meisel.

graphs in the Italian men's magazine *Per Lui,* styled by my good friend Joe McKenna, who is very au courant about the street thing. At Steven's suggestion and not seeing the harm in it, I rang Joe's assistant for the addresses of the stores where I could find those same shapeless sweaters with holes. I succeeded only in upsetting Joe a great deal for not asking him personally if it was okay, though we did eventually make up.

Many of the girls' clothes came from the designer Anna Sui, who, throughout the years, stayed doggedly faithful to that same grungy look. There were no clothes from Marc Jacobs, because this was shot just before he staged his famously controversial "Grunge" fashion show—literally a matter of days earlier—and he doesn't give previews. I didn't use his collection simply because I hadn't seen it yet. This kind of co-incidence happens all the time in fashion, and it's often impossible to unravel where ideas have come from.

In its time, grunge, which emerged from the underground music scene to become a hugely popular youth look, was a major turning point for fashion. It made the flood of bright colors, high heels, and big shiny bracelets look old and out of date, cleansed the palate, and paved the way for the romantic minimalism of designers like Helmut Lang and Jil Sander, and even for the floaty, bias-cut beginnings of John Galliano. It also turned the tide for me. This was one designer movement Carlyne couldn't champion—because she didn't like it.

Not to say that would stop her.

Shortly afterward we were at a Jean Paul Gaultier show in Paris, the one inspired by the traditional dress of Hasidic Jews. The collection was extremely polarizing; people either loved it or loathed it. Some were even deeply offended by it, feeling that it caricatured and made fun of a serious religion. But once you deconstructed the "look," it was undeni-ably beautiful, with jet embroideries and caviar beading on black silks and gray satins. Afterward, Anna asked all of us what we thought. Carlyne expressed herself in her typical forceful fashion. *"Je déteste ça. C'est tous-ce que je déteste,"* she snarled. I had already mentioned how beautiful I thought it was and how much I loved it. So Anna turned around and announced that the show should be given to me to photograph for the magazine, "because Grace loves it." Up until then Carlyne had reserved the exclusive right to photograph anything considered important enough to be called a "designer story," whether she liked it or not. So she exploded. Anna expressed surprise at Carlyne's desire to photograph a collection she "detested" so much. With that, Carlyne completely vanished for four days in the middle of the collections. When she returned, she met with Anna and, by mutual agreement, went freelance.

The pendulum swung further my way with the ascendance of the designer John Galliano, who had a great sense of whimsy and held his romantic shows in Paris after he decided to base himself there. John's earlier collections in London didn't appear on our pages in any significant way because, when he was new to the scene in the mid-eighties, Anna had swept into British *Vogue,* where she was more inclined to devote space to purposeful power suits than to anything nostalgic, wistful, or covered in mud. And John's first big London show—the one after he graduated from Central Saint Martins school of fashion and which upstaged all the more seasoned names of London's fashion week—was as anti–power dressing as you could possibly get. The clothes included long pale cotton nightshirts in striped winceyette worn under huge sweaters riddled with holes, accessorized with dusty, dirty men's work boots, a couple of old broken alarm clocks worn as brooches, and top hats smothered in twigs. For reasons best known to John and his muse, Amanda Harlech (whose admitted inspirations were images of hunting, shooting, and fishing), toward the end of the show one model came out brandishing a large dead fish—a fresh mackerel—which was then tossed into the front row, where it landed unceremoniously in the lap of Mrs. Burstein, the owner of Browns. As the poor woman had recently filled her exclusive shopwindow in London's West End with the designer's entire graduate collection as a major salute to his emerging talent, it seemed a tad ungrateful.

These and other extravagances, like John's designs inspired by eighteenth-century French fops known as *Les Incroyables,* echoed a new enthusiasm among British club kids for dressing up in period costumes. They were called the New Romantics. At the same time, Vivienne Westwood was producing her own brand of piratical men's fashion that I photographed for British *Vogue* on the tail end of a shoot in America with Bruce Weber. Vivienne had insisted on flying someone over with the clothes to show us how to put them on. Bruce then took pictures of them on a group of amazingly hunky male models, some of whom were high school wrestlers. I was so embarrassed asking them to dress up in such feminine looks—I really felt I was humiliating them.

John was a designer whose clothes always formed a narrative, and that, of course, was close to my heart. One imaginative show in a Paris warehouse based on C. S. Lewis's *The Lion, the Witch and the Wardrobe* had the audience entering through the back of a huge wooden armoire to find themselves standing on a set resembling wintry London rooftops, complete with artificial snow falling on their heads. It was particularly magical—and not simply because Johnny Depp was sitting across from us in the audience waiting to see his then-girlfriend Kate Moss model the clothes.

Then there was the show staged while John was once again on the brink of collapse in 1994, after being abandoned by yet another of his financial backers. With only a few bolts of material, mostly black, out of which to produce a collection, he presented one of the most unforgettable fashion shows ever. It was at the shuttered and emptied Left Bank mansion of André Leon Talley's friend, the millionairess philanthropist São Schlumberger, who had recently moved on to even greater splendor in the Champs de Mars at the foot of the Eiffel Tower. The invitation, received by a select group, came in the guise of a weathered old key. Others knew of it only by word of mouth. Few had any idea what to expect—although we at *Vogue* knew more than most because André and Anna had a hand in it, and *Vogue* had exclusive rights to photograph it first.

On entering the abandoned house, we set off to find our seats, sprinkled throughout a series of dusty salons hung with shredded drapes and theatrical cobwebs, and decorated with dried flowers and the occasional glass chandelier that had been dashed to the floor. We came across a rickety cluster of seats in various states of disintegration, which could have come from a Walt Disney castle. *Vogue*'s seats faced the main hall and the grand staircase, so we could see the first of John's black-clad apparitions as she teetered down the stairs on spindly black Manolo Blahnik heels. Because they loved him, all the supermodels of the time had offered their services free of charge. Each was given a single outfit: Christy Turlington tiptoed through the rooms wearing something black and vaguely geisha, tied together with a giant obi; Nadja Auermann's black outfit topped by a cloche looked like it had come straight out of an alternative version of *Cabaret;* Linda, Shalom, and the rest followed like phantoms haunting a ghostly film set, while we sat transfixed. Afterward we poured out into the sunlit Parisian courtyard, and people were heard pronouncing it the best show they had ever seen.

I had been carried away the year before by another of John's collections shown in Paris, in which the theme was bootleggers or buccaneers or some such, and the tale in John's head concerned shipwrecks and booty and young girls kidnapped, held to ransom, and then fleeing, dressed in whatever they managed to grab from the pirates' treasure chests. Which, for the purposes of this show, included lacy lingerie, naughty bodices, and crinoline dresses over huge hooped skirts, the tops of which always seemed in imminent danger of falling down. Some were decorated with rusty pins he had kept for several weeks in a bowl of water in his studio. I found the staging memorable as the girls kept rushing around and then melodramatically pretending to faint, whether from fear or consumption, I can't be sure.

I was happy to take four of John's enormous crinolines on a trip to Jamaica soon after, together with the photographer Ellen von Unwerth, for a shoot inspired by Jane Campion's film *The Piano,* which had recently played to great award-winning success. I took other clothes, too, from designers like Vivienne Westwood, but only John's each needed its own trunk and were so complicated to pack that I was terrified they might arrive mangled and ruined. John wasn't worried at all. He told me that the more destroyed they became, the more he loved them.

We stayed on top of a hill in Falmouth at a Great House called Good Hope. The first stop on our location hunt was the nearby Time N' Place Beach, where we met a couple who owned a little shacklike bar. Tony, the guy, had built the place out of bamboo and assorted flotsam (a skill that came in useful when I subsequently returned to Jamaica for a shoot with Naomi Campbell and the photographer Herb Ritts, and needed someone to build a "castaway" hut).

Tony told us there was a completely deserted beach practically around the corner. So, armed with machetes and with him as our guide, we hacked our way through the undergrowth until we arrived at a perfect horseshoe-shaped bay of turquoise water and white sand, completely empty save for the most extraordinary formations of bleached driftwood washed up by the tide. Soon we were transporting the huge crinolines—it took two people to carry each one—along our makeshift little path to the shoot, which turned out to be an enchantingly easy and simple affair in a way that really doesn't happen anymore.

Ellen is very low-key. She doesn't need an enormous team of assistants, and she uses available light—available everything, in fact. We conscripted an old wooden sailboat found right there, and in the pictures, Ellen's young daughter, Rebecca, played the child of our model, Debbie Deitering. Over the years, I seem to have shot in that same tropical cove with a number of different photographers, including Herb Ritts, Arthur Elgort, Peter Lindbergh, and David Sims. For David's session, Tony was asked to build a raft and make a beautiful bow and arrow. By far the most complicated shoot was with Herb, who insisted on hiring generators, lighting equipment, wind machines, and a load of extra technical paraphernalia all piled high on two enormous trucks, which then attempted to drive down our well-beaten track to the beach. Needless to say, only one made it, while the other became completely embedded in the sand.

It was with images of his crinolines dancing in my head that I recently arrived for lunch with John Galliano, the first time I had seen him since his firing from Dior for making anti-Semitic comments in a bar, an incident regrettable on so many levels. We went to what I thought was a quiet, out-of-the-way restaurant in Manhattan close to the *Vogue* offices and we were both dressed down—which in John's case meant he was wearing a woolly hat and shorts. The next second there was a picture of us on the Internet, probably taken by some spying diner with a cell phone. Modern life! It was so sad, because I hardly ever saw John without an entourage and security, despite having loved his clothes for years and pushed them into the magazine at every opportunity. In the past we rarely spent time together because Anna was the one to take him firmly under her wing, always running backstage before his shows and then whispering to me, "You're going to love it" as she took her seat.

Not being a fashionista, I don't hang out with many designers these days, though I do see Nicolas Ghesquière for dinner quite a lot, and Marc Jacobs, although not as much as I used to when we met regularly at the Brasserie Balzar in Paris during fashion week. Then his Vuitton show was moved to a more inconvenient time on the schedule, so we stopped being able to meet so easily. I have been friends with Karl Lagerfeld since the seventies and always attended those wonderful soirees he threw for Anna at his Left Bank house throughout the nineties. And Helmut Lang I am very close to. We clicked from the moment we first met. Helmut is a very real person with a great sense of humor and, even if it sounds like an oxymoron for an Austrian, he's a lot of fun. It helps, if you are friendly with a designer, to love his or her clothes, and I really loved Helmut's. They were intriguing and unexpected, minimal, but not what the young kids nowadays think of as minimal because they were also brilliantly complicated. . . . Until he gave it all up and became a sculptor instead.

In 1990 I returned to Russia, this time with the photographer Arthur Elgort. Christy Turlington was the model. The difference between this trip and my visit in the seventies was considerable. With the big thaw of glasnost and their newfound affluence, the Russians were more flashy, "designery," and opulent. McDonald's had recently opened, and there were queues around the block. We were accompanied by *Vogue*'s travel writer, Richard Alleman, and I noticed how much less surveillance there was, sparing us that sneaking feeling of being constantly watched.

On this occasion our photos were to include young ballet dancers, skaters, artists, fashion designers, and TV personalities—all representative of the culturally assured new Russia. To this end we were placed in the hands of Vlad, a contact of Condé Nast's Alex Liberman, who was to help coordinate anyone we needed to photograph. But Vlad was really bad. Each day he would greet us with the dreaded words "Do you want the good news or the bad news?" This was inevitably followed by something like "The good news is that lunch will be served at one o'clock." (Pause.) "The bad news is the ballet company has said no to any photos." Variations on this theme continued with the skaters and several others. Thankfully, the artists survived. They lived in a kind of commune-cum-squat. As we didn't have a location van, Christy was obliged to use the bathroom as her changing room. While she was getting dressed, she couldn't help but notice she was sharing it with an extra-large transvestite busily transforming himself into Marilyn Monroe.

The other big difference was that, although I was looking forward to drowning in caviar, there was hardly a teaspoon of it to be had for our entire stay. A shortage meant that anything you would call a decent quantity could be found only on the black market. We were directed to a dubious little square, where we purchased a fair amount to carry back home.

When it was time to fly out, however, the airport customs officials became extremely heated about the impressive haul in our baggage, saying it was not for export and we needed to provide invoices, and adamantly refusing to let us leave with it. At this point I asked if there was any problem with us eating it on the spot. There wasn't. So we sat there, right up to the moment the flight boarded, scooping out caviar from our tins as fast as we could on the blade of Arthur's Swiss Army penknife.

In April 1991 I turned fifty, and Anna and Gabé organized a special birthday party for me. Usually my "surprise" birthday parties are taken care of by Didier, and involve the help of my current assistant and the booking of a very nice restaurant for us and a few close friends.

For my fiftieth, Anna booked the restaurant Indochine, which was the hot and happening spot of the moment. All the people I worked with came. Steven Meisel, who was out and about much more in those days, sat at the head of his own table—rather like Jesus at the Last Supper—flanked by modeling greats Linda, Christy, Naomi, Nadège, Helena Christensen, Susan Holmes, Yasmeen Ghauri, and Veronica Webb. Elizabeth Saltzman, the "it" girl at *Vogue* back then and responsible for the new young designers, turned up wearing twelve-inch heels, a padded bra, and a white-blond wig, which proved so effective a disguise that even her parents had no idea who she was. Bruce Weber and Calvin Klein were there. Two models came in carrying a birthday cake the size of a small table that had my face on it drawn in icing. But Anna wasn't happy with the way the portrait turned out, so she took off her sunglasses and jammed them into the cake, making it appear as if I was wearing them. A salsa band played. Arthur Elgort, who is such a good dancer, twirled me out onto the dance floor. Everybody wiggled away underneath a limbo pole. Anna danced wildly.

Later that year I went on another trip, this time to Marrakech, with Ellen von Unwerth, Oribe, and the Valkyrie Nadja Auermann. Originally, we were supposed to head off to Berlin for this photo session: After the tearing down of the Berlin Wall and the reunification of Germany, it was suddenly the "in" place to shoot despite the ugly building sites on practically every street corner and a skyline bristling with cranes. But Ellen changed her mind, having recently gone to Morocco on a trip for someone else and fallen in love with its exotic romanticism. Our new inspiration was to be Josef von Sternberg's 1930s black-and-white film *Morocco,* starring Marlene Dietrich and Gary Cooper, a fortunate choice because the blond Nadja was perfect to play Dietrich. The series of pictures was remarkable in that not only were the clothes mostly black, but to my amazement, Anna actually accepted having the whole story photographed in black and white, which, as it was held to be so uncommercial, was normally forbidden. We used Oribe's agent, Omar, for our Gary Cooper figure, dressed up in the look of the French Foreign Legion, and found our extras among the local population.

Another extraordinary thing about shooting with Ellen is her luck in casting. We can be just about anywhere in the world, looking for a person to play a specific part in her pictures, when the perfect match will materialize. On this occasion she even discovered a man in a white crumpled suit, the very image of the suave character played in the film by Adolphe Menjou.

In 1993 Anna came up with the idea that I should have a show of my work, which turned into an exhibition of fashion pictures curated by me for the Danziger Gallery in SoHo, a selection of personal favorites taken by the many great photographers I have worked with. As I had been working at American *Vogue* for only four or five years, Anna felt I should include as much material as I wished from British *Vogue,* which was very generous of her—although I was soon shooting everything under the sun to boost the American quotient.

There was heavy lobbying on all sides from those wanting to influence my final choice. Dimitri Levas, who worked for Bruce Weber and was helping me stage the exhibit, wanted Bruce's photographs to be predominant. Raúl Martinez, *Vogue*'s art director, was an avid fan of Steven Meisel's and wanted most to be his. At one point, James Danziger approached me, asking, "Do you think you have enough pictures for an exhibition? Do you have around fifty?" Well, I think the final count was closer to four hundred. I decided in the end that each photographer's work should be individually framed and hung in its own space, but I reserved Bruce's pictures for an extraordinary four-sided easel of his designed by Luis Barragán. I also ordered some running shelves to be built around the gallery walls, then overlapped more of Bruce's photographs on these in a similar fashion to the way he displayed them at home.

The show wasn't meant to be precious in any way. After all, these were just photographs taken for a fashion magazine. The exhibition, which afterward traveled to the Fahey/Klein Gallery in Los Angeles, was called "Short Stories: Celebrating 25 Years of Vogue Fashion by Grace Coddington." The opening was followed by a dinner at Dean & Deluca, right across the street from the gallery. Several people made speeches, because once you enter Anna's world, there is always a speech. Bea Miller, who flew in from London, was due to speak but dropped her notes, picked them up in the wrong order, and was forced to ad-lib. Karl Lagerfeld turned up late with an entourage and wanted to be specially shown around the exhibit, thereby holding up Anna's schedule just at the moment when everyone was expecting to sit down for dinner.

My friend Liz Tilberis had recently been appointed the editor in chief of *Harper's Bazaar.* I was allowed to invite her, but only by the skin of my teeth, and she had to sit at another table together with Patrick Demarchelier, whom she had just stolen from *Vogue.*

The person I probably saw the most throughout my early years at American *Vogue* was the photographer Arthur Elgort. For years, not a month went by without our working together. We shared all my biggest trips, and I could count on him to capture the marriage of fashion and place with unparalleled charm. Whereas someone like Bruce brings his own kind of "Americanism" to a picture wherever he goes, because that's what he is drawn to, and Mario Testino subsumes his backgrounds into the hedonistic party atmosphere going on between himself and his sitters, Arthur takes you there. Bring on the bagpipes! The girls are always pretty and lighthearted. You get to see the clothes and the beautiful locations, and he's up for anything. He likes to eat well, drink a very good glass of wine, and practice playing his trumpet in his hotel room late at night. He loves ballet and photographing anything connected with cowboys, jazz, and travel. He may never stop talking, but he's good with people and can hold a discussion on the many subjects he is knowledgeable about without faking it—even if he does reminisce so much that he sometimes forgets to take the picture! His photographs are utterly beguiling and never dark, unlike those of, say, Annie Leibovitz, whose images demand a strong measure of shadow to maintain their brooding, mythic quality.

Working with Arthur during the early American *Vogue* years took us to so many places, it was as though we were employed by some upscale travel magazine: England, Ireland, Scotland, Wales, Wyoming, Texas, California, the Hamptons, Russia, China, Morocco, and other parts of Africa were just a few of the locations where we (sometimes literally) pitched our tent. In India we arranged a shoot with a hand-painted elephant garlanded in fresh flowers, along with a pair of grand young maharajas to escort our model, Maggie Rizer. But by the time we had everything set up, the elephant had swallowed every last petal of its garland. Little mishaps never fazed Arthur. He merely smiled and took another philosophical puff on his pipe.

For all our far-flung travels, I think some of the most memorable pictures Arthur and I have worked on together were taken on a huge salt lake in California that is somewhat like a giant outdoor studio, with its crusty white surface reflecting a magical light. Here we shot Mad Max, with hundreds of children clad in ragged chamois, and a Wild West story with Stella Tennant and Arthur's two sons, Ansel and Warren, whom I've cast in many of my stories.

Mario Testino is another of those few photographers still willing to go on trips. He's always traveling anyway, so we usually have to work to fit into his timetable. He is essentially at his best going to places he is very familiar with, like Madrid, Rio, or Berlin—cities where he can call on his many friends and put them in the pictures, because he's so great at creating a genuine social dynamic.

I think we first worked together on a collections shoot in New York's Meatpacking District. Then we went to Brazil with Amber Valletta. And then to Naples. Or maybe Naples was first. There we used some strong Brazilian girls—Gisele Bündchen, Fernanda Tavares—and the American Frankie Rayder, and did a very cool picture of them with a bunch of local guys on scooters. Mario is largely responsible for introducing the Brazilian models to our pages.

He is certainly fun to work with (although I personally prefer it when he doesn't make the pictures *too* sexy). The girl always looks pretty, he can fit a lot of people comfortably into the frame, and there is a certain

Chamois clothes, chosen by me and shot by Arthur.
It's not mad — it's Mad Max.

modernity in his work that everyone responds to. It's never threatening, and everyone is always having a good time. And his photographs are hugely collectable in the art world.

In 2002, the same year Karl Lagerfeld published a hefty coffee table book on my work, I was nominated for the Council of Fashion Designers of America's Lifetime Achievement Award. As was Karl. And when it came to the final round of voting, it was neck and neck between us. I found out later how close it was because Anna was on the panel for each stage of the vote. Oscar de la Renta voted for me. Calvin voted for me. Also on the panel, fighting for Karl, was Glenda Bailey, editor of *Harper's Bazaar*. "Absolutely not Grace," she is reported to have said.

In the end it was a tie, so both Karl and I received an award. However, there was still the little matter of the speech. The dinner and presentation ceremony were at the New York Public Library. Anna warned me that I had to be there to accept because, she said, "You can't turn it down." She also suggested that Calvin should present me the award because he was so instrumental in it coming my way.

I arrived on the night in my specially made Calvin suit, but Didier was no longer my escort due to a last-minute job, and I wasn't allowed a substitute. That would be against protocol because Anna

Karl & Oscar dancing the tango at my "Grace" book party

had invited Hillary Clinton to join our table. Seeing as I had such a terrible fear of public speaking and this was my first time doing it, I had devised a cunning let-out. The caricature of me by Michael Roberts from the cover of the Lagerfeld book was animated to speak my words and end with a wink. Which was all very charming, but I still had to stand up to accept the award and stammer out a personal thank-you.

Seven years later I would experience far more of a nightmare at the British Fashion Awards of 2009, held at the Royal Courts of Justice in London's Fleet Street, a building as cold and sterile as an abandoned church. The tables were squashed so close together that you could get neither in nor out. The dimly lit stage faded to black with some strange holographic effects hovering about. I sat at the British *Vogue* table, where there were about ten of us. At the appointed moment, the model Karen Elson, whom I had asked to introduce me, graciously went up onstage, took a step forward, and disappeared head over heels into the orchestra pit. During the ensuing pandemonium, I was asked to say a few words, which is difficult if your friend has just plunged into darkness and is cradling a cracked rib. She did, however, manage to get up and hand me my award—a hefty crystal shaped like a diamond that looked as though it had come from a giant's engagement ring. Today the CFDA statuette, which is a metallic figure a little like an Oscar, holds some of my costume jewelry at home in the bathroom. The British version keeps open the French doors on my balcony so the cats can get in and out and makes a marvelous doorstop.

XIV

ON ANNA

In which
magazines go
faster, *Vogue*
goes global, photo
shoots get bigger,
celebrities rule,
and Anna receives
an unexpected
Christmas present.

I am often heard grumbling about Anna. For instance, whenever I come out of the *Vogue* art room having discovered my photos reduced by a spread or two. Or at the end of a fashion meeting in which one of my most cherished ideas is arbitrarily dropped. Or if I'm required to shoot a difficult celebrity I'm not especially fond of. Or if I'm disallowed from shooting a model I am justifiably fond of. These are all circumstances calculated to make my blood boil, and so woe to anyone—even Anna—who stands in my way as I clomp back along the corridors to the sanctuary of my office.

If Anna doesn't like a set of fashion photographs, they're gone. They disappear off the board where the layouts for the current issue of the magazine first appear. She doesn't offer up any explanation. No re-shoots. You have to come up with another idea. She doesn't like pictures that look too retro, that contain too much black, or that appear too

Even ex-President Sarkozy looks up to Anna as she accepts the Legion d'Honneur

mannered in that arty Italian *Vogue* way. She likes to be involved in a photo session, is pleased to be made aware of the process, and is very happy when the photographer keeps her informed about what he has in mind, although most of them are far too scared to call her.

Funnily enough, I had no idea how cantankerous and argumentative I can seem until I saw myself in *The September Issue.* Small surprise that in the past, Anna has said I am the only person in fashion who can actually grind her down. As the nuns who wrote my school report when I was fourteen put it, "Grace has a very nice way of getting her own will." The truth is, although we do have an occasional fundamental disagreement about fashion, I have enormous respect for Anna both as a person and as an editor. And while I am often approached in the street as a kind of heroine of the film about *Vogue,* to my mind the point of it was to show the creative push and pull of the way Anna and I work together.

I remember Anna from way, way back in the early 1970s, when she was a junior fashion editor at *Harpers & Queen* in London. We didn't communicate much, if ever. She wore layer upon layer of oversize baggy knitwear by the Scottish designer Bill Gibb and many other layered knitwear pieces by the fashionable Italian label Missoni. I don't remember her face so well because she seemed to be constantly hiding it behind layers of hair, too.

After she moved to America in 1976, I would run into her over the years, and she was always very nice to me, although still with that shy little habit of ducking down behind her fringe. Then one day in New York, I received a call from the child psychiatrist Dr. David Shaffer, an old London friend who had relocated to Greenwich Village with his family but had recently separated from his wife, Serena. He said to me,

"I'd really like you to meet my new girlfriend." I joined him at the Algonquin to find him with Anna, who by then was working as an editor at *New York* magazine and seemed far less shy.

"Liberman likes her very much and wants to give her this job with a new title—creative director of *Vogue,*" David said. "What do you think?"

"I think it's great," I said, because it seemed to me at this point in the early eighties that American *Vogue* had become, in contrast to British *Vogue,* very bland. They were a beige and boring crowd, and I thought Anna could really help.

As time went on, I began seeing Anna running around New York with her team of tastemakers, including the high-tech architect Alan Buchsbaum and the discerning interior design expert Jacques Dehornois. And that, I think, was exactly what Liberman wanted from her. She was out and about far more than he was and could supply the magazine with up-to-the-minute information about the latest photographers, cutting-edge design talent, and all that was percolating in the fast-moving worlds of art and fashion.

The photographer Arthur Elgort has another theory. He says, "Alex was always completely overwhelmed by her legs." (Anna is a very flirty, girly person. Whenever she speaks to women, she does so with great assertiveness, but with men she's very seductive, even if they're one hundred percent gay.)

David once said to me, "The great thing about Anna is she doesn't care whether people like her or not." I'm not so sure if this is true, but she never seems to falter when criticized. I care whether anyone—from the mailman to the dry cleaner—likes me. Maybe that is my weakness. But not Anna's.

She does, however, care very, very much about her children. If one of them comes on the phone, I've watched her melt, which is not something you very often see with Anna.

A protégée of the higher-ups at Condé Nast, Anna criss-crossed the Atlantic for a while, taking over as the editor of British *Vogue,* then being brought in to run *House & Garden* in a sort of holding pattern until she took the helm at American *Vogue*. There, her first cover was very different. It was everything *Vogue* hadn't been until then. Shot by Peter Lindbergh, it showed the Israeli model Michaela Bercu, a big blond outdoorsy girl, roaring with laughter in front of a Parisian café wearing a hugely expensive couture jacket by Christian Lacroix and a distressed pair of low-slung blue jeans. (Carlyne Cerf de Dudzeele was the fashion editor here.) The cover endorsed a democratic new high/low attitude to dressing, added some youthful but sophisticated raciness, and garnished it with a dash of confident energy and drive that implied getting somewhere fast. It was quintessential Anna. And the remarkable thing is that it ran. At the time, Richard Avedon had a hefty contract with *Vogue* and he was really pissed. "Oh, I can do that. It's absolutely easy," he said when he saw the picture. Yet this type of cover was the complete opposite of his subjective, tightly controlled photographs, and all his attempts to produce something looser and more spontaneous were doomed to failure.

Avedon and Anna never got along. In the beginning, he wanted to come in to be creative director. When that didn't happen, he approached *Harper's Bazaar* with the same proposition. I heard he even knew in which corner of the office his desk should be situated. But that didn't happen either. From then on he never missed an opportunity to say something snide about Anna and her *Vogue*.

Circumstances were completely different around the photographer

Irving Penn, who for decades had been the magazine's most treasured possession. Anna respected him unequivocally and treated him unlike any other photographer used by *Vogue;* he was afforded a kind of freedom no one else got. Three days to do one picture? Fine. Mr. Penn didn't want to shoot that dress? Fine, too. He was given carte blanche. Mr. Penn didn't like the girl-next-door look? Mr. Penn thought it was terrible. And he found wearable clothes tacky. He was used to couture and to producing iconic fashion pictures.

A reticent, ascetic-looking man who liked to flesh out ideas for his photos in beautifully rendered abstract sketches, Penn always found reasons, when approached with a new project, not to do it. Only Mr. Liberman, and, after a time, Anna, could persuade him to take a photograph, but even then you still got the feeling that it was against his better judgment. Later, Phyllis Posnick, American *Vogue*'s executive editor, went on to become his editor of choice, working with him for nearly ten years. It was an amazing collaboration that led to some of *Vogue*'s most extraordinary images. Their professional relationship became like that of an old married couple.

When I first joined American *Vogue,* I did a substantial number of sessions with Penn because Anna had decided that I was the best person to look after him. I had just worked with him on his powerful photographs against a simple white background of the last collection at Calvin's. In his little studio, the atmosphere was hushed, and everyone kept well back and totally still. Absolutely no music was allowed, nor could anyone—even in those days when everyone smoked—light up. Only the celebrity makeup artist Kevyn Aucoin seemed able to get away with making a sound, standing camply at Penn's shoulder and murmuring approving little noises like "Mmmm," until Penn would say, "Do shut up, Kevyn," and continue to calibrate his lighting. Otherwise we all remained perfectly quiet. It was a wonderful experience, but the rapid pace set by Anna at the magazine meant that there were many other sessions for me to oversee and many trips to prepare. In the end I had to stop working with Penn because my long and involved picture stories were not his style, nor were the available clothes ever exceptional enough to suit him—although not many in modern times could come up to his exacting standards.

More and more over the years, especially in public after Anna became American *Vogue*'s editor in chief, I've come to see her as the possessor of an almost Margaret Thatcher–like, straight-faced control. One spring on her way into a Paris fashion show, for example, after being pelted with some gooey substance by the animal rights people who are always lying in wait, she disappeared backstage, rearranged herself, had her makeup redone, and was still one of the earlier arrivals to take her seat. And when the outrageous Alexander McQueen unveiled his new collection in New York one year, she kept her composure despite his show's deliberately provocative finale. At the time, the fashion world was titillated by McQueen's design for "bumsters"—trousers that barely reached the crotch in the front and hardly covered half the arse. One particularly mischievous model, Dan Macmillan (the great-grandson of a former British prime minister), was wearing them in the show's finale, which found him directly facing Anna in her front-row seat. McQueen stepped onto the catwalk to take his bow, and the entire cast turned to bow back at him. At which point the boy was literally mooning Anna right in the face. And she, unruffled behind her dark glasses, simply stared back.

During each festive season ever since I have been at American *Vogue*, Anna has organized a Christmas lunch. Originally, it was just the two of

The Raccoon Incident

"Gosh, I know Anna likes her meat rare but that's a bit much!"

us, and we would go to La Grenouille, a charming French restaurant on East Fifty-second street that I absolutely loved. Then, as the years rolled by, she began adding people: *Vogue*'s design director, Charles Churchward; fashion director Paul Cavaco, who was eventually succeeded by Tonne Goodman; and fashion market director Virginia Smith.

On this particular occasion Anna arranged for the lunch to be at the Four Seasons, which serves good food but is not what you might call a very pretty restaurant. It has the kind of seriously corporate atmosphere suggesting that global deals and huge financial transactions are being cooked up along with the food. We all piled into a Big Apple Town Car determined to get there first, although we knew that would never happen because Anna is always there before anyone, no matter what.

We then sat through a rather stiff lunch in a big booth surrounded by negotiating businessmen. Charlie was in his new Prada suit and tie, handkerchief billowing out of his breast pocket. Meanwhile, Paul was giving a humorous account of his daughter's escapades, thank God, because he always managed to keep things lighthearted.

During the first and second courses, Anna made small talk, asking what everyone was doing over the Christmas break, then suggesting some of the latest shows to see and things to do. Finally, we got to the coffee. The waiter had just poured it when a girl, smartly dressed in black and carrying one of those fashionable black nylon Prada totes, walked over to the table. She was pretty noticeable because the restaurant was hushed and open-plan. "Excuse me. Are you Miss Wintour?" she asked politely. "Yes," said Anna. With a flourish, the girl opened her bag, took out a dead raccoon, frozen solid, stiff as a board, and a little flattened, rather like roadkill, and whacked it down on the table, shouting, "Animal killer!" or whatever those anti-fur people say. The coffee cups jumped, splashing Charlie's suit. The girl dashed away down the stairs.

People raced over to ask if we were all right, while a waiter glided up with an extra-large table napkin in order to toss it discreetly over the dead animal. We all started to giggle nervously. "Well, that certainly broke the ice a bit," said Anna with a smile, her sangfroid intact.

Fashion magazines have totally changed in my lifetime. If someone like Madonna is a huge success as the cover story of the November issue, next time around there must be someone or something bigger. In the end I think Anna gave up on my styling covers since I'm not good with famous people. We used to use the occasional model, but the sales difference was so marked between them and celebrities that it's now one hundred percent pop and movie stars.

Fashion is just a part of what the magazine stands for today, which may be hard on old-timers like myself but is definitely the modern way. I'm grateful to have lived through the ten years or so I did at American *Vogue* when fashion was the most important element. Since then Anna has broadened our scope momentously. *Vogue* now incorporates the worlds of art, business, technology, travel, food, celebrity, and politics. (You have to remember that she comes from a journalistic family; her father was Charles Wintour, the revered editor of the *London Evening Standard*.) And this is all largely due to her vision.

Vogue's involvement in the opening of the Costume Institute's exhibit at the Metropolitan Museum of Art is a prime example. Ever since she took on the organization of the annual ball to raise funds for the institute, Anna has worked tirelessly to make this New York's night of nights. Harold Koda and Andrew Bolton at the museum do the actual curating, but Anna is the one concerned with every tiny detail devoted to ensuring the evening is a runaway success. And it always is. The lineup of limos is not to be believed.

With Anna at a Versace show. Photo: Arthur Elgort, 1998

There was a period early on when *Harper's Bazaar* and *Vogue* alternated hosting the event, but somewhere in the mid-nineties the responsibility fell squarely onto *Vogue*'s shoulders, and it's been that way ever since. How closely is Anna involved in the whole thing? Completely. She supervises everything from the flower arrangements to the table settings, the color scheme of the decor, and the seating arrangements for dinner. She even chooses from the swatches of material suggested for the tablecloths. Months are spent on the seating plan. Anna leaves nothing to chance and always works out who should sit next to whom, the names moved around and around on bits of paper, pink for girls and blue for boys.

There are endless food tastings and meetings about the after-dinner entertainment, which she always wants to be current—this past year it was Bruno Mars and the Italian opera singer Vittorio Grigolo. Before that was Florence Welch of Florence and the Machine, Kanye West and Rihanna, and Lady Gaga, who came onstage terribly late, which played havoc with the planning and upset Anna very much. This year there was also a film made by her friend the director Baz Luhrmann, showing an imagined dialogue between Miuccia Prada and Elsa Schiaparelli (played by the Australian actress Judy Davis), excerpts of which were shown throughout the exhibit.

I suppose if you are a big-name designer or an industry bigwig who has spent thousands of dollars for the privilege of a table, you might think you can invite whomever you want, but things don't work like that. In my early days, if I hadn't already been invited by someone, one of Anna's assistants would ring the designers and say something along the lines of "Anna thinks it would be great if you had Grace at your table." If that didn't happen, as a last resort there was always "the extra *Vogue* table," usually over by the door and en route to the powder room.

I've certainly sat there in my time, but these days I'm positioned better and, happily, nowhere near the toilets.

For the party, *Vogue* dresses just about everyone. Of the clothes, bags, shoes, and jewelry that appear on the red carpet every year, I would say about ninety percent comes through the magazine. In the run-up to the evening, a constant stream of celebrities heads into the *Vogue* fashion closet for fittings, with our fashion market director, Virginia Smith, and our alterations man, Bill Bull, on call around the clock. And these days even the men pour in to be fitted for their tuxedos because Anna really wants the place and the people to look their best.

On the night, every junior and intern at *Vogue* is pressed into service to show people to their seats, take their coats, or help them on their way to the exhibit. These young women are asked weeks beforehand to choose their clothes from the racks provided—this season, to accompany the exhibit's theme, they were all in several shades of shocking, since Schiaparelli was known for her love of pink—and then photographs are taken of them in their dresses and sent to Anna for approval.

Despite all this careful planning, there can be some unfortunate sartorial moments. Those same juniors, having been sent off to spend hours in the hair and makeup room, can emerge rouged, mascaraed, and tonged to within an inch of their lives, with their hair in sad, droopy ringlets and none of their freshness intact. Usually, at this point I walk by and tell them to wash it all off. And then there was the year when the majority of attending women decided it was far newer to wear tight and short instead of graceful and long, with the result that from the back it looked like a convention of hookers. Another time a beautiful girl turned up at the opening of the *Liaisons Dangereuses* exhibit in full period costume complete with white wig. She soon looked most uncomfortable—almost as much as those models and personalities who arrive wearing dresses with hugely annoying cumbersome trains.

In the end it is couples like Gisele Bündchen and Tom Brady who come across the best, mainly because they keep things relatively simple. Naturally, it doesn't hurt that they are both unbelievably good-looking.

The first sign of *Vogue* moving on from its traditional role of fashion magazine was, for me, when Anna thought up the idea of Seventh on Sale back in the nineties, an inspiration for shoppers to spend and spend, and the forerunner of today's annual Fashion's Night Out, which galvanized retail spending after the recession hit home in 2009. Now it's a worldwide phenomenon, with China being the latest country drawn into Anna's axis. She even went there to drum up support for the event. It's fascinating to see Anna focus on China, and to witness a whole country waking up to the force she is. There is no doubt that *Vogue* is a global brand thanks largely to her efforts. Nevertheless, a little nostalgia for the days when fashion came first doesn't do any harm.

In the early days Anna and I would sit down to discuss a shoot, work things out, think of things together. She would have an idea she wanted me to do, and I would ask, "How do you think I should approach that?" The *Alice in Wonderland* story with Annie Leibovitz, for instance, which ran one Christmas, started out as something completely different. Anna had just seen the award-winning musical version of *Mary Poppins* on the London stage, loved it, and returned to New York eager to base our seasonal special on that children's story. But when I sat down, I thought, "Mary Poppins wears black throughout, which really isn't going to work for Anna in the end," and so I said, "What about *Alice in Wonderland* instead? It could be just as much fun, and I can then ask the designers to make up all the dresses in blue, like the illustrations in the book." Anna thought about it overnight and the next morning said, "Yes. We'll do *Alice* and cast all the designers as characters from the book," which was the most brilliant idea. The resulting pictures, with their enchanting resemblance to John Tenniel's drawings from the classic original, are some of my all-time favorites.

When I started shooting with Annie Leibovitz, my eye matured and we did great work. Anna signed her up to do portraits and fashion shots for *Vogue* after she'd spent years being tied exclusively to *Vanity Fair*. Some of the early pictures we did together, particularly a group shot of models wearing Comme des Garçons outfits, arranged to appear as if they were walking on water, are more than great.

Annie would do huge amounts of research to help construct each image, paying attention to every fine detail. However, the more confident she became about fashion—her great love is for vintage clothes or any item that looks beaten up, muddied, and destroyed—and the more she voiced her strong personal dislikes about the clothes I chose for the shoots, the more uncomfortable I became. We could get overheated, but then she would say, "You're the one who really knows about fashion. You are the most incredible fashion editor in the world." And everything would settle down into a fragile truce. Until the next time, that is.

Anna and Annie are the best of friends. Anna is always excited by the prospect of an Annie shoot. She loves the idea of a journalistic point of view, which is the way Annie handles celebrities. She is also aware of Annie's volatile personality, but ultimately the pictures are always worth the battle.

It was Anna's decision, the moment Hollywood talk turned to *Zoo-*

lander, the comedy film in which Ben Stiller plays a knuckleheaded male model, that he should be taken to Paris and shot by Annie for a couture story (besides vintage, Annie absolutely loves shooting couture). I have to say, I hated the idea, not merely because I respect Paris couture for its purity and exquisite workmanship but because an advance screening of the film revealed it to be a crass and truly mind-numbing experience. I think it was decided upon, really, because Anna had a crush on Ben. (She gets these occasional crushes—Ben, Puff Daddy, Roger Federer.)

Annie wanted Ben wearing clothes resembling his costumes from the film, which were so incredibly vulgar and nasty that I had to put my foot down and say how much better he would look in a dark suit. Even then I had reservations about the whole project. So when it came to choosing the models, I secretly went for the tallest ones around, girls like Stella Tennant, Oluchi, and Jacquetta Wheeler, beanpoles who would effectively show up his short stature.

Annie then became obsessed with getting the tiny actor into a tiny pair of swimming trunks in order to spoof a Helmut Newton photograph. He refused. She tried again. He ever so reluctantly agreed to wear them. On the day the photograph was to be taken, as if by some mysterious act of God, he was given incorrect directions to the location. His chauffeur-driven car took him off for two hours the wrong way out of Paris, came all the way back, and set off again for two hours in the opposite direction. By the time he arrived in the correct place, his patience was tried, but somehow Annie cajoled him into doing the picture.

Overall, the end results, thanks to Anna's justified insistence on Ben, were, I have to admit, quite hilarious. Annie's wittiest decision was to reference key couture shoots of the past, even paying homage to the famous 1963 series by American photographer Melvin Sokolsky, who suspended his models in strange futuristic plastic bubbles over the Seine and above the cobbled streets of Paris. Ben Stiller's frozen, panic-ridden expression, trapped inside his duplicate bubble, was priceless. He was a really good sport throughout for allowing us to mercilessly poke fun at him.

Puff Daddy with Kate Moss was another of Anna's highly successful pairings. It was a couture story photographed by Annie in which we shot the famous rapper and the model being pursued dramatically all over Paris by paparazzi and film crews. As a highlight, we were to photograph them in a party situation at a restaurant surrounded by other models in couture along with all those responsible for the creations—John Galliano, Karl Lagerfeld, Jean Paul Gaultier, etc.—plus any others who could add to the fashionable scene. Annie's idea was to stalk the party, popping up and shooting away as though she were a hardened paparazzo herself. Invitations were sent out that read something like "Anna Wintour and Puff Daddy invite you to a party." The location was so tiny that the girls' changing room ended up being the passage linking the kitchen to the main dining area. Panic was in the air, but that was only the half of it. Anna had told her friends not to worry about arriving by the front entrance, where the general public would be in mass hysterics over Puff Daddy, because it was much easier for them to slip in through the back. But we were dressing six models plus Kate Moss in that entrance.

Anna arrived with a film crew and Patrick O'Connell, *Vogue*'s self-effacing new press officer, and installed herself right in the middle of our tight little spot. "And what do you do?" Patrick asked me, trying to make harmless small talk in the middle of mayhem. "Look at the masthead," I snapped, my already snippy mood even snippier. Waiters juggling trays of champagne flew around or genuflected before Anna, while more and more guests poured in. I remember thinking, "It's insane that we are trying to make fashion photographs in this situation."

Annie Leibovitz, who is not exactly the happy partyish type at the best of times, looked like thunder. All the designers had telephoned to ask how late they might arrive for their photograph, each one wanting to be the last. John Galliano, who was working out regularly in those days, wanted to pose topless. Kate was totally drunk, as was my assistant Tina Chai, who normally doesn't drink at all but had been sent to drag Kate out of the Ritz and ended up joining her for a glass of the extra-potent "Kate" cocktail that Colin the barman had created especially for her in the Hemingway Bar.

The designer Oscar de la Renta arrived unexpectedly just as Annie was preparing to shoot the couturiers, and Anna insisted that he quickly join the group. Annie went apeshit. Because her pictures are so intricately worked out in advance, there was no space for him. I turned to my fellow *Vogue* editor Hamish Bowles for help. "Hamish, you've got to get Oscar out of the picture, because Annie's going berserk," I pleaded. "I am not going to go and remove Oscar," sniffed Hamish, flouncing away. Meanwhile, in the group shot of couturiers, John Galliano was saying he would prefer to be photographed standing up rather than sitting down, to show off even more of his new body; Gaultier was looking a bit fat in his matelot T-shirt with its horizontal stripes because he had pulled it on over whatever he came in wearing; Karl was madly fanning himself and being super-grand, while the white powder he daily shakes into his ponytailed coiffure was sprinkled all over his dark jacket and looking like a severe case of dandruff; and Puff Daddy, who thought the whole thing was purely about him, wanted to be placed in the exact center of the photograph. Annie pointed out that if he was in the middle, he would disappear in the deep V where the pages of the magazine are bound together. But he was not inclined to grasp this technical talk and, despite Annie, planted himself front and center.

Finally, when I had taken all I could of this chaos, I started to walk away from the entire thing. On my way out, I said to Patrick, "You'd better get all these people out of the dressing room or I'm canceling the job and taking the next flight back to New York." Unbelievably, he did. When I returned, the rear entrance was practically empty. Anna had vanished and even the models had gone, leaving the hair and makeup people, Julien d'Ys and Diane Kendal, standing there not knowing what to do.

On the day after 9/11, I walked into the empty *Vogue* offices and found Anna sitting there alone. "Where is everyone?" she asked. "We've got to get this city up and running again!" Gradually, people started arriving at work. Everyone was still dazed and horrified from the previous day, when we had all watched the events unroll on the television in Anna's office. But before they had time to think, the staff was dispatched to find out who was giving blood, what Calvin Klein and Michael Kors were doing to help the situation, and who was helping to feed the exhausted rescuers down at Ground Zero. All the fashion ideas dreamed up for the magazine's next issue were summarily dropped in order to accommodate staunchly pro-American stories.

It was the middle of fashion week. Anna wanted to instill a feeling of "the show must go on," so she persuaded the young designers to get together and the more senior designers to show in their showrooms because, as she put it, "We can't allow the terrorists to think they have won." Finally, we did our fashion shoot, which had flags flying everywhere. In the photos, the supermodel Karolina Kurkova was shown waving one while standing on the roof of a skyscraper. And the background of the cover, which featured Britney Spears, was Photoshopped to contain the Stars and Stripes.

The bane of Anna's life is *The Devil Wears Prada*. Even ex-President Sarkozy mentioned it semi-jokingly in his speech at the official Élysée Palace ceremony in Paris before awarding her the Légion d'Honneur in 2011. But it's not a joke. After seeing a few clips, I never looked at the movie again. I thought it made our business look laughable. Even more so than *Prêt-à-Porter,* one of the worst movies Robert Altman ever made, which caused chaos one summer at the Paris collections when people like Sophia Loren and Julia Roberts were filmed playing characters from the fashion world attending the shows.

When I first heard that a former assistant of Anna's had written the book, I thought, "How disgracefully disloyal" and "What a horrible thing to do." Basically, she was making money out of making fun of Anna's character.

I don't remember the girl at all. Anna has quite a large turnover of assistants who sit in the office outside hers. They don't mingle and are usually just a voice on the phone saying, "Can you come and see Anna?" or "Scheduling meeting," so you don't really have a conversation with them. However, when it came to the movie, as usual, Anna had the last word. She went off to the premier with her daughter, Bee. Both dressed head to toe in Prada, of course.

XV

ON
PUSHING AHEAD

In which
Grace embraces
new faces,
falls down
a rabbit hole,
and runs into
Madonna.

I s fashion art? I think it's sometimes very creative, but I'm not sure I would call it art; that's pushing it a bit. I certainly don't think fashion photography is art, because if it is art, it's probably not doing its job. Obviously, there is photography that sets out to be art, but that's another story altogether. In fashion photography, rule number one is to make the picture beautiful and lyrical or provocative and intellectual—but you still have to see the dress. Of course, I like to push the boundaries; I think that's the most interesting element much of the time, when you walk the line. But you can't forget to show the clothes and, in the end, not alter them beyond recognition; to pretend a dress is something it is not is unfair to the reader, too.

I am, however, happy to put certain fashion photography, framed, on my wall. The 2003 shoot I worked on with Annie Leibovitz based on

"Okay Marc, what's that you're smoking?"

Alice in Wonderland was conceived to bear a close resemblance to the book's original drawings. After Anna suggested putting the designers in the shoot as some of the book's famous characters, she didn't involve herself much further, and my discussions became about the fashion and the look of the pictures. But even if we weren't making art, there was an art to the casting.

Annie and I agreed that the designer Christian Lacroix should be the March Hare and the milliner Stephen Jones was a natural to play the Mad Hatter. Jean Paul Gaultier sitting in a tree wearing his signature matelot jersey was a perfect choice for the Cheshire Cat. And the Russian model Natalia Vodianova, with her wide-eyed innocence, couldn't be a better fit for Alice. Having the designers Viktor and Rolf as Tweedledum and Tweedledee was my idea because I remembered how they always came out wearing identical suits at the end of their shows. They also acted in a slightly prissy way, not letting anyone apart from them arrange the ruffles on the dress they made for the shoot. Ruffles became an issue, too, for Nicolas Ghesquière, at that time fairly new to the fashion world, who was cast as himself to represent the future while Alice pushes herself through the looking glass. The only problem was, the dress Nicolas had so exquisitely made for the story had asymmetrical rows of ruffles all concentrated on the wrong side of the body for Annie's composition. Outrageously, and to my horror, Annie suggested we either put it on backwards, or he remake it. Without a murmur, Nicolas and his seamstress politely obliged, reconstructing the dress to be a mirror image of its former self.

The final cast list also included Donatella Versace and her close friend Rupert Everett as the Gryphon and the Mock Turtle; the designer Olivier Theyskens as Lewis Carroll; and John Galliano in drag as the Red Queen, accompanied by his boyfriend, Alexis, as the King, illustrating the part where the characters play croquet using flamingos as mallets. These were stuffed, although Annie seriously considered using live ones, which you couldn't get and, in any case, wouldn't be allowed to play croquet with.

This mammoth shoot was spread over four days and took place both in Paris and an hour and a half outside the city, in the fairy-tale woods surrounding the Château de Corbeil-Cerf. The first problem for Annie was Marc Jacobs's hair; he had been drafted in to play the Caterpillar. He looked rough, and although Annie usually likes a certain roughness, in this case he clearly looked too rough for her as he sat there on his mushroom puffing on a hookah. So she rounded on Julien d'Ys, the hairdresser, who was staunchly defended by Marc. A three-way dispute erupted.

Once the air settled, there was the situation of the White Rabbit. I had wanted this character to be played by Karl Lagerfeld because I had seen a picture of him wearing a white suit and thought him ideal. Annie, however, was not thrilled by the thought of Karl, as she had been the recent butt of his withering sarcasm. Instead she saw him as the Duchess, who in the book has a face so grim that it could sink a battleship, and famously holds a baby that turns into a pig.

Karl, who had naturally read the book, wanted to play himself—wearing dark glasses—rather than any fictitious character. Because he didn't really want to participate, he set the time for his photo at the impossibly early hour of five a.m. in the little wood outside Paris, which meant the entire crew had to get up at two. Meanwhile, a tiny pig was ordered and hidden in the woods on standby, squealing away, with the idea of digitally inserting it into the picture after Karl had left.

At the appointed time, Karl was chauffeured to the set, got out, and stood with Natalia. After five minutes of shooting, Annie asked him to remove his sunglasses. He refused, said, "That's it," returned to his car, and headed straight back to Paris. The pig, which had been loudly squeaking nonstop, was placed in Natalia's arms as she stood close to where Karl would later appear thanks to the wonders of Photoshop. And for the first time it magically stopped making a din. "You have to press it to your heart so it hears the beat," Natalia explained sweetly. "That way it thinks I am its mother."

Tom Ford was the one to step up to the plate as the White Rabbit—a role he had wanted to play from the start, as he considered it really sexy. And he was immaculate. Not one button, cuff link, or pocket handkerchief was out of place as he arrived on set, only to be informed he was to be photographed falling down the rabbit hole. A piece of black velvet had been rigged up on a slope. And so, without more ado, Annie's prop man, Ricky, picked Tom up, swiveled him around, and plopped him on the background upside down. Too startled to say anything, Tom regained enough composure while Annie was snapping away to ask if I could arrange his tie, which was flapping in front of his face, and to check that he wasn't showing too much sock. And then it was all over.

Not long after he departed, we discovered that Tom had been in difficult talks all week regarding his future at Gucci Group. The result was that he resigned the day after doing our shoot.

Sooner or later it was bound to happen: I would find myself once again working with a challenging subject from my past. And of course this would have to be Madonna. It was 2005. She was now married to the English filmmaker Guy Ritchie and enjoying a very English life between homes in London and the countryside. The usually toxic British tabloids had embraced her to the point of fondly calling her "Madge," as her current husband did, and expending miles of newsprint commenting favorably on how she wore tweeds, had taken up riding, and had been seen several times at the local pub. All the dismissive sneering concerning her involvement with Jewish kabbalah had been replaced by approving articles on how its influence had turned her into a much more agreeable person with a plausible English accent.

Our photographs were to take place at her country house, Ashcombe, once upon a time the estate of the multifaceted English artist/photographer/writer Cecil Beaton, whom I had worked with toward the end of his life. Our photographer was to be Tim Walker, a nostalgia-loving character whose body of work looked like he had conjured all his images from children's fairy tales.

Tim had traveled down early to Wiltshire to discuss all the ideas, which he usually puts into drawings. He and Madonna met in the pub, and when I and the rest of the crew arrived a day later, he ecstatically reported that she had embraced every detail he had suggested. All of which surprised me, as some of his ideas were pretty extreme.

Our first shot of her was in the drawing room wearing a pair of jodhpurs, and that went well enough, although she was a little bit wary when Tim started pinning roses all over her and the chair she was sitting on. Then came a picture in which she was supposed to wear a dress with a very full skirt. She balked at it, saying, "This makes me look like a fifties debutante," which, of course, was pretty much the effect we were after.

Things went comparatively smoothly with our next two setups. We took a picture of her in bed reading the newspapers with her children; Tim's brilliant prop girl, Shauna, had entirely redecorated the bedroom by wrapping it in pages of newsprint. Next we took a shot of Madonna out riding with Guy. Galloping back to the stable, she couldn't have failed to notice that we had started to turn all her sheep pretty shades of pastel in readiness for a picture later on. Then she started to grow testy.

"I'm going to do the picture of her in the martini glass next," Tim told me enthusiastically while Madonna was upstairs changing. I do remember asking if he was absolutely certain she had agreed to this, because we were now walking on eggshells. "Oh yes," he said as she came down, looked out the window, and saw, on her lawn, an enormous martini glass with a giant cherry in it and a ladder propped at its side waiting to carry her up.

"I'm not doing that. No way," said Madonna grimly. Tim began acting like a dog with a bone. He became obstinate and absolutely would not let go of the idea—but she, being Madonna, was totally adamant and ultimately the one calling the shots. She firmly vetoed the image, and when he suggested another that involved her wearing a hat that looked like a cream cake, she angrily refused that, too.

Finally, she calmed down a little when we set up a photograph reminiscent of a Bruce Weber portrait of Debo, Duchess of Devonshire, feeding the chickens on her country estate at Chatsworth. But after that, even though there was another day to go, the mood was far too negative and the session was, for all intents and purposes, over. Sadly, the extraordinary dress—a huge crinoline—that John Galliano had made specially for the shoot was caught in the cross fire. She looked so gloomy in it that the photograph was never used. Despite all the problems, however, we ended up with a really charming evocation of Madonna's English interlude.

For me, the thrill of what I do comes from realizing a look I had imagined in my head. For which you need the right photographer. In the last ten years, the tight circle I work with has expanded to include edgier people like Steven Klein, the Englishmen David Sims and Craig McDean, and the Turkish/Welsh duo Mert and Marcus, as well as old friends like Bruce Weber, Steven Meisel, Arthur Elgort, Peter Lindbergh, Mario Testino, and Tim Walker, all of whom bring their own individual strength and charm to the images.

Mert and Marcus are very funny. They often take the pictures in turn, overexcitedly snatching the camera away from each other. On set I imagine it to be a bit like it would have been working with Laurel and Hardy. M and M, as they are referred to, used to be situated on the Balearic island of Ibiza, from which they refused to move, which made a photo session a bit of a stretch, but they are now more prepared to travel. And although I am usually skeptical about the merits and modernity of digital photography, there's no doubt they are brilliant at it, manipulating forms and saturating colors to produce pictures of ravishing glamour. Their approach is totally different from that of other photographers: Using their technique almost like an art form, they create their own image through the digital process as it is happening, rather than perfect it afterward, as others do. In so doing they are redefining what fashion photography is in the digital age. If cameras ever replace cosmetic surgery, their practice will be the most popular in the world.

The equally idiosyncratic David Sims lives in Cornwall, is surfing crazy, and prefers working close to home—even if he attends a sophisticated dinner in Paris, or the Met ball in New York, you can still sense the straw in his hair. David really knows how to light a picture. He's meticulous about everything, a complete perfectionist; with him, it's not at all about the happy accident. He can talk for three hours straight about the precise tone of gray background he wants to use.

Craig McDean, meanwhile, is always directing the girl in an oddball fashion. He wants everything to look wacky or off-balance. He's constantly searching for a movement you haven't seen a hundred times before. "Do it like this," he'll say, acting like a praying mantis or jumping in a crooked manner. He thrives on creating fantasy and keeping himself amused.

I can't put my finger on what makes Craig's and David's photographs so modern, but I think it's because they are so experimental. David plays around a lot with the color, sometimes almost completely leaching it from the picture. Annie Leibovitz also does this, but for her it is part of a process she goes through in order to make her pictures much darker and richer.

Steven Klein is very intense. You can often find yourself still working with him at midnight, having been there since seven in the morning. If you're lucky, that is. These days, like Annie Leibovitz, he needs to have a prelight day with a stand-in. It's all part of dealing with the pressure we put on the photographers, since tight budgets and even tighter schedules—often due to celebrity subjects—have condensed the time they have to get it right. His pictures are close to art photography, and his collaborations with Phyllis Posnick produce the most amazing single images that are required to illustrate certain beauty or health features.

For editors like my colleague Tonne Goodman, it's fine. She much prefers to completely assemble her shoots in advance, to the point where she has it all accessorized down to the last hairpin. Every outfit is admirably worked out in the office and then bagged up, ready for the studio. She is the one who also has to work with the many celebrities we've negotiated to feature on the cover and in the magazine, so her shoots tend to demand considerable preparation, and the clothes usually have to be fitted beforehand. She has endless meetings with photographers like Steven to talk about what they are doing. She even goes herself on the prelight day.

When she worked in her previous job at *Harper's Bazaar,* there was apparently a dummy kept in the closet that she and her fellow fashion director, Paul Cavaco, liked to dress up and accessorize before a shoot.

I prefer to leave things a little more to chance. However, Tonne is truly brilliant at bringing to life a coat or dress that may not in itself be prepossessing. By tweaking it here and belting it there and adding a little this and that, she puts it into a whole different class. And her shoots can be truly visionary, like the brilliant, futuristic story she shot with Steven Klein for our bumper September 2012 issue at Virgin Galactic's spaceship company.

Recently, I worked hard to bring the photographer Peter Lindbergh, whom I'd worked with at British *Vogue* and in the early days at American *Vogue,* back into the fold. Then he had been lured to *Harper's Bazaar* by Liz Tilberis, and he remained there for a long stretch. A couple of years ago I finally succeeded. Peter's storytelling style had been sorely missed. It works perfectly for the cinematic narratives I have been doing lately in place of the children's tales, like *Little Red Riding Hood* and *The Wizard of Oz,* that I had so much fun with—a little too much fun, perhaps, which made it time for a change.

Peter makes a woman, however young she may be, look grown up and mature in a great, sophisticated way, so that the stories we construct with a model and, say, an older movie star are believable. He's very good with male actors, like Aaron Eckhart, for example, whom we paired with the model Lara Stone; and Ewan McGregor, whom we cast in a story with Natalia Vodianova. In this scenario, he was the husband she left for a waiter, played by a wispy male model, whom I personally never would have left Ewan McGregor for in a million years! In both situations, the girl had children and was cheating on her husband, a narrative that Peter seems to repeat endlessly, despite my misgivings. This causes some consternation among *Vogue* readers, who feel we shouldn't be representing such an immoral situation.

But without a little drama, how can it look like real life?

Working with Didier in the English countryside before we were dating, while he still probably didn't like me. Photo: Barry Lategan, 1981

Me flanked by a couple of clamdigger models and Barbara Dente, with (front row from left) Howard Fugler, Dave Hutchings, Rowdy (Bruce's dog), and Tristan, at Bruce's house, Shelter Island. Photo: Bruce Weber, 1980

With Didier on a bicycle definitely not built for two. Photo: Bruce Weber, 2007

In Jamaica with the photographer's daughter, Rebecca Forteau. Photo: Ellen von Unwerth, 1994

Front row at a Chanel show. Photo: Ben Coster, 1993, Camera Press London

XVI

ON
LIZ

In which best
friends become
rivals, life deals
its harsh
blows, friendship
triumphs,
and Princess
Diana dances
at the Met.

L iz Tilberis, who went on to become the editor in chief of *Harper's Bazaar,* was a very, very dear friend of mine. For nineteen years or so, throughout the beginning of our careers, we spent most days in each other's company. She was like a sister to me. When we both lived in London and worked on British *Vogue,* we would have dinner together two or three times a week. She was always relaxing to be with and a good, sympathetic listener. I treasured this immensely because, being reserved, I rarely feel comfortable revealing my innermost thoughts to anyone. But I always felt comfortable with Liz.

If you saw us walking down the street together, you might have found us an incongruous pair, me in my attenuated, sophisticated version of vintage and she much shorter and chunkier, with tomboyish hair and haphazard outfits. What united us entirely, though, was our love of

"pass the bottle Liz, it's been a long day"

clothes. Although I was always considered the cold, unfriendly, and un-emotional one, while she was much more open and warm, beneath it all we complemented each other. We were as cozy together as an old pair of shoes.

In 1967, just before I joined *Vogue,* Liz won the British *Vogue* talent contest for fashion writing. She was still at art school in Leicester, so she interned for a few weeks in the fashion room, where she occasionally assisted me. She then returned to college, but always with the prospect of a future at *Vogue.* Having become absolutely hooked on magazine life, she returned to us full-time when she graduated.

Liz was so much fun to work with, one of those jolly English girls who likes a joke. In the beginning she was far removed from my world and that of my cool group of peers, who were mostly wedded to the Parisian chic of Yves Saint Laurent and impeccable grooming. Liz had a much more down-to-earth personal style, with a passion for big sweaters, dungarees, tweeds, and bargains in army surplus. But soon her boundless energy and enthusiasm as an assistant endeared her to us all, and as the fashion department of British *Vogue* had a small staff at the time—perhaps ten people in all—we became really close.

She was devoted to making things happen. If you needed a giraffe for a shoot, Liz would find it. She didn't mind lifting and carrying and was never too grand for any task. In her magazine photographs, she was far more adventurous than I. Whereas I was happiest working with a nice, well-made dress, Liz embraced the new-wave, avant-garde Japanese designers in the mid-eighties, with their formless black dresses and sweaters with holes. She loved their complicated, cerebral way of turning fashion on its head. Equally, she loved the wild and crazy creations of English labels such as Bodymap, whose clothes resembled madcap versions of dancers' rehearsal wear, complete with odd-looking leg warmers and leotards. She was also an early champion of masculine/feminine looks such as those created by the British designers Paul Smith and Margaret Howell. In this way she fit in with the photographer Bruce Weber's aesthetic, which was why they adored each other and loved working together. Liz also liked working with boys. Whenever I was on a job with Bruce, I consistently tried cutting down on the number of boys in the pictures. But Liz always encouraged him to book as many as he liked. Bruce was happy with Liz because with her, it was always a case of "more, more, more."

Liz's maiden name was Kelly. Her parents lived in Bath, where her father was a respected eye specialist, though the family originally came from Cheshire. Liz became famous for her whitish-gray hair, which I would guess went that way sometime in her twenties, although when we first met, she took to coloring it a dark plum, so I could never be sure. She wed Andrew Tilberis early in her career, while she was still working as an assistant. Andrew had been her teacher, a tutor at her art college, which shocked a few people when their relationship leaked out. Tutors, then as now, weren't supposed to date their students, so they tried to keep their affair secret until Liz graduated. Andrew then spent his week-days working at the college in Leicester and at weekends drove down to London to pick Liz up and then head off to Eastbourne, on the South Coast, where his parents owned a Greek restaurant. He had taken over their little enterprise in order to manage it more efficiently, with a view to selling it off so they could retire. Whenever I visited Tristan, whose boarding school was situated nearby, I took him there for lunch, a slap-up meal of moussaka, with baklava to follow.

For the longest time, Liz continued to assist the senior fashion edi-tors. Any shoot she arranged was, in the beginning, overseen by Sheila Wetton or some other senior editor, who went along to ensure that she got it right. I, too, sometimes stopped by, although it is incredibly awkward to supervise or comment on a shoot under your friend's watch. So I just whizzed in and out with a few bright words of encouragement.

Liz was eventually placed in charge of the section known as "More Dash Than Cash," in which the photographs—many of them done by either Willie, my ex-husband; Barry Lategan; or occasionally Alex Chatelain—were normally spoiled by the crude price tags printed splashily across the pages featuring the bargain clothes. Liz dressed like that, though, and the section came to life because of it.

As her work matured and her style developed, she quickly became responsible for some major *Vogue* shoots and "lead" stories that appeared at the beginning of the fashion well and defined the theme of the month. Soon we were taking turns doing this very important section. Liz worked with the photographers Bruce Weber, Hans Feurer, Alex Chatelain, and Albert Watson, all pals who had supported her from the start.

When we attended the New York collections, Liz and I spent our free evenings hiding away in my room at the Algonquin, tucked up in bed together, ordering room service and watching TV. Or we'd discuss the collections and drink a lot of wine. Zack Carr from Calvin Klein would visit us, and Didier would drop in on his way home. Alex Chatelain would pass by or occasionally take us out, which was good news for our tiny British *Vogue* budget, because he would treat us to sushi. And boy, did we eat ourselves ill!

It was on one of these trips that Liz—who lived quite healthily in London and regularly played squash—decided we should begin jogging for exercise. "Every morning," she enthused. "It's really good for you." She dragged me off to Paragon, the huge Manhattan sports emporium on Eighteenth and Broadway, to buy track pants and sneakers, which, although sporty, were not, in my opinion, at all attractive. I was made to

With Liz Tilberis on holiday on the Isle of Skye, Scotland, 1974

Liz breaks out the champagne for Bruce and me in her room at the Paris Ritz. Photo: Bruce Weber, 1997

run around first one block, then another and another, until we progressed as far as circling the entire four blocks surrounding our hotel before staggering back and collapsing into the arms of the bell captains, Mike and Tony.

Despite all the travel, fashion work, and companionship, life always contained such a huge void for Liz because she so wanted to have children and seemed unable to conceive. She subjected herself to a series of in vitro treatments at a time when the method was in the early stages of development. The only other option was adoption, and after several in vitro attempts failed, she took it.

In order to adopt, the British agencies needed to know that you had withdrawn from an in vitro program and had enough money to raise a child properly. To assess your suitability, they interviewed you, your family, your friends. I was asked to vouch for Liz. Were they kidding? She would make a dream mother!

Soon afterward Liz and Andrew's tiny adopted baby son, Robbie, arrived. It was a very emotional time for them because the birth mother hadn't yet signed the papers, but finally, Liz and Andrew were awarded full custody. After this, our evenings were spent mostly at their house, marveling over Robbie and practicing changing his nappies (Liz was absolutely opposed to having a nanny). Not yet being nimble at this, we were forever stabbing ourselves with the large nappy pins.

A couple of years later, Liz and her family were down at her parents' house in Bath when a terrible accident happened. Andrew was burning leaves in a garden bonfire, and there was a backdraft. He was wearing only a swimsuit, and his entire body caught fire. Liz threw a blanket over him to put out the flames, and he was rushed off to hospital. He remained in the burn unit for quite some time but was very lucky and eventually healed completely.

A few days after the accident, Liz was scheduled to go to the Paris couture for a story with Bruce Weber. She couldn't go, of course, so I went instead. It was a chaotic shoot, full of crazy confusion and tons of boys because this was supposed to be a Liz production and she had okayed them all. A circus theme had been decided on, which included several trained poodles—found, oddly enough, thanks to Didier through the veterinarian's practice where his mother worked—and this led to a memorable picture of the model Talisa Soto supporting a trained toy poodle on its hind legs in the palm of her hand. It was a male dog, and so, to ease the sensibilities of *Vogue*'s readers, he was retouched in his nether regions.

On the domestic front, while Liz and Andrew were busy acquiring Robbie, Tristan came home to live with me, and I restarted my own adoption saga (funny how our lives seemed to run along parallel lines). Tristan loved Liz, and she quickly became as much a part of his life as she was of mine. Every year, as a birthday treat, I took him to the celebrity restaurant San Lorenzo in Beauchamp Place, and Andrew and Liz (whose birthday was three days later) would join us. As soon as they were seated, Liz and Tristan would commence a furious food fight, during which she kept him fully fueled with enormous quantities of Champagne until he became quite drunk. Inevitably, he threw up when I got him home. Liz did everything to oppose discipline and authority, while Andrew did just the reverse.

They soon adopted a second little boy, Christopher. (You can imagine the chaos.) As soon as their dad was out of sight, Liz would allow them to bounce balls off the wall and skateboard or Rollerblade along the corridors of their home, all the while stuffing themselves with M&M's and potato chips. At work, on the other hand, Liz was extremely disciplined and determined. And ambitious, as I was beginning to discover.

On our famous maiden trip to China, while I was in charge of the magazine's main editorial photo shoot, Liz directed the *Vogue* "promotion"—the name given to pages where all the featured clothes and accessories are chosen by advertisers requiring the glossy sheen of editorial. We had a huge disagreement over which of us had the right to use the Great Wall as a location. Because we shared a bedroom throughout the trip, that only intensified the situation, and the argument ran on and on until finally I felt obliged to pull rank, but to no avail. Even though editorial pages should always have the pick of locations no matter who is paying an advertising fee, she won anyway, evidence of Liz's tenacity over things she believed in.

Exiting some shows in Paris once, my friends the photographer Terence Donovan and the television personality Clive James, there to make a British fashion documentary, accosted me with questions. "I don't do interviews," I told them, briskly attempting to walk off. "I'll do it! I'll do it!" said Liz, hurrying over. I stayed to watch—and it was a revelation. My best friend was throwing out statistics and all kinds of complicated circulation numbers that I neither knew nor cared about. When the cameras stopped rolling, I congratulated her on knowing all those facts and figures about *Vogue.* I told her I had no idea she kept such things in her head. "I don't," Liz said with a smile. "I just made it all up."

When I quit my job to go to Calvin Klein and moved to New York, I departed in the sure knowledge that Liz would be stepping into my shoes as fashion director of British *Vogue.* But in the end, Liz wasn't happy. Each subsequent long-distance communication over the next few months seemed to confirm this. Not only did we miss each other, but Andrew was eager to move to the States, too, as he felt England was not a great place to raise their kids. So I set about finding Liz a job in New

York, finally succeeding in securing her a position with Calvin as design director of his less expensive CK line. However, since that would place her somewhat below me in the hierarchy, and because she was concerned with guarding her position, I think she felt it would be something of a step backward.

"Are you sitting down?" Liz asked the next time we spoke, "because I have some good news and some bad news." "And?" "Well, the good news is, I'm definitely coming to America. But," she added, "the bad news is I'm not coming to Calvin, I'm coming to work for Ralph." It appeared that Ralph Lauren was so keen to have his own English fashion editor, just like his rival Calvin, that he had offered Liz an equivalent position to mine as design director of collection at Ralph Lauren, Inc.

Whatever. It was fine. Not worth losing a friend over. Still, having pleaded Liz's cause to Calvin only to discover she was running straight into the arms of the competition, I felt rather silly. But Calvin is like Anna. He never harbors a grudge. Without missing a beat, he filled the position with someone else.

As expected, and at roughly the same time, Anna was summoned to New York. It was common knowledge that she was meant to become editor in chief of American *House & Garden*—and thus would be positioned to take over the big job at American *Vogue*. With her imminent departure, the job of editor in chief of British *Vogue* fell vacant.

Later I learned that several emergency talks had been held at British *Vogue* about whether they could afford to lose Anna as well as both me and Liz in so short a period of time. Ultimately, the powers that be thought that the magazine would be considerably diminished. So, although her family's belongings were already packed up in crates, when she was offered the job of editor, with Anna's blessing, Liz made the decision to accept it and remain in London. (Anna, meanwhile, landed in New York and promptly renamed *House & Garden HG,* which some snippy media commentators delighted in calling "House & Garment," because of Anna's predilection for fashion content.) The rest is history.

The money Liz received in her new post was by no means spectacular. A certain snobbery colored British *Vogue*'s attitude with regard to somebody rising "through the ranks," as opposed to someone glamorous and high-profile like Anna, who had been flown in from America. But if it rankled, Liz never allowed it to show. She took to her new position like a duck to water. Terence Donovan once said, "When you get a job like that, go in there and fire a few people so they know who you are." Liz was far more strategic. She won Princess Diana over to her side by immediately commissioning Patrick Demarchelier to take her portrait for the cover—a major coup. Afterward, the princess and Liz became firm friends, often calling each other to chat about their children late into the night.

As well as doing the work and making the decisions, Liz loved being the public face of the magazine, as well as the socializing that came with it. When she became editor in chief, life changed: She went from spumante to real Champagne. And it was flowing; she and Andrew were now living the good life. From the beginning, Liz must have wanted the top job, even while encouraging me to go for it as well. I discovered she had put herself up for the position secretly, when Bea was leaving. I wish she had told me; I would have been fine with it.

I was very lonely in America without Liz. She, Andrew, and the kids would sometimes come to stay with me and Didier in the Hamptons. But we lacked the immediate closeness of a work situation and the camaraderie of being on the same team and living in the same country.

At this point, headhunters in New York contacted me about "a very,

very important job in fashion." I knew it had to be American *Harper's Bazaar* because for years Hearst, the parent company, had been desperately attempting to revive that magazine's illustrious past. When I spoke to them, I suggested that Liz would be the perfect person for the job. "Funnily enough," they replied, "we are talking to her, too."

Several years previously, I had been courted by *Harper's Bazaar* when the fashion editor was Carrie Donovan, one of Manhattan's most indomitable industry mavens. "You have to come in for an interview," she occasionally boomed at me when we crossed paths in New York. Finally, I gave in and went. But on that day, the Manhattan traffic proved especially terrible. I couldn't find a cab and arrived an hour late. They declined to see me. I was too late for the brass at *Bazaar,* who punctually and firmly closed my window of opportunity.

At the end of the day, *Vogue* for me carries far more weight and breadth. It's so sturdy and strong, and with such a tradition and history behind it, I don't doubt it will always survive. But the *Bazaar* that Liz produced afforded powerful competition. She didn't want a "happening" magazine, she wanted a magazine that was classic and beautiful. She enticed Patrick Demarchelier and Peter Lindbergh away from American *Vogue,* and smartly found and nurtured new photographers like the British duo David Sims and Craig McDean, whom we used much later. Everyone in our business admired how glamorous and serenely beautiful *Bazaar* was becoming under Liz's stewardship. The art director Fabien Baron, who had performed amazing transformations at Italian *Vogue* and *Interview,* had come on board at the start and helped her achieve much of this thanks to his spare, airy layouts and innovative use of type, which cleverly echoed the trailblazing 1950s work of the legendary art director Alexey Brodovitch.

Soon the rivalry between *Vogue* and *Bazaar* heated up to the point where, yes, I did feel the friendship between Liz and me become really strained. And there was a feeling of nervousness in 1992, when the photographer Steven Meisel was rumored to be off to the revitalized magazine. Would he jump ship or stay with *Vogue*? For months, the question of whether or not he would renew his contract with us developed into something of a magazine-world cliffhanger. Fortunately, he decided to stay. Meanwhile, Liz and I made a kind of pact never to talk about work, and this eased the situation, even if I did have to do a certain amount of diplomatic juggling.

December 1993 was the anniversary of Liz's first year in New York. I, along with 250 others, arrived at her New York town house to attend a glittering celebration and Christmas party. By now she was basking in the unquestionable success of her sophisticated-looking *Harper's Bazaar,* which, in the spring, had won two National Magazine Awards and been roundly acclaimed. The first families of New York social life were all there: Trumps, Lauders, Hearsts, Gutfreunds, and Kempners, as well as Seventh Avenue's leading lights: Donna, Ralph, Calvin, and Isaac Mizrahi. It was a hugely glamorous evening. But as I was about to leave, Liz took me to one side and said, "They just discovered I have ovarian cancer. I'm going into hospital tomorrow for exploratory surgery."

I was in shock. My friend had cancer?

Liz went through surgery a couple of days before Christmas, then endured the first of many rigorous courses of chemotherapy. After much research, she came to believe that the drugs she had taken when she was younger for her in vitro treatment might have contributed to her illness.

She was given at the most seven or eight years to live. Months passed. Every day she thought she was winning the battle for survival only to be told the cancer had returned and she needed to submit to another round of chemo. Her love of life was fierce, and she wouldn't let go easily. No matter how weakened she was during these periods, she insisted on living as normal a life as possible. The Hearst Corporation, which owns *Bazaar,* was completely supportive and kept her totally involved. Every day she was in hospital, the magazine sent the "dummy" of the upcoming issue over to her for approval.

When the cancer was in remission, Liz would be up and about and, remarkably, traveling to the Paris collections. She shed a huge amount of weight, and Karl Lagerfeld was now dressing her in the finest Chanel couture. She looked incredibly chic. Didier trimmed her hair into a flattering elfin cut while it was growing back. All traces of her former mumsy bob completely disappeared. She also hosted the gala for the Costume Institute exhibit at the Metropolitan Museum and even managed to once again snag Princess Diana, this time as her star New York guest, a spectacular triumph that generated huge headlines around the world.

Liz with Princess Diana, collecting her C.F.D.A award

Most important, Liz believed in educating women about ovarian cancer and was very verbal about it. She involved herself in the Ovarian Cancer Research Fund and held its first fund-raiser at her house in the Hamptons. She and Donna Karan inaugurated a huge summer charity event called Super Saturday, which became an established tradition.

Inevitably, Liz fell terribly ill again. In 1998 she bravely agreed to a bone marrow transplant, an extremely harrowing treatment. She couldn't see anyone for weeks except her close family and me. When the doctors needed more bone marrow, I volunteered to give her some of mine, but for all the ways we were compatible, alas, in this one crucial way we were not.

Liz rallied for about a year but never really regained her strength, and in April 1999 she was back in hospital. I had just returned from a trip to India with Arthur Elgort when she died. I saw her the night before. Andrew had warned me that it wouldn't be long. She was so very weak and had the look of death on her face. Early the next morning he called to say she had gone.

Half an hour later, Anna called. "Why didn't you tell me? Why didn't I know she was so close to death?" she asked, clearly distressed at the news. Then, with great compassion and respect, she asked if I would write an obituary for the next issue of *Vogue*. She knew how much it meant to me, and though I was in floods of tears, I managed to pull myself together enough to finish it at the office with the help of Charles Gandee, a *Vogue* features editor at the time. At home, I looked through all the snapshots of our good times together and, again in tears, added these to the page.

There was a small funeral with only Liz's immediate family and housekeeper in attendance, along with Patrick Demarchelier, his wife, Mia, and Didier and me. Her two boys were so brave, it was heartbreaking. Later there was a huge memorial service at Lincoln Center. I remember Andrew's speech for its eloquence and tenderness. Many others spoke as well, though I did not. Andrew asked me, but I just couldn't have held myself together. Even six months after her death, I was too raw. I miss her still.

XVII

ON BEAUTY

In which
makeup is
removed, looking
older is no bad
thing, allergies
are acquired, and
hair is molded
with clay.

As soon as I joined British *Vogue,* I pretty much stripped off all my makeup, with its clever little tricks and flourishes carried over from my modeling days. Out went the professional touches like fake freckles or eight-hour cream on the lips, which became the big thing after the late, great Diana Vreeland recommended it as a way of giving the mouth a modern, glossy look—but it was so thick and gluey, you stuck to the pillow all night if you put it on.

First to go was my heavy black eye shadow and the doll-like lashes I painted below the eye socket. From then on I used nothing, not even a hint of mascara; just a little foundation on my eyelids for that pale, bald Renaissance look. I think it was because I was getting back to reality, to being me rather than a model, who is generally called on to play someone else. I hate a lot of makeup in my fashion pictures now, too. I

"Running to a show is far from my mind, girls"

mean, cover a pimple if you must, but it's fine to have bags under the eyes and a few lines on your face. It's who you are. Nor am I terrified of looking older. Besides, seventy isn't seventy anymore; they say it's the new fifty.

Every day I wash my face with soap and water. Only recently have I begun to use moisturizer, because as I grew older, my skin started to dry up noticeably. After all those years of ignoring beauty routines and not listening to anyone's advice, expert or otherwise, I'd like to say my skin is beautiful. But it isn't. Not taking enough care while sunbathing or working outside has left me with considerable sun damage.

In those teenage years when I used to go drifting about in my little sailing boat, suntan lotion was thought of only as an aid to getting a tan, not something that could contain ingredients to protect your skin. We even used pure olive oil for those occasional periods when the sun broke through the island's banks of costal cloud. And in the sixties, while I was lolling on the beach in Saint-Tropez, I used to splash on lots of coconut milk, under the illusion that it would turn me brown. But it didn't, because I don't have that kind of skin.

The allergic reactions I first experienced as a child became much more severe in my late twenties. On a photo shoot with David Bailey in Peru, we were taking pictures on Machu Picchu when he, being a bit macho, challenged me to race him to the top. It didn't appear to be that hot up there, but the air was so clear that the sun's rays were unexpectedly powerful. By the time I had climbed halfway up, my face was as red and round as a toy balloon. But nothing was as ghastly as the day at British *Vogue* when I found out I was suddenly allergic to oysters, a seafood that, until that unhappy moment, I had thoroughly enjoyed.

After a delightful lunch with *Vogue*'s ex–travel editor Martin O'Brien at Scott's in Mayfair, known for its fine fish, I was discovered collapsed in a toilet cubicle back at the office and carted out of the building on a stretcher, which is very embarrassing because you meet all kinds of people you know on the way down.

These days I use as little foundation as possible, mostly to cover the scars on my left eyelid and match it to my right, and to mask the dark circles under my eyes. These are telltale signs of yet more allergies that I contracted after I turned fifty. I was staying in Italy at the house of my friend Carla Sozzani, owner of the Milanese designer store Corso Como. Much to my delight her dog, a chow chow, slept on my bed. When I awoke, however, I couldn't open my eyes. They were incredibly swollen and stuck together. I've had allergies to practically everything ever since, except, strangely enough, cigarette smoke. Perhaps all my years of smoking in London have left me immune.

The only makeup I really use now is lipstick. I have to first make an outline with a pencil to stop it from running because of the deep wrinkles around my mouth. I don't have eyebrows anymore. I had heavy ones in my early modeling days, until Eileen Ford ripped them out. They've grown back higgledy-piggledy ever since, so I keep them plucked.

I do spend a lot of time on my hair. If it weren't for that, I would be totally unrecognizable. It needs to be recolored every two weeks, not the six to eight it used to be. Louis Licari, my brilliant colorist, says red hair is the most difficult to work with. Because it requires so much maintenance, I've been thinking of just letting it go gray.

Steven Meisel told me on a shoot recently that I couldn't leave his studio before having a trim, and I must admit my hair was looking quite raggedy and unkempt because Didier—who has a lot of hair, and very good hair, too—had been away for a while and he is the only person I allow to cut it. Although I might think of going gray, I'm never cutting it short again. I need a big frame around my head because it helps to make my body look smaller. At least that's what I like to think.

Each day I wake up as stiff as a rake. I hate going to the gym. The instructor always says, "You'll grow addicted to it," but I never do. I'm English, and English people always hate going to the gym. I like Pilates, though. I go two or three times a week, and it does help to stretch. I walk in hunched, come out much straighter, and find I can breathe much better, too.

I don't believe in face-lifts. Besides, after my car crash all those many years ago and the five operations on my eyelid, I've had enough plastic surgery to last me a lifetime. And to be honest, I think people look much better before than after. I've seen what happens to them—they all start looking the same. What's wrong with a few wrinkles, anyway? Breast implants? I think they throw people out of proportion. Liposuction? I've seen it on TV, and it looks so terrifying I could never go there. This Botox thing is indecent, too. Willingly putting poison into your face and losing all your facial expressions? That's mad!

My favorite bit of beauty pampering nowadays is my "mani-pedi," the manicure and pedicure session I regularly indulge in at Think Pink, my local New York salon. The entire staff is Korean. And they love me. "Glace! Glace!" they shout when I walk in. They used to like sitting me near the window so passersby could see me. Pedestrians looking in often came up to the glass. When they realized I couldn't hear them, they mouthed things at me like, "I love *The September Issue*. I love your work." Because of all these interruptions, the therapists now discreetly seat me at the back so I won't be disturbed.

My job brings me into contact with beauty practically on a daily basis. After all, I do work for a magazine dedicated to beautifying people's

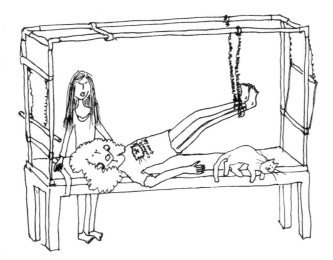

Stretching out at Pilates with Kayoko & Lovie

lives. Beautiful people, beautiful objects, beautiful clothes, all shown in beautiful photographs. Not to mention on beautiful models—although it is well known that my notion of a beautiful girl is not exactly the same as that of most other fashion editors. I prefer a much quirkier kind of beauty. And I learned early on, as far back as the seventies in London, when everything was based on silver-screen glamour, that a great hairdresser or makeup artist can make a picture better, even when it looks as though they have done very little. They can enhance whatever image is being attempted. I have undoubtedly worked with a few who are considered geniuses at this.

The first time I found out about the makeup artist Pat McGrath was by listening to two great models, Shalom Harlow and Amber Valletta, sing her praises. "She's amazing," they told me. So I booked her for a job with Helmut Newton in the South of France. It was a bit of a test, because working with Helmut was always a little challenging. The pictures were with the blond German model Nadja Auermann, and it was the shoot that included the infamous picture of Leda and the swan.

We had never met before, and I didn't see Pat arrive at our hotel—she came with one little bag and no assistant—but once she was there, she called my room and said she would love to come over right away to discuss the shoot. When I opened the door, a big, beautiful black woman was standing there smiling at me, so open and friendly, in a way that is far from inevitable in the fashion world.

Pat did an amazing job. Even Helmut was impressed. Nadja had never looked more dewy and luminous. From then on I worked with her whenever I could. Soon afterward she began collaborating with Steven Meisel. It was love at first sight, and they ended up working together virtually every day. Pat is very loyal to him. Once, in the middle of the international collections (she does practically every single show), she flew from London to New York to work with Steven and me for the day, then flew back the same night, the instant she finished. She would do anything for him. If he can't get her for the makeup, I know he often doesn't take the job.

Pat is famous for traveling with upward of fifty bags, big black canvas holdalls of makeup and reference materials. At hotels she has to book an extra room solely to keep them in. Extra cars are ordered to carry them. In Paris she hires a special delivery van to transport them from job to job and show to show, while she speeds off to the same venues on the back of a hired motorbike, which enables her to nip through the traffic at high speed.

Everything in Pat's bags is immaculately filed and carefully labeled. One might contain beige foundations 1 through 100 and another might have orange lipsticks 15 through 50. She takes two to three bags filled with books: film books, books on the thirties, forties, and fifties. Then there are the Polaroid albums that contain every look she has ever done, documented with each product she has ever used. So on any given day, she can turn to an assistant and say, "Now, what was that very pretty pink lipstick we used two years ago for such-and-such magazine on so-and-so?" and the assistant can look it up and locate that exact thing. Lately, Pat has lightened her load a little by putting much of this documentation on her iPad.

Normally, Pat works with between six and eight assistants. Meanwhile, she's developing new makeup and shades of color for the industrial giants Procter & Gamble, cajoling the photographers she works with, and giving interviews. Throughout, she's never, ever in a bad mood. She has even developed a beauty video game; it's remarkable. Nowadays at fashion shows, she mainly directs. She will make up a

Pat McGrath   Guido   Di Kendal

Julien d'Ys   Stephane Marais   Gucci   Gawen

model's eye and an assistant will copy it, filling in the other. Each of her assistants has a specialty. One will do lips and another will shape the eyebrows, though they can all do skin. Before Pat arrives at a show, the assistants will prepare the girls' faces so that when she walks in, there's a perfectly blank canvas for her to work on. She can be creative and extreme, but she's never torturous. And she cares about everything, every last eyelash.

I met another brilliant makeup artist, Gucci Westman, on a job with Bruce Weber, who does not like a lot of makeup on the skin. In fact, for many years he would work with only a hairdresser, leaving the models' faces bare and natural, a groundbreaking move in beauty at the time. It says a lot that Gucci could enhance without intruding, so Bruce felt comfortable with her.

Gucci is very easy to work with. A good traveler, she is great to take on a trip because she never complains about her room. She makes people feel at ease. Actresses like her a lot. And she's a very pretty girl herself. I love what she does—it never overwhelms the girl or makes her appear heavily made up or "draggy." Gucci can do theatrical makeup as well. I once wanted her to have one of Bruce's cute boys look wounded on a shoot, and she did a fantastic job reproducing the effects of blood and bruising. On another occasion she managed to completely conceal my black eye and stitches when I fell over just before my appearance on *The Martha Stewart Show.*

As for the hairdresser, I sometimes think of them for a shoot before I even decide on the photographer. In the sixties it was all about the cut. Vidal Sassoon would do the actual cutting himself, but once that was done and the hair had been ironed dead straight, there was no need for him to physically attend the photo shoot. It wasn't until much later that hairdressers styled hair solely for photo sessions and salon work took a backseat. Leonard, who graduated from Vidal Sassoon's academy and opened his own salon, was the stylist I worked most with when I started at British *Vogue*. Although he had trained at Vidal, his style was somewhat opposite—very curly and romantic.

The permanently in-demand hairstylist Guido works in much the same way as Pat, except he employs an extra person called "Production" who coordinates everything for him. It is the modern way, and they—he and Pat—are a great team.

Guido creates fashion in hair. He is extremely versatile and has a light touch, so the hair doesn't look as if it's been "done." He adapts his style to both Steven Meisel and David Sims, who likes to pair him with Diane Kendal. Di does gentle makeup, beautifully applied, the kind where you can't tell whether the girl is wearing any. Extreme is not her thing; to me, her work is very truthful. She is also soft-spoken and self-effacing, which is occasionally a disadvantage, such as when Guido, who is extremely assertive, attempts to dictate the shoot—telling her to remove or bleach the eyebrows, which is a particular hate of mine, by the way. Stéphane Marais, on the other hand, is noted for doing really heavy brows. He and Peter Lindbergh have owned this look since back in the early eighties, together with smudgy black eyes. Stéphane and Julien d'Ys collaborate brilliantly. When booking a team for a shoot, choosing people who work well together and complement each other can make a huge difference to the harmony on-set.

Guido recently told me that both he and Pat have been asked by their respective sponsors to tweet during every fashion show they work on. How crazy is that? It is another insane condition of modern-day working that has been added to their contracts—as if it isn't enough that they do amazing hair and makeup.

Julien is very romantic. He is also French, complex, and artistic. For photographs he likes to give hair a certain texture—it could be with either a clay paste or salt or sugar water—so that he can mold it. He's a little like a sculptor, except he doesn't like things to look "finished." For him, it's better when the hair looks rough or tousled. When he arrives on a session, he brings a great many references, all to do with paintings (not other people's shoots). He is brilliant with wigs and fearless with color. As he goes along, he fills the huge scrapbooks he carries around with all sorts of ideas for the shoots he is working on—newspaper clippings, Polaroids, and masses of sketches of the way he sees the hair. He also watches a great many films and gathers stills to add to his inspirations.

I like to book him with most any of the photographers I work with, but especially Annie Leibovitz. They have a very good relationship and a mutual respect—and he is the only one who can stand up to her, although it can blow up every now and again. You have to treat Julien gently, because when he takes offense, he shows it. Also, his kind of styling lends itself well to display of all kinds. He has worked on several exhibits for the Met, and once a year, when I am asked for Fashion's Night Out to design the windows for Prada, he always helps me out with something really surprising.

Didier makes women appear real, touchable. They look as though they have been discreetly fooling around. And they are believable and sexy. He can do extreme, but it looks plausible. For example, he never does straightforward retro, but his modern version of it. The styles he creates in photographs of women are the kind you could quite happily wear in

Didier does really BIG hair

"By the way, do you like cats?"

the street. The men's hair he did for Bruce Weber's fashion editorials in the eighties and nineties—heavily combed glossy wedges and waves—were so intrinsic to the photographs that it gave them a strong style, completely identifying them in the history of fashion. As did the way he merged hair with nature in our groundbreaking photos for Karl Lagerfeld and the British *Vogue* series in an English garden, which are still popular and hugely influential reference points today.

Didier is old-school, like the brilliant Garren—a hairdresser who started in the seventies and whom I worked with a lot in earlier days. They are hands-on, whereas others might get their assistants to fill in for them. They can do a great chignon or cut because they had the sort of training that doesn't happen now. When Didier began his career in Paris in the sixties working at the hairdressing salon of the Carita sisters, he learned all the traditional techniques. The salon was popular with Catherine Deneuve and many of the French film actresses of the day. When he left, he went to work at Jean Louis David, where he was persuaded to abandon those techniques and become much more spontaneous. His studio work commenced there. When Jean Louis decided he wanted more publicity for his salon, he put together a band of young stylists and sent them out to the studios to do editorials. This was way before hairdressers were even part of a photographer's team.

Didier has always preferred being completely independent and free, so he doesn't have hugely lucrative hair-product contracts like many of the others. Nor, like some, does he ever dream of having his own hairdressing salon. For him, an unpredictable work schedule is something to relish, an approach that couldn't be more different from mine. But like Jack Sprat and his wife, we muddle through just fine. At least I know my hair will be in good shape, however old I get.

XVIII

ON CATS

In which
our heroine has
cats up to there,
cats in her hair,
a few cat-astrophes
in the country,
and goes cat-crazy
with Martha
Stewart.

D o I dream very much? Do I dream predominately about fashion? No. I dream much more about cats.

Cats are such special animals. They feel your emotions and are incredibly calming. If ever I've had a bad day, Bart, my blue Persian, will lie on my bed purring and massaging my head in order to soothe me. (Sometimes, however, he forgets to retract his claws, and that can get a bit painful.)

Having said that, both Bart and Pumpkin, my orange-and-white Persian, are extremely high-maintenance. They have highly sensitive stomachs, so each has an individual diet, and I have to wash their eyes every morning and evening. As their long fur gets easily matted, they also need combing and brushing at least twice a day. Luckily, they have their own live-in hairdresser.

I must say, I like the independence of cats. You can't make them do

"Just a little too cozy Bart"

anything they don't want to. And they're funny. They get themselves into all kinds of wacky situations and behave in a really silly way. Persians have fairly short legs and aren't able to jump high or climb trees, so they spend a great deal of time earthbound. Bart, for instance, will sit on our bed for hours with his paws crossed or pressed together in the posture of a meditating Buddha. (He also has a strange habit of jumping on my lap when I'm sitting on the toilet, which is really annoying, as it means I could be stuck there for hours.) Pumpkin, when the weather's hot, will lie on her back on the cold bathroom floor like a wanton harlot, waving her legs in the air. When we are in the country and it is time to come in from the garden for the night, she likes to play catch-me-if-you-can, hiding in the ferns and running this way and that, any way but through the door, with me in hot pursuit.

In New York, I'm cat central: Absolutely everyone calls me for advice. They call me if they need to find a vet or discuss their cat's symptoms or get the telephone number of my cat psychic. She's brilliant, by the way. Her name is Christine Agro, and I was introduced to her by Bruce Weber. Christine lives in upstate New York with her artist husband and their son. When she was still quite young, she discovered that she had an exceptional ability to communicate with animals; she also treats them holistically. Whether or not you fully subscribe to her findings, the insights she reveals about the inner world of your pets are so charming—and conjure such compelling images—that they're impossible to ignore.

I have loved cats ever since I was a child, even though we didn't have any at home; my mother kept dogs. Still, there were a few of them around—feral mostly, wild ones that hung about the hotel grounds, scavenging for scraps. The first cats I ever remember owning came my way when I was modeling in the early sixties. They were a pair of pedigree Siamese given to me by the Armenian photographer Peter Carapetian, whom I worked with a great deal and who, in 1962, shot my first *Vogue* cover.

Cats didn't figure during the period I was with Michael Chow, my first husband, because he was allergic to them. My next pair, Brian and Stanley, you could call my divorce settlement after the collapse of my marriage to Willie Christie. When I moved out of his house in Gunter Grove, they accompanied me to a new apartment down the road. There they made friends with a grumpy old cat called Miss Puddy, who belonged to a neighbor.

Sadly, a couple of years later, I arrived back in England from my summer holiday to discover I had lost Brian. He had been run over by a car in the Fulham Road. Andrew Powell, the *Vogue*

me and my pussy

travel editor who was cat-sitting for me at the time, was mortified. I, of course, was devastated. Sobbing, I fell into his arms for comfort—and we ended up having a two-year affair. Meanwhile, Stanley, who never recovered from the loss of his brother, abandoned me and my apartment to move in next door with Miss Puddy.

When I became a New York resident and settled down with Didier, we acquired three new kittens: Coco, Henri, and a little later, Baby. I discovered them on a visit to the cat show at Madison Square Garden. All three were a French breed known as Chartreux and were very fashion-conscious felines. Coco, we named after Coco Chanel. Henri was originally meant to be called Yves, after Yves Saint Laurent, until Didier pointed out that in France it was considered a very common name. So we settled instead on Henri, after the champion tennis player Henri Leconte. Baby was originally to be called Madame Grès, after the couturier, but that was a bit much, so she became Baby, since she was the youngest of the group.

Chartreux are a great breed to have as pets: loyal, perfect lap cats, and in contrast to Persians, easy to look after—and I just love their dense gray fur and chubby faces. Each of my trio had a distinct personality and appearance. Baby had a wonderfully thick, long tail but suffered from weight problems. Coco had a kink at the end of her tail, and Henri's tail was very, very short.

When they were about four years old, while I was away on a fashion shoot, Didier kept passing the downtown pet store around the corner from where we lived. He spotted a red-haired kitten in the window and went inside for a closer look. (I think he was missing me.) Almost as soon as I got off the plane, I was marched off to check the kitten out. When he was taken from the window and placed on the counter, he strutted up and down with real attitude. He obviously had great character. He was a "marmalade cat," just like Orlando in the books I had read as a child. I couldn't resist, so we took him home straightaway in a little cardboard container and named him Puff. At first we called him Puff Daddy Junior, but this proved a bit of a mouthful, so it was shortened to Junior and finally to Puff. On meeting P. Diddy himself in the course of a photo shoot

Puff goes "walkies"

one day, I told him about our Puff, but I think he wasn't too impressed with having a cat named after him.

Puff kept us all entertained and was as exasperating and endearing as a naughty boy. Like Didier, he was a huge Knicks fan. They would sit together watching the play-offs each season, carefully following the ball around the screen. If the team lost, both of them would be in a really bad mood.

When Puff grew up, he became the alpha cat in our family, and he liked to take charge of everyone. For instance, when we set off on a Friday evening for the Hamptons, Puff usually wanted to drive and insisted on sitting on Didier's lap and getting his tail in the way of the controls. Occasionally, he got bored with driving and preferred to navigate, sitting between us in the front and keeping a keen eye on the road. As soon as we turned off the highway toward our house, he would become wildly excited, and the second we opened the car door, he would shoot out like a scalded cat to reclaim his turf.

Puff would become severely depressed if we didn't go to the country every weekend. He was never happier than when we spent our entire August in the Hamptons. He stopped any other cat from entering his territory, which grew larger by the day, and I had to fend off the complaints of neighboring cat owners about his aggressive behavior.

Later still, he became independent, a totally outside animal. But at night I didn't like him to stay out, because the woods on Long Island can be full of creatures dangerous to cats, like raccoons, foxes, owls, and hawks. There was even a rumor of a coyote spotted in our neighborhood. When he went on his long expeditions and we weren't able to find him for hours, however much we called him, we asked Christine for help. She spoke to him (psychically, of course), explaining how worried we were and that he must come home. Finally, she heard from him, and he told her something like, "Yeah, Yeah, just another ten minutes." Ten minutes later, there he was, sitting on the doorstep, ready to be welcomed like the Prodigal Son.

At one point we tried putting a leash on him to go for a walk after dark, and he loved that. From then on he would become so happy whenever we pulled the leash out of the drawer that taking Puff for a stroll became our regular routine each night in the country before turning in.

With age, however, he developed faulty kidneys, and eventually, he had a stroke that left him with a paralyzed leg so that he couldn't even struggle into his litter box. It was heartbreaking: He was such a proud old feline that this wasn't at all how he saw himself. On Christmas Day 2007, we finally had to let him go. For a long while afterward I found it difficult to return to our house in the country because I felt his presence everywhere. He was the most important cat in my life.

One day, when all our Chartreux had finally passed away (but Puff was still with us), I was preparing a photo shoot with the English photographer Tim Walker, who is famous for including cats in his pictures. I spotted Bart—an unbearably cute fluffy gray kitten with a squashed-looking Persian face—for sale on the Internet. His picture popped up as if he were searching for me, rather than the other way around. Although it is not usually a good idea to find a pet in this fashion, I fell instantly in love.

I picked him up from some highly dubious Russians in Atlantic Beach whose house was filled with tons of Persian carpets and hundreds of Persian cats. Most likely, it was an illegal cat farm. Grabbing Bart as I handed over a fistful of dollars, I jumped in my car and headed straight for the Hamptons. When we arrived, Puff, who was outdoors as usual, at first refused to come inside. For the next week, to keep the cats

In bed with my favorite cat, Puff, at home in Wainscott, Long Island. Photo: Didier Malige, 2000

Stanley & Brian

Baby

Coco

Henri

Puff

Bart

Pumpkin

separate and the new kitten safe, I slept in the spare room with Bart while Didier slept in the main bedroom with Puff. At the beginning of the second week, I moved back in with Didier. We woke the next morning to find both cats sleeping peacefully at the end of the bed.

Originally, Bart was called "Little Boy Bart" and Pumpkin was known as "Girly." She also came from the cat show in Madison Square Garden, which has to be one of the craziest events around. It's completely different from a dog show, where the animals are seriously put through their paces around a ring. Here the cages can be decorated in leopard print or pink satin with little four-poster beds inside, and each cat has an owner fawning all over it. The cats are there to compete, but there are also kittens for sale. You can put your name down for the next boy or girl cat, as I had done twenty years earlier with Coco, Henri, and Baby.

Pumpkin was in a cage with some other kittens waiting to be sold. She was the smallest of the litter. During the two days of the show, I kept walking past and chatting with her breeder, Pam Rutan, who had a couple of champions and several other cats in the event. Frankly, I was nervous about getting yet another pet, afraid that Didier would think I was overdoing it to bring a third cat home. But once I'd seen Pumpkin, I wanted her desperately. Although she was shy and cowered in the cage when a stranger came near, if Pam put her in my arms, she would purr at top volume. And how she could move! Pam would hold up a feathery stick, and off she'd cha-cha, back and forth like a contestant in *Dancing with the Stars*. Again it was love at first sight.

I arranged to pick up the newest and littlest member of our cat family the next day on our way out to the Hamptons. Didier was driving. Puff and Bart were also in the car. It was my intention that we should all come to know one another on the long drive down. But in her box, Pumpkin started screaming blue murder. We hadn't even left the city when Didier

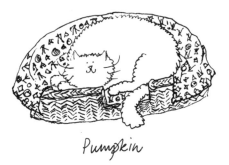

Pumpkin

shouted, "This isn't going to work. Take the box out and leave it on the sidewalk. She's so cute, someone is sure to give her a home." "Absolutely not!" I screamed, outraged. And so we drove on through the suburbs and into the Hamptons, arguing all the way to our home in Wainscott, with Pumpkin relentlessly screeching the entire time.

When Pumpkin arrived at the house, both Bart and Puff began spitting and attacking her. It was a nightmare that carried on for a full week. Finally, we called Christine. She came over, and the cats were soon all sitting around her in a circle, hissing. Afterward she explained what was bothering them: Bart was worried that there wasn't enough love to go around for three cats. Christine reassured him there was, and we went out to dinner. When we returned, all three cats were calmly lying together, snuggled into the sofa.

As for Pumpkin's traveling troubles, her breeder suggested a mild dose of valerian. A friend of ours, the fashion editor Alex White, gave us a CD of Beatles lullabies to play while we drove. Neither worked. My assistant, Michal Saad, opted to conduct a methodical series of experiments with different homeopathic drops—Panic Stop, Rescue Remedy, and so forth—as we drove my car up and down the West Side Highway after work each day, with Michal at the wheel, and me taking care of Pumpkin. We tried putting her in the back, the front, on my knee, but every time, she screeched. Out of her carrier, back into her carrier, still she screeched. I would call Christine, who occasionally had a serious "talk" with Pumpkin, and she did calm down. But only for a moment.

In the end we discovered that the latest addition to our family remained reasonably quiet only if we attempted the entire journey in day-light, which in wintertime, as darkness fell so early, cut our weekends down considerably.

My cats are not only loved and comforting companions, but they also provide me with a constant source of inspiration: Row upon row of framed sketches I have made of them hang on the walls of our Hamp-tons house, and these are a fraction of the hundreds I have drawn over the past twenty-five years. As Didier and I both travel a huge amount, and because expensive phone calls at odd times of day and from differ-ent time zones are never a good idea, we became dedicated senders of faxes. Didier wrote his because he can actually write. I, because I cannot write well at all, drew mine. And what I chose to draw was the funny idea of our cats acting out scenes loosely based on our fashion careers and domestic lives—they would go to fashion shows in Paris, trick-or-treating in New York at Halloween, or spend Christmas in the Hamptons around the tree, opening presents. In the summer they would sail, learn to swim with water wings, and gorge themselves on buttery corn. Also, they were best friends with all the photographers and trav-eled to all the places we did.

In the beginning, the drawings were rough. But as time went by, they became more refined. Karl Lagerfeld saw them, and although he was neither a cat nor a dog person back then, he thought them charming, and we agreed that I should make them into a book that he would pub-lish.

The Catwalk Cats was launched in the autumn of 2006, with a sign-ing at Marc Jacobs's shop in Greenwich Village. Marc was amused by the book; he, too, is a great animal lover. (He owns two dogs, Alfred and Daisy; whenever we meet for dinner, we always talk about our pets, rarely fashion.) He also had T-shirts manufactured to celebrate the book's publication, to be sold in his stores both at home and overseas, the proceeds of which went to an animal charity of my choice: City Critters, a small organization that I felt would feel the most impact from the money. For the Paris shop, the T-shirts carried my drawing of Bart holding a baguette; for Tokyo, Bart was dressed as a samurai warrior; and for New York City, there was a bulky, padded, all-star quarterback Bart. The night of the signing, Marc must have been feeling a little combative himself, because he turned up in a T-shirt with "If it ain't stiff, it ain't worth a fuck" printed on it. He proceeded to put his arms around me and Anna, to be photographed by the world's press.

Cats led me to my ultimate television moment—on the air with Martha Stewart.

Vogue's annual Age Issue traditionally spans the decades with features on women at different stages of their lives. For 2008 an idea came up to have each fashion editor dress a model in a way appropriate to the editor's own age. However, both I and my colleague, Tonne Goodman, who is much younger than I, misinterpreted this to mean we should turn the models into literal look-alikes of ourselves. So while Tonne was busily transforming her girl, Tanya D, into the epitome of thin blond minimalism that she is, I re-created my model, Karen Elson, as my doppelgänger—same shock of frizzy red hair, same pale face, same clothes, all black. I decided to take the idea even further and put my cats in the picture, too. However, after realizing how stressed they would get under the studio lights, I asked Pumpkin's breeder, Pam, if we could use the cats from her company, Top Shelf Persians, because they are all so well trained.

When Martha Stewart saw the issue, she fell head over heels in love

Anna, Marc Jacobs & me at my "Catwalk Cats" book signing

Karl with his new kitten Choupette
he too finally has become a cat person.

with the cats captured in Steven Meisel's photographs, crawling charmingly through Karen's hair and flying through the air. She rang, asking me to put her in touch with the breeder, and subsequently bought two kittens, which, I heard, she often allowed to accompany her into the bath.

Later, Martha called me again, saying she was about to do a program dedicated to cats and wanted to invite me to take part. Of course I accepted. The entire studio audience for the show consisted of cat lovers. All had been asked to bring their cats along (I didn't bring mine; they would have been too freaked out) and arrived with them on leashes. The studio doors were firmly locked, and they held their pets up as soon as they were given the cue "Everyone put your cats in the air."

To be surrounded by all those felines was awesome. I thought it was ambitious of Martha to invite so many that didn't know one another to be in such close proximity, and I never thought she'd get away with it. But the thing about cats, if you take them to a strange place, is that they tend to become quite subdued. Martha mentioned my book, and I was proud to see Pam up onstage with all the cats that had appeared in my pictures with Karen Elson, which was how it all started for Martha and her new Persians, Princess Peony and Empress Tang. Having always been reluctant to go on TV, I was in cat heaven this time and hardly noticed the cameras when they were turned on me.

After the show, which I thought went really well, Martha asked if I could dress her for her future programs. In the end I steered clear of that. I was perfectly aware that she had strong ideas about how she wanted to look, and so, to avoid any conflict, I declined. We have remained friendly, though. There's always a certain friendship between cat people, a pronouncedly personal understanding.

XIX

ON
THEN AND NOW

In which the
past becomes
the present,
the present flies
past, and our
heroine goes
digital and makes
peace with
computers at last.

Before I arrived at American *Vogue* in 1988, while I was still at Calvin Klein, Didier and I went in search of a weekend getaway outside New York. Like so many other foreign professionals living and working in Manhattan, we were well acquainted by now with the sheer awfulness of summer in the city: The air outside becomes so hot it scorches your lungs, and to be confined to an office all day means to virtually risk frostbite from the full-throttle air-conditioning. So many of our friends would return refreshed and renewed from weekends spent at their bolt-holes upstate or their rentals in the Hamptons that we decided to try it, too.

It took some searching—we didn't want anything that was too lengthy a car trip from town, or too expensive, as we didn't live the lifestyle of many other people in fashion—until eventually, we found the perfect

"Eureka! I just opened my first email"

place in the Hamptons, not too far from the sea, because Didier loves to sail. He's more passionate about it than even I was when I was young.

The house was brand-new, in the little town of Wainscott, hidden away at the end of a cul-de-sac with a small garden backing onto woods. The building was unremarkable, to say the least; to be truthful, I had always hoped for something much more charming, like one of those old, beautiful clapboard houses you see in the movies. But many of these are a fortune nowadays and can be found only by the side of busy, noisy highways—which put them way off-limits for me, Didier, and our cat family.

Over the years our country house, which we initially saw as a stopgap on the way to something better, has become an essential part of our extremely private life (we hardly ever socialize), a treat for the cats, and when it comes to the garden, which is landscaped in a freewheeling, rambling manner, very much my way of keeping hold of a little piece of England and its glorious greenery. Early on we planted a few bamboo shoots at the back, which now, when I happen to look out of my kitchen window, seem to have grown into a thick forest surrounding the two small wooden, ivy-covered cabins we built at the end of the garden, one for occasional summer dining and the other for stopover guests.

Inside the main house, which I try to keep under control despite Didier's propensity for buying books, my one major indulgence has been to entirely cover the walls with rows of shelves supporting layers of original framed photographs—mostly in black and white—by my favorite photographers past and present. Because these pictures have taken up every square inch available, a few years back I started storing them, packed in their bubble wrap, in our spare room. Then I had an entire row of cupboards built along one wall. Gradually, as their numbers grew even larger, to be joined by several big oil paintings, some Native American rugs, my antique dressmaker's dummy, and my sewing machine, I suddenly found myself with a space almost exactly like the junk room that had so embarrassed me as a child back at our family home in Wales.

I tried recently to tackle the confusion in that room again, with its stacks of photographs so tightly wedged together that I cannot prise them apart, along with random items like an obsolete fax machine and a giant book on Muhammad Ali bought by me as a birthday present for Didier and still in its box, and an even bigger one, *Sumo,* by Helmut Newton, which came with its own table to sit on. I wondered if I would ever fulfill my dream of building something, not unlike a little barn, on the small piece of land we bought across the road, in which to curate and store in an orderly fashion all the beautiful images and objects that it has been my good fortune to collect over the years. But then, as always happens, my zeal for tidying became waylaid by the lure of reminiscence as each photograph drew me back down Memory Lane and made me stop what I was doing. . . .

Fashion has changed so much in my lifetime. Today I find myself at the collections, asking, "Who are all these people?" They appear to come from anywhere and everywhere, and ninety percent seem to be uninvited hangers-on. Sometimes I think I'm the last remaining person who goes to the shows for the pleasure of seeing the clothes, rather than desperately wanting to be there for the social side—which is the part of things I have always had to be dragged to, kicking and screaming. And everyone has an opinion! Before the television interviewers and film cameras came along, people kept themselves to themselves. But now, when they turn up to fashion shows, all they want to do is talk and talk. Or be filmed answering inane questions.

Everyone has a cell phone or camera, including all the models getting ready behind the scenes, so everyone knows exactly what's happening in real time. There are no secrets anymore—everything has been texted, tweeted, or e-mailed all over the world way before the show has even begun.

During the time I worked at Calvin Klein, Carrie Donovan, formerly of *Harper's Bazaar* but by then elevated to the powerful position of fashion editor of *The New York Times,* attempted to send her photographer backstage at one of our fashion shows. I threw him out. Then Calvin came running over, demanding to know why I had done it. I said I thought that seeing what we were doing ahead of time would ruin the surprise, and besides, the guy was in the way. "No, no," he said. "It's for Carrie Donovan. You've got to allow it." That was the beginning of the end. Now it is complete mayhem back there, with probably more pictures taken behind the scenes than of the models on the runway.

I used to see every show in the New York collections, but these days I'm much more selective, partly because the experience has become so trying. Giveaway gossip papers like *The Daily* are constantly being pushed in your face, and cheap champagne is handed out at nine o'clock in the morning—with the English fashionistas being the first to gulp it down. As you dodge the movie cameras on your way in, there is usually some starlet of the moment surrounded by photographers and planted in the middle of the runway, hindering everyone else from getting to their seats. I can't stand it, so I usually put the blinkers on and rush straight through. Before the show, there is that intensely irritating moment when the photographers yell out, "Uncross your legs!" What I usually think is "Screw you!" because if my legs were really in the way, I would know it.

Each ready-to-wear season, I usually fill one sketchbook per city—Paris, Milan, New York—plus one for each season's couture, resort, and cruise. So that makes twelve sketchbooks a year, and they can all get pretty full. My system at the shows is to draw, sketch, put down everything—every single outfit—and worry later whether I liked it or not. Occasionally, I will put a star next to a favorite. Because I don't write about fashion, I don't take notes. I find it faster and easier to draw a dolman sleeve, for example, than to describe it. It was simpler in the old days, when there weren't so many collections and most people showed a maximum of thirty outfits.

I do become terribly intense when I'm drawing anything complicated or intellectually challenging, such as the Prada or Balenciaga collection, and I get extremely irritated if I'm in the middle of it and people talk to me, disturbing my concentration. Most other people these days don't take notes, because they look at the Internet, with its bloggers and instant information, and most freelance stylists don't even bother coming to the shows. But I have to see them. They're easier for me to absorb if I'm there. On a flat screen, things look flat. I don't think I could recognize a great collection if I just saw it on a screen or in a look book.

I'm not exactly a technophobe—even though I learned how to text only recently and still have a problem writing e-mails—but I've never been that fascinated by the computer age. I got my first cell phone in 2006, and it was pure peer pressure. That and not being able to find Jean-Louis, my driver, whenever I was in Paris for the collections. Cell phones and texting are a curse and a blessing at the same time. How ridiculous is it that I have to text people to ask them to turn on their phones because I wish to call and have a conversation with them? I text as little as I can. For me, it's far slower than a conversation, and so impersonal. I liked it before, when you could snuggle down with the telephone and feel like the other person was in the same room. You could carry on whole relationships through the receiver. Before I began using a cell phone, I needed to make all my arrangements prior to leaving the house, adhering strictly to a timetable. There was no texting, no tweeting. No nonsense.

It's hard for me to define what is modern, because I am not. At work I have a computer because I must. Am I glued to it all day? Never. For several years it sat there on my desk at *Vogue* before I opened it up and turned it on. By which time, unbeknownst to me, I had accumulated millions and millions of e-mails, which remained unanswered. Now all my messages are picked up and printed out by my ever-patient assistant, Stella, who is young and cute and gets rid of the reams and reams of spam that appear every morning. She has tried to teach me how it all works, to no avail—I just don't seem to have the knack.

I think that I am probably the last surviving fashion editor who actually dresses the girl rather than leaving it to an assistant. It is so important to me. The dressing room is the only place you have left to communicate with the model and get your opinion across as to how she should stand and what mood should be conveyed, without interfering with the job of the photographer. I'm told other stylists sit down and direct from behind the camera, preferring to have their assistants tug the clothes straight, turn up the collar and push up the sleeves.

I guess I'm pretty critical of fashion and always concerned about whether something is well made. The first thing I do in the showroom when I go back to look at a collection is to turn whatever I'm looking at inside out. Designers like Peter Copping at Nina Ricci, Marco Zanini at Rochas, and particularly Marc Jacobs always think about the inside of a garment, which is something I rarely found working in England, where the finishing was dreadful and most designers seemed content with any old lining. However, I was fascinated to read—in the Metropolitan Museum catalog of his show, perhaps—that Alexander McQueen liked having things sewn inside his clothing to give it a backstory in much the same way a nineteenth-century gentleman would have a lock of a prostitute's hair sewn into his jacket as a memento or trophy.

To me, fashion falls into one of two categories. It can be instantly appealing and you would like to wear it; or it is something you wouldn't necessarily wear but it is driving fashion forward. For that reason, I like Comme des Garçons. Whatever the designer Rei Kawakubo thinks up is intriguing. You often see some creation of hers and wonder how she thought of it, how she could turn a particular political situation into that sort of dress. At other times, she makes something that is heartbreakingly beautiful, such as her "Broken Bride" collection. When I went backstage after that show, I cried: such accessible romanticism after all those years of experimentation, of seeing strange padded things that distorted the body.

I do not have enough space to keep my collection of photographs, let alone fashion. I haven't kept any of my old clothes. Unlike my colleague Hamish Bowles, *Vogue*'s international editor-at-large who, if you mention any name from Poiret to Schiaparelli, has it; he lends pieces out to museum exhibitions. He used to keep racks of rare pieces in his office until he couldn't fit himself in there anymore. But I do appreciate vintage clothes and could kick myself for not keeping some of my amazing old Saint Laurents and Azzedines.

The thirties and the forties are my favorite eras. Part of the fifties, too, which were romantic. I hated the exaggerated shoulders of the eighties; they were hideous. Power dressing was hideous, too. (The film *Working Girl* with Melanie Griffith is a reminder of one of fashion's ugliest moments.) The original forties look was a squared-off shoulder, which is not the same thing at all, and the only person who did that properly in modern times—by which I mean captured the spirit of the forties—was Yves Saint Laurent. I loved what Karl did early on for Chloé and, later, at Chanel couture. I loved watching those early Japanese shows as well. They were like the most beautiful theater. I loved the craziness of the Kenzo shows in the seventies, so colorful and youthful, although he didn't make Japanese clothes; his was a Japanese eye on European clothes. The English designer Ossie Clark made incredible things in the sixties and seventies, brilliantly cut and slightly driven by the thirties.

I always love bias cut. It's incredibly flattering, never looks tight, and falls perfectly when done correctly. Like Ossie, John Galliano is a master of that. Azzedine Alaia is a genius, and I don't use that word lightly. I love Nicolas Ghesquière's clothes. His shows for Balenciaga are very, very uncompromising, but there is always a reason behind every pleat and fold. He is a perfectionist and an inspiration. Daring to take chances, he is endlessly copied by others who lack his courage to take the first step.

Although it says "creative director" next to my name on *Vogue*'s masthead, I'm not creative in any other part of it than fashion, so if you asked me for my job description, I guess I would have to say "stylist." That term can seem a bit redundant when the mood changes, and it changes as we speak.

Every so often I have lunch with Anna at her request. These days, though, I get worked up beforehand, usually thinking, "This is finally the time she'll say, 'You're getting on a bit. You're looking tired. I think you should take it easy,'" as a prelude to gently asking me to step down. In fact, the last time we went out, I dared to say, "I thought you were going to tell me to leave." At which point Anna laughed and said, "No, as long as I'm here, you will be, too."

I never had an actual birthday party when I was a child. As with any other social happening, it was the sort of thing that made me far too nervous. Sure, there would be cake and a few presents, but a noisy gathering of friends and balloons? That just couldn't happen. Whatever anxieties I felt at seven, however, were magnified tenfold when I reached seventy and people started to mention the possibility of a large-scale birthday celebration.

As the day approached in the spring of 2011, Anna said, "Your big birthday is coming up, and I'm going to give you a party. Have it where you like and however many people you like." (Funny how she likes celebrating other people's birthdays but ignores her own.) Twenty years had come and gone since she had organized my fiftieth at the restaurant Indochine during our early days at *Vogue,* when we could laugh about retiring together.

Anna approached Didier and said she would like to host the party with him, possibly because she knew it was the only guaranteed way of getting him to show up. I designed the menu, the cake, and the invitation, the cover of which was a cartoon-like pen drawing of Anna wearing Prada and Didier wearing a suit. I was compelled to add some sketches of our cats dressed in their party finest, with Bart in a suit like Didier's and Pumpkin wearing Balenciaga. Which, coincidentally, turned out to be the same dress Anna wore to the festivities.

At the office Anna said she hoped I didn't mind, but I would have to celebrate my birthday a week early because she didn't want my event to clash with that of the annual Costume Institute gala at the Met. She didn't want there to be "two big parties back to back." I agreed, of course. But I started to get anxious. Exactly how big was she expecting my party to be?

Everyone kept suggesting very new restaurants. Some might not have been new enough, because Anna likes nothing more than to take over a place that hasn't opened yet. But finally, just as it had years before, it came down to Indochine. The restaurant was experiencing a big revival and the food was great.

The party was a roaring success. Everyone came, including Condé Nast's proprietor, S. I. Newhouse; Carey Mulligan, an actress I adore; Helmut Lang, who rarely leaves his home on Long Island; my old boss Calvin Klein; Seth Meyers, who had made me laugh so much on a shoot once that my sides ached; Arthur Elgort; Bruce Weber; Craig McDean; tons of designers from New York and Europe; all my favorite models; everyone from the fashion and art departments; and ten of my former assistants from British and American *Vogue*. I was so overwhelmed, it all went kind of blurry, as it does every time I'm the center of attention.

Hamish Bowles and the model-turned-singer Karen Elson sang "Happy Birthday." Bruce, Marc Jacobs, Didier, and Jessica Diehl (one of my ex-assistants) all said a kind word. Didier made some drily amusing comments about me, telling everyone, "It took a long time for me to be acknowledged by her." And "Grace is always right, as her many friends and assistants will attest."

Naturally, Anna made a speech. "Grace," she jokingly began, "this is going to be your favorite part of the evening, when we all get to talk about you." Then she continued, "To me you will always be the heart and soul of the magazine, its guardian at the gate, its beacon of excellence. For about as long as I have edited *Vogue,* one person, Grace Coddington, has made me excited to come into the office every day . . ."

Menu, invitation, and place cards for my seventieth birthday party, 2011

I was speechless. This from a woman who normally never pays you a compliment to your face! How could I possibly respond? I could click my heels in the air or turn cartwheels, but my regular sessions of Pilates were not quite that effective. I could laugh and cry at the thought that so many painstaking years of toil were held in such esteem. I could shimmy across the dance floor knowing I still had some life in me yet.

While these thoughts were running through my head, I looked at the many photographers, hairstylists, makeup artists, art directors, fellow editors, and ex-assistants around me, and realized I don't really have a single friend who isn't in the business. Which is perfectly fine by me.

So am I still that completely fascinated by fashion? In many ways, yes. Having worked in it for over fifty years, I gratefully accept that my world has expanded with time, not contracted. Fashion has opened up many opportunities for me beyond the printed page, and the future is alive with diverse possibilities: illustrations (I had so much fun drawing the pages for this book); a chance to make an animated feature based on my cat sketches; directing a series of documentaries (and yes, it most likely would be about fashion.)

Whatever it is, I would hope my work will always be created with the personal touch that several modern aspects of being a fashion editor no longer afford me. For instance, I was recently involved in a photo shoot where the subject was to be replaced by a stand-in. Only the real subject's head would be featured, grafted onto the stand-in's shoulders thanks to the science-fiction wonders of Photoshop. Unbelievably shocking.

But I've grown to realize that life doesn't stand still and it's no good being sad about it. For me, one of the most important aspects of my work is to give people something to dream about, just as I used to dream all those years ago as a child looking at beautiful photographs. I still weave dreams, finding inspiration wherever I can and looking for romance in the real, not the digital, world.

All I know is that if I continue in fashion, no matter what, my head will always remain firmly attached to my body.

SELECTED WORK

————————————————

BRITISH VOGUE

1968 — 1987

Norman Parkinson, 1973

Norman Parkinson, 1973

THE
SEYCHELLES

*in which
she happens upon
a footprint
on the shore,
comes upon a Dog Friday
wins his friendship
and feeds him upon oysters*

Norman Parkinson, 1971

Norman Parkinson, 1971

Guy Bourdin, 1972

Guy Bourdin, 1975

Guy Bourdin, 1971

Guy Bourdin, 1977

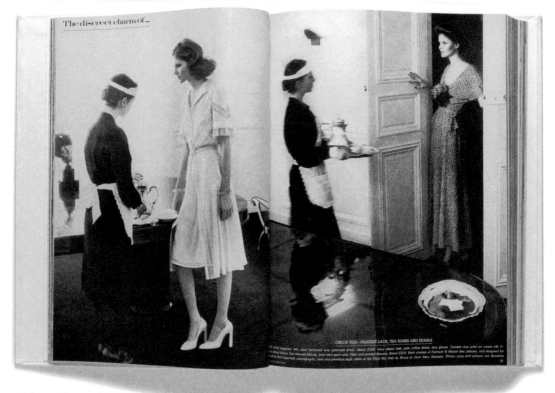

Helmut Newton, 1974

Helmut Newton, 1974

Helmut Newton, 1973

Helmut Newton, 1973

Alex Chatelain, 1979

Alex Chatelain, 1979

Barry Lategan, 1983

Barry Lategan, 1983

Bruce Weber, 1984

Bruce Weber, 1984

Bruce Weber, 1981

Bruce Weber, 1981

AMERICAN VOGUE

1988 — 2012

Arthur Elgort, 1991

Arthur Elgort, 1995

PETTICOAT
JUNCTION
Her broad lines shelter
behind her enormous
taffeta skirts. Make-
gray gown with gigantic
black tulle petticoat,
Vivienne Westwood
Gold Label, Bergdorf
Goodman; Vivienne
Westwood Boutique,
NYC. Details, see In
This Issue.

Arthur Elgort, 2001

M.
dogs and Englishwomen.
With his sights set on
Mary Quant, Michael Kors
designs a jacket and
matching skirt in the softest
pastel pink wool. Jacket
(about $1,295) and skirt (about
$455) by Michael Kors.
Barneys New York; Bergdorf
Goodman; The Gazebo,
Dallas. His suit from Prada.
Details, see In This Issue.

473

Arthur Elgort, 1995

Steven Meisel, 1992

Steven Meisel, 1992

Jean Paul Gaultier:
Devoutly Irreverent

In keeping with the spiritual overtones of fall's plain,
monastic silhouette, French bad boy
Jean Paul Gaultier offered his own religious take—
a Hasidic send-up complete with payess and
platter hats. "It's an homage to
the Jewish religion," he explains,
"but it's also quite punk"—a street style
that's coming around again.
Hair, Orlando Pita for Bumble & Bumble.
Details, stores, see In This Issue.

Steven Meisel, 1993

MRS. MINIVER
"Her heart belongs
to Tangerine," sang
the Jimmy Dorsey
Orchestra. On today's
home front, subtly
"off" hues are chic
again: faded orange,
putty, mustard. On
Sasha, *near right:* Etro
wool coat, $3,340,
Etro, NYC. Dries Van
Noten skirt, $589,
Capilto, Charlotte NC.
Verdura earrings.
Martin Katz bracelet.
Prada heels. On Karen:
Dries Van Noten silk
jacket ($1,153) and
skirt ($649), Blake,
Chicago. Siegelson
earrings and bracelet.
On both: Cartier
brooches. Details,
see In This Issue.

Steven Meisel, 2009

Ellen von Unwerth, 1992

The
Piano Lesson

Call it a case of fashion following film. Chic of the most acclaimed movies of late, *The Piano*, had all of Europe talking at precisely the time designers were sketching their spring collections. Now its influence comes to light as evening dresses sail into more romantic territory, echoing the full, classically feminine silhouette seen on the screen. Photographed by Ellen Von Unwerth

Ellen von Unwerth, 1994

jean seberg

Breathless made actress Jean Seberg a star in 1959—
here she's the inspiration for Christy Turlington

The story of two lovers on a crime spree, Jean-Luc Godard's *Breathless* had a revolutionary look, due in part to camerawork that Roger Angell in *The New Yorker* called "jumpy, bold, and irritate." THIS PAGE: A portrait in the same rough style. Turtleneck by Marc Jacobs for Perry Ellis. About $590. Saks Fifth Avenue; Nan Duskin, Philadelphia; I. Magnin. OPPOSITE PAGE: His part in *Breathless* as a small-time hood was the first starring role for Jean-Paul Belmondo, a former boxer. Here, another boxer turned actor—Stephane Ferrara—takes the part. Christy wears a contemporary version of the *Herald Tribune* T-shirt Seberg wore (photo on page 366). Turtleneck (sans logo, about $130) and pants (about $295), by Isaac Mizrahi. Saks Fifth Avenue; Adaris, Birmingham MI; Liberty House of Hawaii. In this story: hair, Didier Malige for Jean Louis David; makeup, Laurie Starrett for L. Rossi and C. Shack, Paris. Details, more stores, last pages.

Fashion Editor: Grace Coddington
Photographer: Ellen Von Unwerth

365

Ellen von Unwerth, 1990

the great plain

Harking back to centuries-old traditional Amish work wear, this almost panoramic view of fashion reduced to its bare, functional essence. LEFT: Calvin Klein Collection wool jacket (about $780) and wide-leg pants (about $480), Miss Jackson, Tulsa; Neiman Marcus; the Calvin Klein stores. I. Goldberg, Philadelphia shirt, about $10. RIGHT: CK Calvin Klein pants, about $300. Barneys New York; Macy's Herald Square; Neiman Marcus. Agnès B. Homme shirt, about $90. Agnès B. Homme, NYC, Los Angeles. Details, see in This Issue.

Ellen von Unwerth, 1993

Peter Lindbergh, 1991

Peter Lindbergh, 2011

Peter Lindbergh, 2010

Peter Lindbergh, 2011

THE MAD TEA PARTY

"Your hair wants cutting," said the Hatter. He had been looking at Alice for some time with great curiosity. "You should learn not to make personal remarks," Alice said with some severity: "It's very rude."

Annie Leibovitz, 2003

TWEEDLEDUM AND TWEEDLEDEE

"I know what you're thinking about," said Tweedledum, "but it isn't so, nohow." "Contrariwise," continued Tweedledee, "if it was so, it might be; and if it were so, it would be: but as it isn't, it ain't. That's logic."

Annie Leibovitz, 2003

Annie Leibovitz, 2005

"Bang on my chest if you think I'm perfect. Go ahead, bang on it!" says the Tin Man. "It's empty. The tinsmith forgot to give me a heart"

Annie Leibovitz, 2005

Annie Leibovitz, 2001

Annie Leibovitz, 1999

Annie Leibovitz, 2009

Annie Leibovitz, 2010

Bruce Weber, 1989

Bruce Weber, 1989

Down on the farm, THIS PAGE: Nadège in a city-slicker-goes-Dolly Parton dress. By Chanel Haute Couture. Boots by the Justin Boot Company. Hat from the Alamo of Nashville. Even with a hat, one needs a sun block on the face: here, Chanel's Total Protection Moisture Cream SPF 15. OPPOSITE PAGE: Sunset near Nashville. Details, last pages.

180

Bruce Weber, 1990

No matter what the script holds for the future, no way do the Seven Dwarfs want to let Snow White sleep. The perfect tease for our leading lady—Prescriptives' new Soft Matte Makeup in Cappuccino. In this story, hair: Didier Malige for Frédéric Fekkai at Bergdorf Goodman; makeup, Denise Markey, Aretha's makeup, Lanier Long for Fashion Fair Cosmetics.

Fashion Editor: Grace Coddington

Snow White and the Seven Dwarfs

Once upon a time, not so long ago, photographer Bruce Weber and a few lambs decided to give Snow White a hip, even hip-hop, twist. Model Beverly Peele takes the lead, rap group Another Bad Creation are the seven small guys, Aretha Franklin plays the queen (of course), and L.L. Cool J, well, what a prince.

Bruce Weber, 1991

Mario Testino, 1997

Mario Testino, 1998

STAY STILL
Playing himself in the small painting studio, Condo studies his subject, fantastic and impossible in her beauty. Abuela ocean-teal, white and black cutout swimsuit, $280; Hilary Rush, Los Angeles. In this story: hair, Julien d'Ys; makeup, Stéphane Marais; set design, Mary Howard. Details, see In This Issue.

"When the muse appears, suddenly you become creative—and that moment comes through in the painting," says Condo

Mario Testino, 2007

COOL CUSTOMER
Waitressing at the famous Katz's Deli will pay the rent while she waits to be discovered. She hopes a pretty floral frock will make her stand out. Before Jimmy Fallon joined the cast of Saturday Night Live and went on to host Late Night with Jimmy Fallon, he worked his fair share of unglamorous jobs, from video store clerk to grocery bag boy. "I would do the whole Cha-Pup in aisle three thing," he remembers. Burberry Prorsum sequard dress, $4,995; Burberry.com. Details, see In This Issue.

Mario Testino, 2009

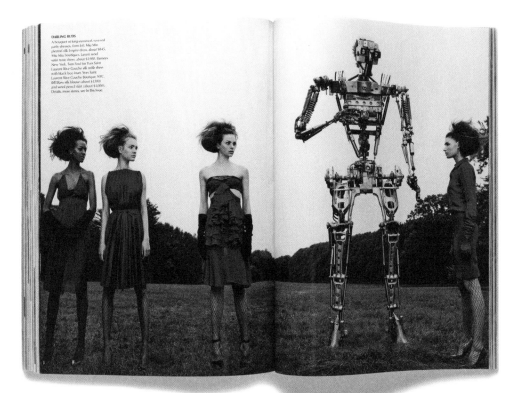

Steven Klein, 2003

Steven Klein, 2003

Steven Klein, 2003

Steven Klein, 2003

Mert & Marcus, 2009

Mert & Marcus, 2009

Sweater Girl

Model Lara Stone cozies up to the season's oversize knits, form-fitting cardigans, and prim crewnecks. Photographed by Mert Alas and Marcus Piggott.

CABLE READY
When temperatures dip, you're prepared in a classic fisherman's sweater with thick braid stitching. Prada wool sweater ($1,315) and slingback heels; select Prada boutiques. Details, see In This Issue. Fashion Editor: Grace Coddington.

Mert & Marcus, 2010

FULL CIRCLE
Mad Men-era swing skirts, now making a comeback, amplify both a slim waist and a trim knit. Miu Miu wool sweater ($565) with Peter Pan collar; select Miu Miu boutiques. Louis Vuitton silk taffeta skirt ($2,785) and pumps; select Louis Vuitton boutiques. Details, see In This Issue.

Mert & Marcus, 2010

David Sims, 2010

David Sims, 2011

David Sims, 2007

David Sims, 2010

Craig McDean, 2007

Craig McDean, 2002

Craig McDean, 2012

Craig McDean, 2012

INFORMATION

Norman Parkinson

Barbados 1973, Apollonia van Ravenstein

Barbados 1973, Apollonia van Ravenstein

Seychelles 1971, Apollonia van Ravenstein

Seychelles 1971, Apollonia van Ravenstein

© Norman Parkinson Limited/
courtesy Norman Parkinson Archive

Guy Bourdin

Paris, 1972, Aija. Hair: Didier Malige

Normandie, 1975, Carrie Nygren, Kathy Quirk

Normandie, 1975, Carrie Nygren,
Kathy Quirk, with Grace Coddington

London, 1971, Sue Baloo. Hair: Oliver Bond

France 1977, Kathy Quirk, Audrey,
Carrie Nygren. Hair: Valentin.
Makeup: Heidi Morawetz

Helmut Newton

France, 1974, Kathy Quirk
with Julie Kavanagh. Hair: Bruce Libre

France, 1974, Kathy Quirk. Hair: Bruce Libre

France, 1973, Danielle Poe and models,
with Grace Coddington. Hair: Jean Louis David

France, 1973, Danielle Poe and models,
with Grace Coddington. Hair: Jean Louis David

Alex Chatelain

China, 1979, Esmé. Hair: Kerry Warn

China, 1979, Esmé. Hair: Kerry Warn

Barry Lategan

Venice, 1983, Elisabetta Ramella.
Hair: Didier Malige

Venice, 1983, Elisabetta Ramella.
Hair: Didier Malige

Bruce Weber

England, 1984, Victoria Lockwood.
Hair: Didier Malige

England, 1984, Victoria Lockwood.
Hair: Didier Malige

New Mexico, 1981, Jon Wiedemann,
Sloane Condren. Hair: Howard Fugler

New Mexico, 1981, Jon Wiedemann,
Sloane Condren. Hair: Howard Fugler

AMERICAN VOGUE

Arthur Elgort

Scottland, 1991, Linda Evangelista.
Hair: Didier Malige. Makeup: Sonia Kashuk

Long Island, 1995, Stella Tennant.
Hair: Didier Malige. Makeup: Sonia Kashuk

California, 2001, Stella Tennant.
Hair: Julien d'Ys. Makeup: Gucci Westman

England, 1995, Donovan Leitch
and Kirsty Hume. Hair: Didier Malige.
Makeup: Mary Greenwell

Steven Meisel

Paris, 1992, Linda Evangelista, Kristen McMenamy.
Hair: Garren. Makeup: François Nars

USA, 1992, Kristen McMenamy, Nadja Auermann.
Hair: Garren. Makeup: Denise Markey

Paris, 1993, Jean Paul Gaultier Group:
Nadja Auermann, Daniel Baylock, Nadege, Amber
Valletta, Kristen McMenamy, Linda Evangelista,
David Boals, Shalom Harlow, Naomi Campbell, Jay
Littlewood, Christy Turlington. Hair: Orlando Pita.
Makeup: Denise Markey

New York, 2009, Models: Sasha Pivaverova, Karen
Elson. Hair: Julien d'Ys. Makeup: Pat McGrath

Ellen von Unwerth

Morocco, 1992, Nadja Auermann.
Hair: Oribe. Makeup: Laurie Starrett

Jamaica, 1994, Debbie Deitering with Rebecca
Forteau. Hair: Peter Savic. Makeup: Laurie Starrett

France, 1990, Christy Turlington
with Stéphane Ferrara. Hair: Didier Malige.
Makeup: Laurie Starrett

USA, 1993, Christy Turlington, Jaime Rishar,
Keith Martin. Hair: Peter Savic

Peter Lindbergh

Brooklyn, 1991, Helena Christensen, Stephanie
Seymour, Karen Mulder, Naomi Campbell, Claudia
Schiffer, Cindy Crawford. Hair: Odile Gilbert.
Makeup: Stephane Marais

Palmdale, 2011, Daria Werbowy with
David Strathairn. Hair: Julien d'Ys.
Makeup: Stephane Marais

Long Island, 2010, Natalia Vodianova with
Ewan McGregor. Hair: Didier Malige.
Makeup: Stephane Marais

Los Angeles, 2011, Lara Stone with
Alexander Skarsgård. Hair: Didier Malige.
Makeup: Stephane Marais

Annie Leibovitz

France, 2003, Natalia Vodianova with Stephen
Jones and Christian Lacroix. Hair: Julien d'Ys.
Makeup: Gucci Westman

France, 2003, Natalia Vodianova
with Viktor Horsting and Rolf Snoeren.
Hair: Julien d'Ys. Makeup: Gucci Westman

USA, 2005, Keira Knightley with Brice Marden.
Hair: Julien d'Ys. Makeup: Gucci Westman

USA, 2005, Keira Knightley with John Currin.
Hair: Julien d'Ys. Makeup: Gucci Westman

Paris, 2001, Stella Tennant, Jacquetta Wheeler,
with Ben Stiller. Hair: Julien d'Ys.
Makeup: Stephane Marais

Paris, 1999, Kate Moss with Diddy.
Hair: Julien d'Ys. Makeup: Diane Kendal

New York, 2009, Lily Cole with Andrew Garfield,
Lady Gaga. Hair: Julien d'Ys. Makeup: Gucci
Westman

Nashville, 2010, Karen Elson with Mark
Watrous, Jackson Smith, Rachelle Garniez,
Olivia Jean, and Marc Fellis. Hair: Julien d'Ys.
Makeup: Gucci Westman

Bruce Weber

USA, 1989, Naomi Campbell with Mike Tyson and Don King. Hair: Didier Malige. Makeup: Francois Nars

USA, 1989, Naomi Campbell with Mike Tyson. Hair: Didier Malige. Makeup: Francois Nars

USA 1990, B.B. King, Nadege. Hair: Didier Malige. Makeup: Bonnie Maller

Bellport, N.Y., 1991, Beverly Peele with Another Bad Creation. Hair: Didier Malige. Makeup: Denise Markey

Mario Testino

Italy, 1998, Gisele Bündchen, Fernanda Tavares, Frankie Rayder. Hair: Marc Lopez. Makeup: Kay Montano

Rio de Janeiro, 1997, Amber Valletta. Hair: Orlando Pita. Makeup: Tom Pecheux

New York, 2007, Daria Werbowy with George Condo. Hair: Julien d'Ys. Makeup: Stephane Marais

New York, 2009, Daria Werbowy with Jimmy Fallon. Hair: Julien d'Ys. Makeup: Linda Cantello

Steven Klein

New York, 2003, Liya Kebede, Natalia Vodianova, Elise Crombez, Eugenia Volodina. Hair: Orlando Pita. Makeup: Polly Osmond

New York, 2003, Liya Kebede and Natalia Vodianova. Hair: Orlando Pita. Makeup: Polly Osmond

New York, 2003, Natalia Vodianova with Justin Portman. Hair: Luigi Murenu. Makeup: Gucci Westman

New York, 2003, Natalia Vodianova with her son Lucas. Hair: Luigi Murenu. Makeup: Gucci Westman

Mert & Marcus

England, 2009, Natalia Vodianova. Hair: Julien d'Ys. Makeup: Charlotte Tilbury

England, 2009, Natalia Vodianova. Hair: Julien d'Ys. Makeup: Charlotte Tilbury

New Jersey, 2010, Lara Stone. Hair: Luigi Murenu. Makeup: Lucia Peroni

New Jersey, 2010, Lara Stone. Hair: Luigi Murenu. Makeup: Lucia Peroni

David Sims

Cornwall, 2010, Stella Tennant. Hair: Guido. Makeup: Diane Kendal

Cornwall, 2011, Arizona Muse with Jeremy Irvine. Hair: Guido. Makeup: Diane Kendal

Paris, 2007, Raquel Zimmermann. Hair: Guido. Makeup: Peter Philips

Jamaica, 2010, Daria Werbowy. Hair: Guido. Makeup: Diane Kendal

Craig McDean

New York, 2007, Raquel Zimmermann. Hair: Eugene Souleiman. Makeup: Peter Philips

Paris, 2002, Maggie Rizer. Hair: Luigi Murenu. Makeup: Diane Kendal

Toulon, 2012, Natalia Vodianova. Hair: Julien d'Ys. Makeup: Stephane Marais

Toulon, 2012, Natalia Vodianova with Michael Fassbender. Hair: Julien d'Ys. Makeup: Stephane Marais

Still lifes of magazine spreads by Tim Hout

ACKNOWLEDGMENTS

Given that I've barely read two books in my life that aren't picture books, no one is more surprised than me that I have produced a memoir. For that, I owe a debt to R. J. Cutler for getting anyone intrigued enough in me to read it because of his film *The September Issue,* and to my publishers, Susan Kamil and Clara Farmer, for the leap of faith they made in commissioning it. After listening to me for so many years, my former assistant Tina Chai convinced me that I have had a life worth talking about, and pushed me to go forward. I thank her for her friendship and encouragement—and also for being my companion to all the movies that have given me so much inspiration.

Huge thanks go to my lifelong friend Michael Roberts for taking on this assignment and bringing my voice to life with his wicked wit, as well as for jogging my memory on the things I had forgotten. It's tough to live so closely with someone over an extended period, but I hope he will agree we had a hell of a laugh. To Eve MacSweeney for her English ear and humor as she thoughtfully edited the book into shape, and for keeping me calm in the final stages when I believed I was losing my mind. To Anna Wintour for allowing me a free hand to write about how our lives have been entwined through all our years together at *Vogue,* and to Beatrix Miller for recognizing my passion so early on and giving me my first chance to express it.

My assistants past and present will be my friends forever. To Anne Christensen, a fellow redhead whom I always call my daughter. To Jessica Diehl, who taught me to be tough, and Michal Saad, who taught me to be positive. And to Stella Greenspan—without whom I absolutely could not have done this project—for patiently typing in all the corrections (remember, I don't use a computer), advising me when I went too far, and reading my stories a hundred times and still laughing at them.

To Didier for suffering for three years while I was working on the manuscript reading it over and over again—very slowly—instead of, say, making dinner, and for being so complimentary when he finally read it himself, despite the mention of all my ex-boyfriends and husbands and the insults I directed at his people, the French.

To everyone in the *Vogue* art department: Martin Hoops for giving up his weekends to work on layouts, the nimble scanners Daphne Taranto and Amanda Camodeo, David Byars for stepping into the breach, Desirée Rosario-Moodie for tracking down photographers and getting permissions, and Julie Bramowitz for valiantly correcting my muddled memory on the facts.

To my agents, Elyse Cheney and Natasha Fairweather, for taking me on, guiding me, and backing me up, even when I stubbornly declared I knew best about something I had never done before. To Jay Fielden, who introduced me to Elyse and got the ball rolling.

Finally, thank you to everyone who has been part of my life. To all the many designers, photographers, models, hairdressers, and makeup artists, who are really the ones that create the pictures. And to my partner in crime Phyllis Posnick, who has put up with me for the last half century while I complained about everything, and who I failed to mention in the book is one of my dearest friends.

ABOUT THE AUTHOR

Grace Coddington lives in New York City and Long Island with her partner, Didier Malige, and their two cats, Bart and Pumpkin.

CONTRIBUTORS

DESIGN DIRECTORS
GRACE CODDINGTON AND
MICHAEL ROBERTS

EDITOR
EVE MACSWEENEY

ART DIRECTOR
MARTIN HOOPS

ARCHIVAL RESEARCH
DESIRÉE ROSARIO-MOODIE

COORDINATOR
STELLA GREENSPAN

Michael
Roberts

Sally
Singer

Susie
Menkes

Franca
Sozzani

Tabitha
Simmons

Camilla
Nickerson

Elissa
Santisi